The Future
as an Academic Discipline

The Ciba Foundation for the promotion of international cooperation in
medical and chemical research is a scientific and educational charity established by
CIBA Limited – now CIBA-GEIGY Limited – of Basle. The Foundation operates independently
in London under English trust law.

Ciba Foundation Symposia are published in collaboration with
Elsevier Scientific Publishing Company, Excerpta Medica, North-Holland Publishing Company,
in Amsterdam.

Elsevier/Excerpta Medica/North-Holland, P.O. Box 211, Amsterdam

The Future
as an Academic Discipline

Ciba Foundation Symposium 36 (new series)

1975

Elsevier · Excerpta Medica · North-Holland
Amsterdam · Oxford · New York

ISBN Excerpta Medica 90 219 4040 x
ISBN American Elsevier 0444-15184-2

Published in September 1975 by Elsevier/Excerpta Medica/North-Holland, P.O. Box 211, Amsterdam, and American Elsevier, 53 Vanderbilt Avenue, New York, N.Y. 10017.

Suggested series entry for library catalogues: Ciba Foundation Symposia.
Suggested publisher's entry for library catalogues: Elsevier/Excerpta Medica/North-Holland

Ciba Foundation Symposium 36 (new series)

Printed in The Netherlands by Mouton & Co, The Hague

Contents

Participants

Symposium on *The Future as an Academic Discipline* held at the Ciba Foundation, London, 6–8 February 1975

C. H. WADDINGTON (*Chairman*) Institute of Animal Genetics, West Mains Road, Edinburgh EH9 3JN

Lord ASHBY   Clare College, Cambridge, CB2 1TL

J. N. BLACK   Bedford College, Regent's Park, London NW1 4NS

Y. DROR   Department of Political Science, Hebrew University of Jerusalem, Israel

H. W. ELDREDGE   Department of Sociology, Dartmouth College, Hanover, New Hampshire 03755, USA

J. M. FRANCIS   Heriot-Watt University, Research Park, Riccarton, Currie, Edinburgh EH14 4AS

F. R. JEVONS   Department of Liberal Studies in Science, The University, Manchester M13 9PL

A. KING   The International Federation of Institutes for Advanced Study, 168 rue de Grenelle, 75007 Paris, France

I. F. KLIMES   *Futures*, IPC House, 32 High Street, Guildford, Surrey GU1 3EW

K. KUMAR   Keynes College, University of Kent at Canterbury, Kent CT2 7NP

A. LUNDBERG   Department of Physiology, University of Göteborg, Göteborg, Sweden

F. OLDFIELD   School of Independent Studies, University of Lancaster, Fylde College, Bailrigg, Lancaster LA1 4YF

Sir WALTER PERRY   The Open University, Walton Hall, Milton Keynes
MK7 6AA

J. R. PLATT   Mental Health Research Institute, The University of Michigan,
Ann Arbor, Mich. 48104, USA

Sir HUGH ROBSON   Old College, University of Edinburgh, South Bridge,
Edinburgh EH8 9YL

H. G. SHANE   School of Education, Indiana University, Education Building,
Room 328, Bloomington, Indiana 47401, USA

Sir FREDERICK STEWART   Grant Institute of Geology, University of Edinburgh,
West Mains Road, Edinburgh EH9 3JW

R. D. UNDERWOOD   School of the Man Made Future, University of Edinburgh,
15 Buccleuch Place, Edinburgh EH8 9LN

K. VALASKAKIS   Département des Sciences Economiques, Université de
Montréal, Case postale 6128, Montréal 3, PQ, Canada

M. H. F. WILKINS   Department of Biophysics, University of London King's
College, 26–29 Drury Lane, London WC2R 2LS

Sir ERNEST WOODROOFE   The Crest, Berry Lane, Worplesdon, Guildford,
Surrey GU3 3QF

J. M. ZIMAN   University of Bristol, H. H. Wills Physics Laboratory, Royal
Fort, Tyndall Avenue, Bristol BS8 1TL

Editors: G. E. W. WOLSTENHOLME (*Organizer*) and MAEVE O'CONNOR

Introduction

C. H. WADDINGTON

Institute of Animal Genetics, University of Edinburgh

We are here to discuss whether universities in general and British universities in particular should take account of the problems that mankind is obviously going to face in the next few decades, and, if universities are to do this, how should they do it? It is only because the situation in the next few decades is clearly going to be unlike what it was in our grandfathers' days that I think the question arises so seriously now. We all recognize that we are facing a series of crises which can't be completely separated from one another. Each one of them—atomic warfare or the population problem or the environment problem or the energy problem or what have you—is a considerable threat. The whole set together form what the Club of Rome has called the *problèmatique*.

How far should universities do anything specifically in connection with this? It seems to me there are two aspects to this. One is the question of incorporating into the universities any of the pure scholarship that is going on in these fields. That is relatively simple for universities to do, even if the scholarship doesn't fall into any previously well-defined disciplines. A great deal of profound thinking of an academic kind is going on in these fields now, at the highest levels of academic scholarship. There is some high-level thinking about the methodology of dealing with complex systems—things like the stability theory, the catastrophe theories of Thom and derivatives of this. Many of these developments can, if you like, be regarded simply as mathematics, but they are a type of mathematics that applies specifically to dealing with complex systems such as confront us historically in the social sphere. They are not only mathematics in the abstract.

There are also scholarly studies on the precise and detailed economic, political and industrial questions. For instance, the economist Jan Tinbergen is working on a project for the Club of Rome which he originally called 'Renewing the world system', and which he has now given the slightly more modest

1

title 'Reviewing the world system'. In it he is considering how all the economic, industrial and natural resources with which the world is working at present should or could be made to work in a more equitable manner. This is a major work of imaginative scholarship.

Most of these things are at present being done outside the universities and I think universities should make a bigger effort to bring in some of these studies, or at any rate be closely connected with them. They constitute one of the most significant types of academic scholarship in the world today. It is not too difficult for universities to bring them into their existing structure, which is always rather flexible in relation to research and postgraduate aspects. But we need to think seriously about the undergraduate aspect of this problem. Until a short time ago universities were basically there to provide a general education. It is less than a hundred years since a man had to be in Holy Orders before he could be a Fellow at Oxford or Cambridge. And about a hundred years ago the basic purpose of the universities was to produce either clerics or well-educated generalists. The idea that the universities are there to turn out highly-specialized professionals is a recent change in their purpose. I think many university people have found it upsetting. I read the other day that a questionnaire sent to some physicists asked them whether they were high energy particle physicists, and if so were they working on hadrons or kleptons or something else. Not only that, but were they working on positive or negative hadrons? The physicists were not really allowed by this questionnaire to take an interest in anything more than one hypothetical subnuclear particle, and some of them complained about this.

Universities are in some danger of finding themselves fossilized into these sorts of divisions. There are a lot of young men who badly need to understand how the world is working and who realize that they don't really do so. So far as they get taught anything about the processes of thinking, they get taught about linear sequences of cause and effect: A causes B, B causes C, C causes D, and so on. It is quite clear that that is not the way the world works now. In the past, when man's industrial resources were such that he could only scratch at the surface of the world, any particular scratch could probably be considered relatively independently of any other, and one could maybe get away with thinking of everything as happening in isolated linear cause–effect sequences. Now that we are dealing with the world in a more profound manner, going much deeper, where everything we do runs into everything else we do, we can't escape from a whole lot of feedback circuits, interactions and non-linear effects. Thinking in terms purely of cause and effect in the old-fashioned way is totally inadequate in our present situation. I think most young people realize this and know that they are not being taught any of the newer ways of dealing with the problems. The methods don't fit into any standard curriculum. Possibly engineers have to learn a bit on one side, and possibly economists will learn another bit, but nobody in general knows all the different types of thinking of this kind, and most people go through university never having heard of them. I think possibly something should be done about that.

Secondly, in this great complex of problems any single problem is itself complex. We may think that the food problem is easy enough, but nobody actually knows how much of any sort of food we really need, or when food starts doing more harm than it does good, and so on. The population problem also sounds simple until, again, we look into it and find that it is extremely complex, depending on the age structure of a population, how fast it is going to reproduce, the social aims, the rate of material progress that is likely if the size of the family is limited, whether it is economically better to have six sons on the basis that at least one will be left alive when his parents are old and unable to work, and so on. In any one of these problems we find that we are hitting against the fringes of the others. We don't try at present in ordinary universities to give anybody a general overall picture, and it is my belief that we ought to do this.

I have been trying to introduce this type of undergraduate teaching in Edinburgh, on a voluntary basis, for a year, and I hope that we shall soon be able to turn it into one of the options in various courses. I thought that the only way of convincing people that this was an academically respectable course for undergraduates was to write the textbooks and thus explain what I think ought to be in the course. I have written two textbooks for half-year courses. They are at second-year level; that is to say they really are going to skim over everything, with nothing gone into in any depth, but the aim is that if you take the course you can't avoid rubbing your nose in everything: you won't know much about it but at least you'll know it is there. One book is called *Tools of Thought about Complex Systems*. It could also be called 'A Child's Guide to the Fashionable Jargon'. It aims to show what methods people are developing about how to think in more subtle terms than linear sequences of cause and effect. Then I have a more factual book called *The Sources of the Man Made Future*, on the components of the world's *problèmatique*, under twelve headings. Both books will be published by Cape and Paladin Books in 1975. This is just an approach to what I think is a genuine gap in the education we are at present providing for our young people. I have some experience of the way they react to being offered such a course, and I think they feel they need this. There are very few places they can get it from. It can be, and is, an academic discipline in the sense of being a scholarly pursuit. It can or should be—and is, in a few places— part of the educational opportunities which we offer to students.

Professor Eldredge has for some years been making surveys of what courses are being offered and he should be able to tell us what other countries and universities are doing about the future.

The Mark III survey of university-level futures courses

H. WENTWORTH ELDREDGE

Dartmouth College, Hanover, New Hampshire

Abstract Six years of information-gathering and three reports on some 500 university-level futures courses give rise to the following generalizations. Most academic disciplines and fields are to some degree alerted to the future implications of their research and teaching. The numbers of future-oriented courses in many varying forms have increased; but individuals seem to come and go in the field. There appears to be a somewhat negative intellectual image of futurism and futures studies today; the need to define the field, upgrade methodology and recruit wisely is clear. Societal forecasting (especially values forecasting) based on valid sociocultural change theory is the weakest aspect in the futures complex, along with fumbling attempts at creativity training. 'Futurizing' existing courses appears the most valid operational ploy for introducing future dimensions into university curricula at this point. Technological forecasting joined to technology assessment offers the most promising methodology (excepting perhaps cross-impact matrices), especially if joined to modelling, and it is certainly backed by powerful government and private forces. Informal educational systems may be extremely efficacious in futures studies. The delivery of insights and knowledge (such as it is) about the future in a cybernetic policy-studies fashion is the most pressing next step.

After collecting information (primarily by questionnaire) for six years and writing three critical analytical reports [1,2,3] on university-level futures courses, with information now in hand on about 500, I venture to say that futures studies, as a quasi-discipline at least, are tolerated on the academic scene. The enormous shock to western society of the 'surprising' energy crisis (although more or less precisely forecast in physical terms for at least a decade), coming after the generally heightened public consciousness on environmental questions, has had its overspill in academia. The rapidity with which the underdeveloped Muslim nations internalized political compact-making and cartel-design (societal technology) of the western type convinced even the most obtuse that the world was on the move at an accelerating pace and that we might be witnessing one of the major revolutionary breaks in history.

Triage—whom do you allow to die by starvation? [4,5]—and 'the lifeboat theory'—whom do you throw overboard to save the others?[6]—are the questions that now face the affluent societies, and especially the United States. Has our vaunted humanitarianism merely been the result of a once teeming plenty or are we Americans as 'selfish' as Europe and Asia—not to mention the developing areas and the communist bloc—have of necessity always been?[7] Trapped by the Marshall Plan and our own 'bleeding hearts' are we doomed to feed the foolish globe to its own Malthusian destruction? It would seem that all systems may be 'no go'.[8,9] In fact Frank Davidson of early Chunnel fame gives a course on 'failure' with the System Dynamics Group at MIT's Alfred P. Sloan School of Management. All this has now been sharply punctuated by India's detonation of a 'peaceful' nuclear device as well as Israel's frank admission of military nuclear capability. In the late 1960s, the youth revolt and ethnic unrest dramatized the smouldering discontent of large segments of the populations of western civilization with the lack of human depth in our life patterns. This upheaval certainly forced the young clients of North American universities to wonder about what their future had in store for them. Could they anticipate long and drab lives or fiery extinction? And, on a more optimistic level, could they have some say in creating possible alternative futures of quality? In view of all this turmoil it is hardly surprising that an increasing number of university researchers/teachers have attempted to forecast the future for their students in university-level courses.

This attack on the future has come from a number of directions and is of varying quality. *Demography*, long interested in extrapolation (initially egged on by profit-minded insurance companies), continues to plod ever more wisely into the future. *Utopianists* (literary or design-oriented) reach back through a long tradition linked to the legends of primitive man and spin possible futures which criticize the present or prefigure a better world. This latter group are joined by the *science fiction* enthusiasts who seem to feel that all global ills can be solved by a 'technological fix', although increasingly they prefigure far-out psychological and behavioural technologies. Big business and big government, immensely serious, have inspired assiduous *technological forecasting* in the business administration schools; and latterly, brought up short by shifting social values (for example, environmental concern led to the cut-off in the supersonic transport programme and the near-stoppage of nuclear power plant construction in the United States), business and government have become increasingly involved with *technology assessment*—still in its infancy. *Educationalists*, who fancy that they hold the future in trust through their manipulations of the young, show spots of inventive futures techniques in education (as do others), in addition to 'futurizing' their course contents. *Sociologists* are among the strongest supporters of futures studies, at least among the younger social change/operational types intrigued or horrified by the *Brave New World* cleverly glimpsed by Huxley.[10] *Political scientists* are getting into the act increasingly and if all the members of the future-oriented Policy Studies Organization (80 programmes are run by members) were added to the political scientists offering futures courses, they would possibly be by far the most numerous social science group. I do not pretend that Table 1 which lists by discipline those giving futures courses who reported to the Mark III Survey, is a valid sampling of discipline/field interest—here are recorded merely those course-givers who fell into my net—but it may be instructive as to interest.

The techniques for learning/teaching futures studies rest quite obviously on what exists to learn/teach. It would appear that there is little that is excitingly fresh to be discovered (*a*) in reliable knowledge in the futures field, except in technological forecasting/technology assessment, systems dynamics and the policy sciences, (*b*) in new teaching techniques, or (*c*) in people-oriented experiential learning (except Syncon, a highly complex form of group dynamics). It should be noted that technological forecasting/technology assessment, systems

TABLE 1
Future course-givers, by discipline, reporting to the Mark III Survey

	1973–1974 Reports	Cumulative 1969–1974
Anthropology	4	9
Business administration	32	57
Computer science (modelling, etc.)	24	27
Demography	2	2
Economics	7	10
Education	28	40
English	5	10
Engineering	17	26
Geography	7	10
History	5	8
Humanities (overlap with English)	16	19
Law	3	4
Natural sciences	13	25
Political science	19	33
Psychology	3	3
Sociology	50	77
Theology	5	10
Urbanists (including architecture)	15	28
Miscellaneous	58	78
	313	476

Note: Science fiction, policy studies, peace studies are not included in these totals.

dynamics, and policy studies in general tend to eschew the label of 'futurism'. The standard methodological ploys that I explored in my 1970 and 1973 surveys are still with us, adding little to the twelve that Daniel Bell staked out a decade ago.[11] These standard methods may be conveniently grouped under five headings:

Type A: Intuitive methods ('genius forecasting') and codified intuition or Delphi; now enriched by cross-impact matrices;

Type B: Trend extrapolation;

Type C: Ideal state and/or alternative possible futures and scenarios;

Type D: Dynamic models;

Type E: Social (societal) indicators and Quality of Life (QOL) indices, which constitute an adjunct methodology crucial to the delivery of futures research.

The total evidence in hand indicates that in late 1974 all the standard futures research and teaching methodologies (conventional wisdom?) were still in use, with little firm evidence at hand to verify the reliability or heuristic value of any! The *validity gap* faces all futures study, it would seem. In five general directions, however, there appears to be some purposeful activity in the development of research/teaching methodology, at least in these significant areas: (*a*) technological forecasting/technological assessment; (*b*) general systems theory and systems analysis/dynamics, (*c*) Delphi/cross-impact analysis, (*d*) creativity and experiential learning, (*e*) policy studies. I shall examine the first four of these in turn.

(a) Technological forecasting (TF) and technology assessment (TA)

Long firmly based in advanced military hardware planning, TF is making increasing inroads into both governmental and corporate planning. No nation wants to be caught short by an enemy's gadget or by resource depletion (or resource cornering), although almost everyone seems to be caught sooner or later. No private corporation wishes to be lapped by a competitor's *nouvelle vague* product or crushed by a value shift (as supersonic transport was). The penalties for sleeping at the switch are national extinction and corporate bankruptcy. Inadequacies are painfully evident and painfully penalized. Thus the unemotional vigorous schools of business administration with their generally highly motivated students appear to be testing both the concrete and the general outlines of the future. A leading sage of technological forecasting berates all sociologists (through me) unceasingly and probably quite correctly: 'The important point to convey to the sociologists is that we are receiving continual pressure from industrialists to get them some help on predicting the interaction of social change with technological change. In other words, give them some insight on social forecasting' (private communication).

The brilliant paper by Richard L. Henshel and Leslie W. Kennedy[12] has shown that as our skills increase in these directions so will the complications resulting from self-defeating or self-fulfilling prophecies.

The rapid recent growth of interest in TA all over the globe and in trans-economic social (or societal) indicators, with sensitive Quality of Life indices being developed in Japan, Germany, England, and the USA, to cite but a few involved nations, bodes well for an eventual humanistic weighing of TF on a professionalized scale. The key node of this activity is the International Society for Technological Assessment in Washington, D.C.

There is in this whole TF/TA complex the seed of excellent futures research. With TF stemming from the graduate schools of business administration (originally from Harvard), it is hardly surprising that, in addition to some precise theorizing, the store of *case studies* of both TF and TA in operation is increasing. The finest way to test a method is to examine the results of using it in real-world situations (often neglected by social scientists, who serve usually as mere analysts, *not* operational planners). Actually TF/TA in my estimation will fall far short in practical results unless they are married to systems analysis/ systems dynamics and general systems theory.

(b) General systems theory and systems analysis/systems dynamics/modelling, etc.

While not necessarily so, basic systems analysis tends to be increasingly mathematical. Systems dynamics is clearly dependent on computer storage and manipulation. These rigorous, highly intellectual technologies seem to be at the very roots of the alternative futures game, and they seem of considerable interest to America's mathematical youth. Are we spawning an intellectual technocratic élite as guardians of esoteric processes? In any case, the game must be played; all teacher/scholars are increasingly involved with the computer— like it or not. The variables are too complex for anyone to test out mentally unaided by the planning–forcing techniques of systems analysis—generally computer based—and the game is too changeable in process for us not to include a continuing cybernetic feedback on the values, resources and organizational structure, in an endless chain reaction. Even *intuitive futurists* use mental models. Whether the sophisticated mathematical crutches already available will ever cope adequately with the infinite complexity of future reality is doubtful, but they are already better than the sages' guess-estimates. It is more than likely that all futurists will need to master this difficult bundle of technologies if they wish to produce more than 'hot air'. From the University of Pennsylvania's Wharton School of Business Administration came this nugget: 'I teach a seminar on forecasting methods. It's called "Long-Range Forecasting: From Crystal Ball to Computer".'

(c) Delphi techniques/cross-impact analysis

Based on lumps of 'genius forecasting', Delphi projection techniques in mini or maxi form edge into a great majority of courses in all fields. A clear externality of the use of students as 'experts' in Delphi operations is experiential learning through participation. But Delphi is more than that and the time is now ripe to evaluate its successes and failures after more than a decade of use in increasingly varied fields. The handy time span of a decade is available for testing the validity of its projections and reshaping the format of use so that it can do better in precise prognostication. The development of cross-impact analysis, into which leading Delphi practitioners have moved, indicates a formal awareness that 'everything is related to everything else'. One is reminded of the Kahn/Wiener fifteen-fold interlocking trends from the 1960s and of total environmental planning/holistic planning on the urban/regional/national scene, now almost two decades old. Obviously straight-line and complex extrapolation curves do fit into this cross-impact method. Since both Delphi and cross-impact analysis have clear (formal organizational, too) relations with TF/TA and with general systems theory, systems analysis, and systems dynamics, this complex of research thinking is forming a veritable powerhouse of methodology. The Rand Graduate Institute (RGI) had in 1973–1974 some twenty persons in a doctoral programme—each working in an area tied to a real-world current or past Rand project in policy studies—clearly a new departure in sophisticated extra-university future-oriented education. All futurists should learn to manage mathematical modelling with their left hand as they cleave ahead (hopefully) with their right guided by 'creative intellect' under a holistic systems theory. Clearly there is also a useful and fascinating teaching device in this bundle of skills.

(d) Experiential learning/creativity/scenarios

These enormously varied and vital activities, both in research and in teaching, can hardly be classed as 'hard' technology. But who can gainsay the basic importance of fresh creative insights—'more of the same' promises little. It would appear that a most unusual collection of tricks is available (essential?)

for the well-equipped futurist teacher. Mod and trendy instructors do not 'tell' students anything but serve hopefully as exciting resources, even models, for the neophyte to use in expanding up to his presumably ample God-given potential. Assuredly the educational structure is in ferment, as should be amply evident to readers of the ubiquitous newspaper (not averse in capitalist countries to inflating and to exploiting the spectacular over the drab norm), and quite unlike the pattern in 'socialist' lands where teaching is a solemn authoritative business. 'Doing something sticks in the consciousness better than reading about it' goes the new wisdom. Just how do you 'live' in the 5th century B.C. of Athens or 2000 A.D.? A mock-up could be fashioned, of course, and museums of the future growing in both Denmark and Minnesota are early attempts in the direction of 'living in the future'.

In a rough way, there appear to be two innovative poles of activity in futures studies, one at the hard or 'right' pole: TF/TA, policy sciences, corporate cramming courses of a high excellence and precision in non-standard time formats. In the middle, there are free educational structures marrying futures orientation with 'futurist' educational restructuring and open course management. At the 'left' or soft pole are the intentional communities and the full gamut of often curious experiential learning experiences, as well as attempts at fostering intellectual creativity.

There is a hodge-podge of new directions in this last rubric, many left of centre, difficult to conceptualize in any adequate fashion. Futurist teachers tend to be innovative and iconoclastic, interdisciplinary, and by definition probers of the unknown—not always in any way that could be called planned by any stretch of the imagination. Consciously or unconsciously they do covertly or overtly push for systems breaks. The gamut of educational 'gimmicks' used to stir up client students, presumably to foster creativity as well as culture/future shock, seems endless: simulations; telephone interviews; movies; TV scripts; participatory planning; poetry readings; formation of a collective; expressive dancing; technological cum group-think jamborees such as Syncon and the World Game; a voodoo experience; scenario building/intentional communes for future living; 'happenings'; confrontation/encounter sessions; role-playing; modelling; brain-storming; free-form courses; nature worship; a futures fair; a personal life history projection; visits to 'futuristic' locations such as California; videotapes; survival training and solos; individual obituaries. In my ongoing survey I shall continue to record, often with amazement, the things people do in attempting to make other people think! If such an assault did not unsettle the recipient, it would be surprising, but what does this *ersatz* and slanted experience actually add up to? Obviously all courses do not employ all techniques. But is 'creativity' also a product of such bustle? Do glorious and valuable thoughts emerge—thoughts which are so much needed before rigorous testing and experimentation if viable alternative human futures are to be created for man? In my surveys, no answer has as yet been revealed. In short, there is little or no evidence of any sophisticated controlled development of creativity—a serious gap. An interesting people-involving Open University (England) course, 'Art and Environment', planned to start in 1976, exemplifies neatly the neo-populist faith in the untapped abilities of the common man and exemplifies also certain participatory futures-teaching techniques as well as content.

The impact of futures studies on two important professional graduate fields in the United States can be seen in two courses. The first example is the attempt, at Syracuse University's respected Maxwell Graduate School of Citizenship and Public Affairs in 1973–1974, to link administrative techniques with insight into the future in a course on 'Post-industrial administration and social change'; the second is a similar venture made in a seminar on 'Planning for alternative possible urban futures' offered at Harvard's Graduate School of Design, Department of City and Regional Planning, in the autumn of 1974. Both courses seem to indicate that, although a reasonable *tour d'horizon* can be made in which futures studies are related to existing professional training, little more than that can be expected within the short span of a few months. It proved heartening in the Harvard case to have pre-professionals—with so much operant knowledge to digest in so short a time—still eager for mind-stretching in a futures direction. The urbanists have finally come to future life, heralded by William Ewald's massive editorial job[13,14,15] for the American Institute of Planners—an organization curiously long dormant in the face of the rather obvious fact that at least the physical works of urban planners live long into the future (see the Roman colosseum). BART, San Francisco's Bay Area Rapid Transport System, will undoubtedly be around in 2075, barring a MIRV barrage. Portions of London's Underground were laid out for steam trains in the 1840s! *The California Plan Tomorrow: The Future is Now*[16] offers a California One scenario in which the quality of life becomes seriously impaired before 2000, and a California Two 'which makes possible person fulfillment within an amenable environment'—one hopes! *Hawaii 2000*[17] chronicles the wide participatory planning 'five-ring,' multi-media drive of that state towards human futures, backed heavily by the State Government and the State University, offering at least six 'alternative Hawaiis'. *Inventing the Future Memphis*, a lively effort by Southwestern University's Center for Alternative Futures in that city, has struggled ahead and is now getting ever-better results in public education and realization. Joining *Tomorrow's London* are *Washington 2000*, *Seattle 2000*, and *Atlanta 2000*; the latter city, largely influenced by the private sector, is rapidly building a spectacular and commercially outstanding central city. Is the Quality of Life (QOL) quotient quite so highly served as the profit motive in this spectacular central business district with 'futuristic' glassed construction of high rise and high-cost commercial and transient hotel recreational facilities?

A significant development is the application of Forrester's urban dynamics to the real city of Lowell, Massachusetts, a decaying manufacturing city from the early nineteenth century, buffeted by technology shifts and the movement of the textile industry first to the South and latterly out of the United States.[18] A team from the MIT System Dynamics Center for the past three years has worked closely with the city officialdom and people and, using a computerized mathematical dynamics model as a heuristic device, has upgraded community decision-making in four key directions: (a) values for the future city, (b) final land use (c) property tax and (d) housing policy.

What are the results of this third iteration of my survey of futures courses? Specifically, analysis of the 300 courses collected by the standard questionnaire in 1973–1974 revealed, among other things, these five salient conclusions:

(1) Futures studies *per se* have grown steadily but not spectacularly as university-level courses both at the undergraduate and graduate levels. Other fields, not labelled 'futurism', but with a clear future-orientation (such as: environment/ecology; TF/TA; long-range planning; policy sciences; peace studies; general systems theory; systems analysis and dynamics; even science fiction; black studies and women's studies) appear to have increased more rapidly than futures studies in North America.

(2) The population of course-givers in 'pure' futures studies seems to fall into a sieve from which some old hands drop out each year, to be replenished by a fresh stream of generally young recruits. This suggests the somewhat negative present intellectual image of futurism (an identity crisis?)—an image perhaps derived from its 'pop' manifestations or from disillusionment with its success at reliable forecasting and immediate delivery. It also indicates clearly the necessity of defining the futures field, of upgrading training in the relatively slight corpus of reliable knowledge (including embryonic theory) of futures study, and of stepping up the enlistment and development of fresh young minds *already grounded solidly in some recognized discipline or field*. European universities appear, from inadequate evidence at hand and with the possible exception of technological forecasting and general systems analysis/ mathematical modelling, to have approached futures studies much more gingerly.

(3) Societal forecasting, and especially values forecasting based on valid sociocultural change theory, is the weakest aspect of the entire futures com-

plex. It is to be hoped that experienced anthropological and sociological researchers will contribute here eventually.

(4) Futurizing the content and point of view of existing solid courses in recognized fields and disciplines seems the most valid operational strategy for extending futures studies for the moment. Many physical scientists burned by the now revealed diseconomies of atomic skills do this. Increasingly alert researchers/teachers in varied fields glance 'over their shoulder at the on-rushing future', as do many of their rather pessimistic young clients. This is especially true for those dealing with new medical technologies.

(5) In my personal estimation, technological forecasting for big business and big government is the most highly motivated and successful research-oriented complex on the American and Canadian scene—and has the best methodologists apart from the modellers and the users of cross-impact matrices. Brought up short by value shifts, the TF fraternity is flailing about (with some new environmentalist recruits) in technology assessment. Many of these people tend to see 'technology' much too narrowly, failing to grasp that there are also (feeble, admittedly) societal and behavioural technologies based on the social and behavioural sciences. And that all basic science and the resultant technologies subsist on a burgeoning intellectual technology resting heavily on the 'gadget' assistance of the computer.

Finally, are there further tentative insights that can be drawn from my six years of research in futures' teaching? Here are three:

(1) The folders on 500 course-givers, filling six file drawers, are now too numerous to be handled adequately by a one-person 'team'; a much more rigorous delving is needed into the realities of what actually goes on, rather than what respondents state happens. Questionnaires have clear limitations; follow-up is most necessary. The coverage of the non-North American experience is much too feeble. Data storage and retrieval is inadequate and the detailed interrelationships and interconnections must be subjected to a much more rigorous analysis than one individual's resources in time, energy and expertise permit. Futurism and futurists do seem stuck on a developmental plateau. To these ends a search has been instituted for a powerful research group, public or private, profit or non-profit, who could build on my shoulders.

(2) The future, hanging ominously or looming in an excitingly challenging fashion ahead, is too crucial to be left to amateurs, part-time 'genius forecasters', woolly-headed visionaries (however well meaning), and publicity seekers. The uses made of futures studies by the national governments of France,[19] Sweden[20] and the Netherlands,[21] and the location of these futures bureaus (at least as early warning systems or look-out stations) close to central decision-making, are facts emphasizing that alternative national futures can

possibly be removed from control by the 'hand of God' or conversely from control by capitalism's beloved invisible hand.

(3) Futures studies must link up as a subset with convoluted policy studies or advanced delivery systems[22] if human civilization is to survive or possibly even continue to flourish. If there is to be a systems break in the next decades, no doubt futures studies could serve as a helpful bridge over that chasm. The universities and other types of less traditional learning/teaching centres (with or without walls) have a central role in training societies and their leaders for these alternative *futuribles* (possible futures). It is unimportant whether future-oriented learning is entitled 'futures studies' or not, so long as a man-centred, holistic, operational, long-range, flexible planning effort is forwarded.

Discussion

Waddington: One of the great questions facing us at this meeting is whether we should be teaching about the future as a whole, with everything brought into it, or whether specialists should give specialist courses that look a bit into the future of a particular specialty. For instance, until two years ago the energy experts in the United States were forecasting that the US would consume four times the current amount of petroleum by the year 2000. That doesn't look very convincing if we take into account considerations other than those concerned only with the use of energy. In the whole subject of looking into the future within a specialty, how far can we get without bumping into the future in other specialties? Can we find a way of looking at the futures of all of them together?

Platt: The question is illustrated by the fact that until a year or so ago, demographers and United Nations forecasters repeatedly based their forecasts for world population on expected numbers of children, or on expected dates for the 'demographic transition' to fewer births, totally ignoring factors such as food and resources. But it is only when food and resources are put into the equations formally, or into the thinking, that we begin to see certain limits which have no historical precedents. Instead of forecasts of 7000 million or 12 000 million people after the year 2000, we then suddenly come up with numbers like 5000 or 5500 million people by the turn of the century, with perhaps 1000 million people dying of starvation between now and then. The *Limits to Growth* forecast by Meadows and others in 1972 showed, I think for the first time, that the population would necessarily be a substantially lower number; and this was because they took into account the interaction of these other factors.[23]

Dror: Professor Eldredge's work is one of the most hopeful signs of futures studies. Someone is trying to do some self-evaluation, which is unusual.

Futures-studies teaching faces six main problems or choices. First, many futures classes are based not on any research but only on transferring ideas and on intellectual resources which themselves are still underdeveloped. The relationship between teaching and research is a symptom of the main dilemma of where the dividing lines lie in futures studies. Second, there is too much emphasis on utopian or anti-utopian images of the future, and too little on feasibility and on lines of continuity—on how past and present evolve into one of several alternative futures. Third, in many programmes we do not know how value sensitivity should be handled—that is, how we can achieve clinical detachment towards a subject with which we feel highly emotionally involved. This causes great difficulties, especially with young students who feel very agitated about problems which nevertheless have to be treated on an intellectual level. Fourth, how can we convey a real sense of the complexity of things in a short undergraduate course lasting one year? The danger is that we may sell an over-simple view of reality hidden behind some complexity of words. Fifth, the need for a real interdisciplinary basis for futures studies has to be balanced against the ease of basing a university course on single teachers. Sixth, how can we sensitize students to the problems of the future when they are concentrating on working in depth in their specific fields of study? And how can we, at the same time, prepare futures studies professionals? Also—and this is a fundamental fault which sums up some of my main points—a large number of the futures courses represented in Professor Eldredge's excellent surveys suffer from a serious disease which I call 'well-intentioned naiveté'. What is really needed is a strong dose of sophistication.

Valaskakis: Professor Eldredge's surveys are perhaps too inclusive. It could be argued that all science is really involved with some kind of prediction or other. The distinction I would make between futures studies *per se* and science in general is the long-term versus short-term orientation. This is not just a question of time but also one of approach. The 'long term' is a period long enough to provide for structural change, and this structural change can only be perceived in an interdisciplinary fashion. That is why I disagree with Eldredge's point that futures studies should be considered as part of policy studies. I would say that policy studies should be part of futures studies, the latter being a much larger concept which includes value reorientations, value forecasting and definitions of utopias (in the non-pejorative sense of utopia). A specialized monodisciplinary approach would not be suitable for futures studies *per se*. It may be marginally suitable to have a futures orientation in existing disciplines but this does not go very far.

Eldredge: I probably didn't manage to make myself as clear as I should have in the time available for my presentation. In fact, I am a holistic planner. I do not think that there is just one road into the future, or that there is only one discipline that knows it. I was one of those in the US who played a part in switching urban planning away from physical planning into societal planning as well. Almost all the main American urban planning schools are run now by social scientists, not by physical designers. Futures studies have developed in a haphazard way in most universities, where they now exist with originators and recruits from a great variety of backgrounds. I am quite aware that as a long-term strategy a highly sophisticated and holistic futures operation should be organized in various centres. A number of excellent schools of public adminis-tration, at Syracuse, Berkeley, Harvard and to a certain extent MIT, are keenly interested in the longer-term futures orientation.

Of course, being a good academic, I could nitpick with Dr Valaskakis im-mediately and say that it is not just a matter of long term and short term, but that there is also a medium term. He is implying that we are in a systems break; in my paper I said that almost all futurists are aware that we may be at one of the great watersheds of history. My whole background has been inter-disciplinary and I see that in futures studies the question is whether we should turn a natural scientist into a futurist or a futurist into a natural scientist. Should we turn a social scientist into a futurist, or vice versa? Should we make a philosopher into a futurist, or vice versa? I rather lean towards 'futurizing' an existing scientist, physical or social. I used to say, simplistically, in urban studies, that any 'damn fool' can make a plan, but that then one has to put the plan into operation in a cybernetic way. The old planning formula is: goals, resources, alternative plans, the plan, operations. Then cybernetically goals change, resources change, the plan changes and so on. I am not thinking of policy studies as a tool but as part of the cybernetic system, with values and futures all part of it and with policy studies/'wise' decision-making as the important end to which futures studies could truly contribute.

References cited

1   ELDREDGE, H. WENTWORTH (1970) Education for futurism in the United States. *Technolog-ical Forecasting and Social Change, 2*, 133–148
2   ELDREDGE, H. WENTWORTH (1972) A Mark II Survey and critique of future research teaching in North America. *Technological Forecasting and Social Change, 4*, 387–407
3   ELDREDGE, H. WENTWORTH (1974) A Mark III report on university education in futures study. *Fields Within Fields*, December
4   PADDOCK, W. & PADDOCK, P. (1967) *Famine, 1975*, Little, Brown, Boston, Mass.
5   EHRLICH, PAUL R. (1968) *The Population Bomb*, Ballantine Books, New York

[6] HARDIN, GARRETT (1968) The tragedy of the commons. *Science (Wash. D.C.) 162*, 1243–48

[7] GREENE, WADE (1975) Triage: who shall be fed? Who shall starve? *The New York Times Magazine*, January 5

[8] VACCA, ROBERTO (1973) *The Coming Dark Age*, Doubleday, New York

[9] HEILBRONER, ROBERT L. (1974) *An Inquiry into the Human Prospect*. Norton, New York

[10] HUXLEY, ALDOUS (1932) *Brave New World*, Doubleday, Doran, Garden City, N.Y.

[11] BELL, DANIEL (1964) Twelve modes of prediction—a preliminary sorting of approaches in the social sciences. *Daedalus 93* (Summer), 845–880

[12] HENSHEL, R. L. & KENNEDY, L. W. (1973) Self-altering prophecies: consequences for the feasibility of social prediction. *General Systems, 18*, 119–126

[13] EWALD, WILLIAM R. (ed.) (1967) *Environment for Man: The Next Fifty Years*, Indiana University Press, Bloomington, Indiana

[14] EWALD, WILLIAM R. (1968) *Environment and Policy: The Next Fifty Years*, Indiana University Press, Bloomington, Indiana

[15] EWALD, WILLIAM R. (1968) *Environment and Change: The Next Fifty Years*, Indiana University Press, Bloomington, Indiana

[16] HELLER, ALFRED (ed.) (1972) *The California Plan Tomorrow*, William Kaufmann, Los Altos, California

[17] CHAPLIN, G. & PAIGE, G. D. (1973) *Hawaii 2000*, University Press of Hawaii, Honolulu

[18] SCHROEDER, WALTER W., III (1974) *Urban Dynamics in Lowell*, MIT Urban Dynamics Group, Cambridge, Mass.

[19] CAZES, BERNARD (1974) L'utilisation des études à long terme dans la planification française. *Consommation—Annales De Crédoc*, No. 2, 63–71

[20] ROYAL MINISTRY FOR FOREIGN AFFAIRS AND THE SECRETARIAT FOR FUTURE STUDIES (1974) *To Choose a Future*, Norstedt, Stockholm

[21] NETHERLANDS PARLIAMENT (1973) Law of October 26, 1973 establishing the Scientific Council for Government Policy in the Netherlands. An informal translation. Session 1973–1974–12668 Netherlands Parliament Royal Message No. 1 Bill No. 2

[22] DROR, YEHEZKEL (1971) *Design for Policy Sciences*, American Elsevier, New York

[23] MEADOWS, DONELLA H., MEADOWS, DENNIS L., RANDERS, JØRGEN & BEHRENS, WILLIAM W., III (1972) *The Limits to Growth*, Universe, New York; Earth Island, London

A university experiment in Sweden

KARL-ERIK ERIKSSON and ANDERS LUNDBERG

Centre for Interdisciplinary Studies of the Human Condition, and Institute of Theoretical Physics and Department of Physiology, University of Göteborg, Sweden

Abstract   The Centre for Interdisciplinary Studies of the Human Condition in Göteborg, Sweden, is an official university institution which has existed for almost three years. It functions as a forum for interdisciplinary contacts within the university, mainly in relation to serious problems of a global nature. Membership is open to research workers, teachers and graduate students, and a total of 400 people have joined. Lectures and seminars are sponsored on topics of interest to many disciplines, and the Centre has arranged a number of interdisciplinary undergraduate and graduate training courses which are recognized by the university. Members of the Centre participate in problem-oriented interdisciplinary study groups and the results are usually summarized in reports which are distributed to all members of the Centre. One of the aims of the Centre is to contribute to the factual basis for the process of public opinion formation and for decision-making at different levels in the society. For this purpose many members engage in *external* activity, often utilizing material from the reports from study groups.

This external activity has grown rapidly and its present scale has revealed a desire in society for contact with the universities which previously has not been fully recognized in our country. According to our experience the internal inter-disciplinary work provides a good platform for the external activity.

The Centre depends almost entirely on the voluntary spare-time work of people employed in teaching and research in specialized disciplines.

We must accept that in recent decades there has been a major shift in the public view of science. Many people, particularly the young, are becoming increasingly disillusioned with it. It seems to have lost some of its prestige, and the confidence entrusted in it as a tool for ensuring the progress of mankind seems to be on the wane. This may appear rather surprising to many members of the scientific community, since our time has witnessed so much important progress in science, including a large number of advances of great benefit to man. Nevertheless, there seems to be a spreading public view that science is almost powerless in relation to the major problems facing society. Some even feel that these problems have their origin in scientific and technological advances. This lack of trust in science is in striking contrast to the confidence it enjoyed during the post-war period only twenty-five years ago. At that time few had any doubt that it was a major tool for ensuring progress in western countries ravaged by the war, as well as in underdeveloped countries. Now we are witnessing a spreading disenchantment with what many consider a runaway technology, and even a growing concern for the long-range survival of the human species. Inequality between the rich and poor halves of the world, overpopulation and mass starvation, depletion of natural resources, interference with the balance of the biosphere, and destruction of the environment are some of the components in what is now described as the global crisis.

Since the crisis is at least in part a result of scientific progress, the reaction against science is not surprising. Yet we believe that this reaction is both irrational and temporary. The realization that science has given enormous power to man has created a shock, but if we have any rationality left we shall soon realize that science is of the foremost importance if we are to achieve a solution to man's problems. Science has indeed already played an important role in identifying and measuring the threats which man is facing.

But how can science contribute when the main problem is not science itself but the utilization of scientific results, over which the scientists can exert little influence? The main problem seems to be that society does not have the ethics and the politics to match science and technology. Neither nationally nor internationally do we have governing agencies, political or administrative, which are equipped to face the serious long-term problems. Governments have their hands full, staggering from one crisis to another. Unemployment, social unrest, economic difficulties, etc., are familiar issues requiring remedies which at best—if provided—are only temporary. There is little energy and time left for the fundamental long-term problems, and in any case our political systems—whether parliamentarian or authoritarian—are fit to cope mainly with short-term problems.

If the presentation of global problems given above is correct, it follows that 'the innocence of academic science cannot be regained'.[1] The social responsibility of the scientist—which so tormented the atomic physicists after the Hiroshima bomb—has now become a major concern for a growing number of the scientific community. It concerns above all the academic scientist, since he enjoys a relatively high degree of independence. Chomsky[2] has formulated his views in this respect as follows:

'The university should be a center for radical social inquiry, as it is already a center for what might be called "radical inquiry" in the pure sciences.

It should loosen its "institutional forms" even further, to permit a richer variety of work and study and experimentation and should provide a home for the free intellectual, for the social critic, for the irreverent and radical thinking that is desperately needed if we are to escape from the dismal reality that threatens to overwhelm us'.

The present structure of our universities makes it hard to imagine how the task envisaged by Chomsky should be carried out. The main difficulty is probably the increasing degree of specialization which has been, is and will remain necessary for the production of new knowledge. Although there are some notable examples of individual scientists who applied their knowledge to man's situation,[3,4,5] the scientist's specialization makes it difficult for him to function socially. There is the danger that his outlook is too narrow, so that his attention becomes focused on only one issue of a complex problem. Unfortunately narrowness is sometimes also coupled with specialist arrogance. It is almost a truism to state that virtually all problems facing man and society have many facets and require contributions from many sciences for their solution. And yet who is trying today to make a synthesis of the contributions from the different disciplines? Precious few attempts are being made in the scientific communities themselves. Hence the executive branches of government and industry are left to find their own way in the bewildering stream of information flowing from the scientific institutions. It seems to us that the synthesis of knowledge must become the responsibility of the universities to a much larger extent than is the case at present. Such a synthesis requires close interdisciplinary contacts which may widen the outlook of the scientist by forcing him to view his own field and results in the perspective of knowledge contributed by other disciplines.

If research results are digested in this way they will become more accessible to society than at present. An even more important effect of such interdisciplinary contacts may be to catalyse individual concerned scientists into action. By himself the scientist may be powerless and frustrated, but the combined knowledge of many disciplines may give him a platform from which social action will be more meaningful.

In recent years, there have been many demands for increased interdisciplinary contacts and research and even recommendations for new institutional forms.[6] At the University of Göteborg we have a forum for interdisciplinary contact called the Centre for Interdisciplinary Studies of the Human Condition. Since the Centre has now been in action for almost three years an account of how it came into being and how it operates may be of interest here.

In October 1971, seriously concerned by the increasingly negative effects of specialization, some members of the Faculty of Mathematics and Natural

Science at the University of Göteborg started an integrative science course for their graduate students. The graduate level was chosen for two reasons. First, there is considerably more freedom to introduce new contents in the curriculum at the graduate level than at the undergraduate level. Second, graduate students are more experienced and can contribute relevant information from their own fields.

The course was called 'The humanistic–scientific picture of the world'. The term 'humanistic' was chosen to emphasize an outlook paying due respect to man and human society. This course met with an unexpectedly vivid interest. About ninety students entered the course when it began. Very soon thirty graduate students of medicine also entered the course. With its 120 students this was probably the biggest graduate course ever given in Sweden.

Outside the lecture hours the students met in smaller interdisciplinary groups for studies centred around topics freely chosen by themselves. The written reports produced by these groups turned out to be of high quality. Almost all of them dealt with serious problems of a global nature. When the course ended, in February 1972, a statement based on the group reports was agreed upon and signed by a large majority of the participants. A few days later this statement was published in *Dagens Nyheter*, the largest daily newspaper in Sweden.

A few weeks later a small conference was held to which all faculties and all graduate students of the university were invited. At this conference the idea of an interdisciplinary centre* was put forward. During the spring of 1972 the Centre for Interdisciplinary Studies of the Human Condition was established. According to its charter *the aims of the Centre* are

— to promote interdisciplinary research and training as well as debate and exchange of information;
— to cooperate with different disciplines in the search for new knowledge and in restructuring knowledge already gained;
— to provide a better factual basis for the process of opinion formation and for decision-making at different levels in society.

In order to realize these aims the work of the Centre will be directed towards

— studies of the historical development of the sciences and their theoretical foundations;
— a continuous effort to build a scientifically founded picture of the world;
— analyses of the global situation of man on the basis of humanistic values.

---

* In Swedish university terminology 'Centre' is used to denote an organization for collaboration between departments.

The number of members joining the Centre soon reached 300, mainly from the University of Göteborg and the Chalmers Institute of Technology in Göteborg, but also scholars from other universities, as well as writers, journalists, librarians and administrators. The number of members now exceeds 400. The university has accepted the Centre as a university institution and provides adequate premises and an annual budget, including the salary for one secretary. The Centre is directly responsible to the university council. So far the Centre has arranged a fair number of public lectures. Series of seminars on different topics have been held for members. Members also meet in small study groups or project groups which present their results in seminars and written reports.

The Board of the Centre has appointed several committees to decentralize its many functions. There are committees for planning futures courses, for contacts with the mass media, for library matters, for editorial work, etc. *Ad hoc* committees are often formed to handle specific problems or recommend proper action.

One basic activity of the Centre has continued to be graduate courses of general interest. The courses are recognized by the university and are financed through special university grants. During this academic year (1974–1975) three graduate courses are being given: first, a new version of the 'world picture' course open to students from all faculties; second, a course on 'Malnutrition in developing countries—social, economic, political and medical aspects'; third, a course on the 'Popularization of scientific knowledge'. Since the 'world picture' course this time does not have to meet an accumulated need, as it did in the first course, the number of students is now considerably lower. However, the general interest in the Centre's interdisciplinary courses still remains quite large. During autumn 1974 a course in *human ecology*, open to undergraduate students, was introduced and has met with a lively interest. This course includes not only topics from the natural and social sciences but also a substantial contribution from the humanities.

Starting this academic year, Georg Borgström, professor of food technology and economic geography at the University of Michigan, is attached to the Centre on a part-time basis. Professor Borgström is an internationally renowned expert on the global food problem who has written a number of widely-read popular books in this field. In March 1975 he is to give a series of lectures on the three recent (1974) United Nations conferences in Caracas, Bucharest and Rome.

The Centre has not yet had any capacity for research in the usual sense of this word. However, the constant ambition in the Centre to combine and to restructure available knowledge has influenced the work of some university institutions and has led to definite plans for interdisciplinary research projects.

Two projects concern the planning of a housing area according to ecologically and socially sound principles, using available scientific, technical and practical knowledge. From such studies we hope to be able to assess human needs for land, energy, water, and various materials in a well-planned technically advanced community.

Work in study groups and project groups has led to conferences. So far the Centre has organized five conferences:

(1) In September 1972 a conference was held with journalists on the selection and presentation of scientific information to the general public.

(2) A conference with members of the Swedish parliament in June 1973 discussed economic growth from an interdisciplinary perspective. This conference constituted a first and very valuable contact with national politicians.

(3) In January 1974 artists and writers were invited to a conference on 'Life quality and cultural patterns'. Ways of obtaining contacts and collaboration between scientists and artists were discussed at this conference. Such collaboration may become a source of inspiration for both categories and lead to new forms of cultural activities.

(4) In March 1974 a second conference was held with members of parliament, this time devoted to energy and arranged in collaboration with the Swedish Society of Members of Parliament and Scientists. The resulting report was called 'Energy—not only a technical issue', which illustrates the wish of the Centre to broaden a debate that runs the risk of becoming dangerously narrow.

(5) Our latest conference, in August 1974, dealt with research policies and was arranged by the Centre in collaboration with the Secretariat for Future Studies under the Prime Minister's office. Representatives from the universities and research councils as well as from government and higher administration participated. The title of the conference was 'The planning of research in the face of an uncertain future'. Several problems of vital importance to the role of the university in the society were subject to lively—and at times quite penetrating—discussion.

Sweden prepares for reforms through officially appointed commissions of inquiry. We have the unique system of circulating the reports of such commissions to various bodies in society for their opinion and comment *before* they are brought to parliament. On a number of occasions the Board of the Centre has submitted its comments on such reports. Many members have been active in preparatory work for such comments.

As the Centre is the only institution in the university—and in some sense in the whole country—with truly interdisciplinary ambitions and with the ambition of being available to society at large, the Centre has been overwhelmed by an enormous demand for seminars and lectures, for articles in newspapers and journals, for participation in public debates and for expert opinions. Our most important external activity is directed to school teachers. We provide lecturers for meetings lasting one to three days, which are scheduled in the regional teachers' training programmes. The Centre has also planned and participated in study groups within the previously mentioned society for collaboration between scientists and members of parliament. Some local study groups in different parts of the country are working in constant contact with the Centre and can be assisted when needed.

Our capacity is not sufficient to satisfy all the demands made on the Centre. Yet a large number of members are active, not only in the internal work of the Centre but also in the external services for society at large.

In the general discussion concerning the country's future energy policy, members of the Centre have participated actively. One conference on energy has been mentioned already. Some ten members of the Centre have contributed to hearings arranged by the government's Energy Council, which has the Prime Minister as its chairman.

To keep members informed about the various internal and external activities of the Centre a monthly bulletin is issued. Besides announcing forthcoming events it also includes progress reports from study groups, travel reports, bibliographical notes and sometimes short papers on topics of common interest. It is possible for people outside the Centre to subscribe to the bulletin and the number of such subscribers is rising. The total circulation is now 1100.

Summarizing the experience from almost three years of activity in the Centre for Interdisciplinary Studies, we may state that it has contributed towards a change in our university environment. The possibility for easy contact with colleagues from other fields represents a break with specialization which has increasingly isolated representatives of different fields from each other. We do not know whether this lack of contact is more marked in Sweden than in other countries, but it has certainly been very marked here. The competition for meagre resources within a tight budget may even create some animosity between disciplines: many scientists certainly have a rather childish feeling of prestige regarding their own subject. To meet colleagues from entirely different fields for discussion of common problems, and to share teaching duties in problem-oriented interdisciplinary courses, has been a useful and intellectually stimulating experience for many of us. Joint appearances in external activities and conferences with politicians and administrators have contributed to a feeling of unity amongst us. We do not know whether it has made us more humble but two other effects are clearly evident. First, we have been forced to abandon our specialist jargon which is a great barrier to the exchange of thoughts, and one that is difficult to overcome. Second, it has given us an opportunity to view our own special field from a new angle. Consciously or unconsciously, we are all bound by internal scientific traditions, often specific to each field. It is useful to reflect from another perspective on the criteria which guide us in the daily routine of research and teaching, and to view them in the light of their possible impact on society. It is as yet difficult to know what effect, if any, these interdisciplinary contacts will have on research in specialized fields. We wish to make it clear that so far most members of the Centre do not participate in interdisciplinary research. For all except a few of those who have shared in the limited research referred to above, it has been a part-time activity.

The most significant impact of the Centre has probably been its function as a platform for external contacts. As an almost automatic result of the internal problem-oriented interdisciplinary work there were contacts with individuals and organizations outside the university who were interested in the same problems. As a result we have today an extensive network of contacts which is unique in our country. When word spread about the existence of our organization, we were approached from different quarters with requests for information, advice, assistance or collaboration. These requests revealed that society had a need for contact with the universities—a need which had not previously been paid due attention. Through our organization we can now easily channel a request to an appropriate addressee or call on a group of members if the issue, as is usually the case, has interdisciplinary aspects. If this work has had some success it is probably due to the preparatory work in seminars and study groups which has trained the members to use everyday language, and which has perhaps broadened them by counteracting some of the negative effects of specialization.

Members who participate in this external activity do so because of their belief that the universities should be of more direct use to society, and in most cases also because they have a strong belief that present society needs radical long-term changes which cannot be brought about without an enlightened public opinion. When participating in the public debate with articles in newspapers, or in television or radio broadcasts, each member expresses his own views. The Centre as such has no opinion of its own. However, members are usually introduced as belonging to the Centre for Interdisciplinary Studies and since most members who appear in public hold similar opinions on serious global problems the public may have got the erroneous impression that opinion within the organization is unanimous. However, the Centre should function as a forum for debate and naturally there are considerable differences of opinion among members. For example, while many members are very concerned about Sweden's nuclear power programme—which, measured by expenditure per head of population, is the most ambitious in the world—there are some strong proponents of nuclear energy. On some topics the Centre has issued statements as an organization. The decision is then taken by the Board. The plenary meeting has sometimes exercised its power of criticizing the Board. Our policy in this matter is currently under discussion.

Our activity during the last three years has been an interesting university experiment. It is now time to raise two questions. Should such an activity as ours become an integrated part of life in the university? If so, how can it be maintained? Let us consider the second question first. Opposing forces may be *external*, coming from those bodies on which the universities ultimately depend for funds and for the maintenance of their relatively independent status, but they may also be *internal*, coming from within the university and the scientific community itself. On festival occasions politicians and administrators may talk about the freedom of the universities and urge them to use this freedom for 'radical social inquiry'. But how will they react if such an inquiry yields results contrary to their own convictions and recommends lines of action quite contrary to their own plans? It would be presumptuous to claim that the impact of the Centre for Interdisciplinary Studies of the Human Condition has been so strong in our society that this problem has become a reality. Nevertheless we must keep it in mind. So far, we have met with benevolence and been encouraged by higher authorities in charge of university affairs. Special requests from the Centre for (modest) grants to arrange conferences or to meet occasional emergencies have been promptly satisfied outside the regular budget of the universities. On the whole our work has also been favourably viewed by the mass media: the press, radio and television have all been attentive.

It is interesting to note that our activity is rather in line with some of the recommendations in a report from a government committee. Some years ago the government appointed a committee (or perhaps rather a working party) to enquire into questions related to 'Studies in the future' in Sweden. Their report (abbreviated version in English: 'To choose a future')[7] deals partly with technical questions related to planning but a major part is devoted to the impact of the serious global situation on long-range planning in Sweden. They emphasize the long-range significance of basic research and they contrast 'the precarious state of university research with the buoyant growth that has infused certain investigative and planning functions among government agencies as well as manufacturing firms and trade associations'.

The authors of the report recommend that special support should be given to three new types of research activities:

(*1*) *Critical research*, implying research that challenges or denies the values and priorities that actually govern the direction of planning. In this connection we quote from the report: 'A free society is obliged to ensure that critical research stands a fair chance of working, and it stands to reason that universities make the forum where such research is most readily accommodated'.

(*2*) *Alternative planning*, implying an elaboration of Sweden's investigation-by-commission system. Although the reports by the government commissions are ambitious and often extremely thorough and detailed, they rarely give more than one concretely worked-out proposal. Accordingly they are often unsatisfactory when the issues involved are long-range and they 'afford a pretty frail foundation on which to nurture debate of real long-term alternatives'. The authors of 'To choose a future' propose that when a 'heavy' government commission is appointed, funds should be set aside to finance a small number of critical enquiries into the same problem at the same time.

(*3*) *Long-term motivated basic research*, coming close to autonomous basic research but related to the future according to certain criteria.

The government has adopted the last of the three proposals and parliament has now given funds for 'long-term motivated basic research'. A portion of these funds is at the disposal of the Secretariat for Future Studies directly under the Prime Minister's office; another portion is administered by a more independent committee.

So far our government has not taken any decision with regard to funds for 'critical research' or 'alternative planning'. But the very fact that they were recommended in an official report may have contributed to legitimizing the activities of the Centre for Interdisciplinary Studies. In the report 'To choose a future' the authors also call for external university activity. They write: 'Scientists and scholars the world over, acting as enlighteners, warners and enthusiasts, have been highly instrumental in the moulding of public opinion... this vital critical function must prevail'.[7] They recommend more active contact with the mass media and with the system of voluntary public adult education. Clearly the work in our Centre is well in line with these recommendations.

Let us now consider internal opposition from within the university. Chomsky ends his essay on 'The role of the university in a time of crisis' by stating that one barrier to serious reform and innovation will be 'the fear of the faculty that its security and authority, its guild structure, will be threatened'.[2] So far our activity has been strongly supported by the council of our university. There is little doubt that some faculty members dislike it and find it incompatible with academic dignity and the status of science. So far they have not found the time opportune for voicing their criticism openly—it appears as a general reluctance, perhaps tinged with some contempt. Since the opposition is silent we do not know its extent. In this connection it is relevant to point out that so far we have drawn very little on the monetary resources of the university. All members have their main obligation to teaching and research in their specialized disciplines. A core of highly motivated members has been the driving force, but the results achieved depend mainly on the spare-time work of a large number of members. Nevertheless it is clear that in many cases these activities have 'interfered' with research in the specialized disciplines, because devoted scientists have no spare time. However, a conflict may appear if we request a larger share of the funds available to the university. For different motives powerful specialist interests may then react,[8] and this is not difficult to understand at a time when many departments are desperately short of funds for staff appointments and when resources for basic research generally are shrinking.

It is strange that the reaction against science to which we referred at the beginning of this paper has hit mainly the universities, while other research bodies continue to flourish. Those research bodies, created for direct service to society, government or industry, are often highly specialized. They may be well suited to dealing with short-term problems arising in each sector of society, but hardly to dealing with the incredibly complex long-term problems related to man's future.

The university has not only an important educational function. It is also society's *focal point of learning*. Through both these functions, and through the discovery of new knowledge, it fills a crucial role in society. If the university does not respond to the present crisis, then society will have to develop other institutions to carry out these functions.

Discussion

Waddington: The Centre for Interdisciplinary Studies at Göteborg is a most remarkable development, showing just what a university can do in these fields. At postgraduate level, the Centre is looking at the whole human future, and it has this remarkable series of external contacts with the government on one side, artists and writers on another, and schoolteachers on a third side. But how far have you been able to get an undergraduate programme going, Professor Lundberg? The undergraduate parts of the university are the ones most tied up by legislation and full curricula.

Lundberg: We only started the undergraduate course in human ecology this academic year (1974–1975). Also, in our country more formalities are required at the undergraduate than at the graduate level. We did submit a plan of the curriculum last year, and establishment of this course actually required a special decision by the government. However, our proposal for such a course passed through the higher administration with lightning speed and was approved at all levels. I believe the higher authorities, including the Department of Education, were genuinely interested in the proposals but in any case a refusal was hardly possible in view of the anticipated reaction from an alert public.

Jevons: It seems to me that we are in danger, through insufficiently careful use of the word 'interdisciplinary', of overestimating the novelty of interdisciplinarity. Nearly always when the problems of the real world are being attacked, we have to call on a range of academic disciplines as defined by academic criteria. Engineering, forestry, business management, architecture and so on are all in some real sense interdisciplinary. Do you see your venture in Göteborg as a transitional stage before more permanently institutionalized forms come into being for dealing with problems such as malnutrition in the third world, human ecology, and so on? Or do you see the Centre as a mechanism for continuously injecting novelty into a system which would otherwise be in danger of ossifying?

Lundberg: Rather the latter. It is quite true that problems of the 'real world' require an interdisciplinary approach. But my very point is that many university scientists have become so specialized that they are almost inaccessible to a non-expert. It is our hope that interdisciplinary contacts within the university will bring about a changed situation, making us more ready to apply our knowledge to society at large. I believe this is vital at a time when man's future is at stake.

Dror: I have no doubt about the importance of the work of the Centre, but isn't its usefulness going to be partly a question of critical mass, in the sense that if really solid suggestions are to be provided on complex matters, a group of people working on a full-time basis will be needed? In other words, to provide studies in depth, wouldn't you need permanent staff from different disciplines who would slowly evolve into some kind of full-time 'think tank'?

Lundberg: We cannot sit and wait for such an institute but will have to try our best within the existing framework. If we all seem to agree on the necessity for interdisciplinary work, why not make a start by establishing interdisciplinary contacts? Research projects may grow out of such contacts. Meanwhile let us not forget that we can be useful by making existing knowledge available to society.

Dror: How do you handle the value problems? Do you recommend alternatives so that others make the value judgements, or are your own value judgements expressed in your recommendations?

Lundberg: The value problem is a difficult one but mainly in relation to the internal work. There have been some clashes between Marxist and non-Marxist views but we have learned to live with that. When the organization as such acts externally it has certainly never recommended alternatives to suit different value judgements. However, most external appearances are by individual members who express their own views.

Perry: In the Open University, when we tried to produce multidisciplinary or interdisciplinary courses our experience was that the time and money spent was far greater than that spent on single-disciplinary courses. A striking development at the Open University is that people who came from single-disciplinary studies to work in interdisciplinary ones have already, in a relatively short time, significantly changed their research interests in the direction of the interdisciplinary. Have you seen this in Göteborg?

Lundberg: It is also our experience that interdisciplinary teaching requires considerable effort—in both planning and execution. In our special case the monetary cost is small because we depend largely on voluntary spare-time efforts. A large number of members have now been quite active on a voluntary basis for some years but more financial support will certainly be required in the long run. A few members have switched their research interests but I believe it is still too early to assess the impact of the Centre on research activity.

Woodroofe: Are the universities themselves going to become flexible organizations, with their currently well-defined disciplines less water-tight than they used to be, or will they remain the inflexible organizations that they are now? Here you are already arguing about the discipline of policy studies as against that of 'futures studies'—in other words there is evidence of the beginnings of some ossification even in studies for the future. The idea of study of the future is that it will enable us to take decisions now which will be better for mankind, but it has not been ordained that the problems of the world will be defined in terms of the faculties or disciplines of the universities. To solve those problems we shall need a variety of disciplines. Different problems will require different mixes of disciplines, and different proportions of effort from those disciplines. As we move along the stages of looking at those problems we may need additional disciplines, and others may have to drop out. Could there be some sort of department within a university, an initial central core, which would give continuity and have the ability to draw in teams, loosely structured, which would deal with the problems? Then as the problems changed the teams could alter too.

Waddington: Present financial restrictions may conceivably lead to a situation where the universities can no longer completely man the rigid hierarchies in which they are now arranged. And conceivably these financial restrictions may act as a loosening-up situation, simply because the universities can't man the hierarchies.

Eldredge: Although the US is a completely chaotic country compared to Sweden, which has been very disciplined indeed, some of the situations are quite similar. Having had a lot of experience in problem-oriented work in universities, through urban studies, I see futures studies as a similar sort of opportunity for bringing people together, with all the results that you have suggested and perhaps others, Professor Lundberg.

It is interesting that it is apparently a characteristic of futures studies everywhere that they are started up by lively individuals who use their own free time to talk to others in other universities and in other continents. In the United States, we have 2300 institutions of higher learning, at least 500 of which, someone remarked, 'should be hit on the head'. Nevertheless, with a disorganized situation like that, one can be quite innovative. One doesn't have to go to the Minister of Education for permission to start a course—no one would quite know who to go to. One has to get a little money of course, and though everybody is perfectly willing to have innovation, nobody wants to pay for it. So what happens is that starting a futures course going comes out of some instructor's hide, or free time. I would think that the Cabinet or politicians at a similar level would be the people who should lean on you, work with you, and perhaps make a higher synthesis for application in the real world than the university would. This is a national research opportunity to which the university can contribute greatly.

Francis: Part of my experience has been in teaching a technology foundation course within the Open University. This course leans very much on the approach to futures studies down a perfectly respectable academic path, although it certainly isn't directly described under that heading.

The Open University differs from most other universities in having undergraduates over a wide age distribution. In courses where people with a wide range of industrial experience join others who have had entirely different experiences outside the university, the fusion of ideas takes place much more easily than in undergraduate classes of a more conventional kind. Have you attempted to create a course in Sweden which allows people with a varied cross-section of professional and other backgrounds to come in from outside the university and make their contribution in the 'teaching and learning' situation? This seems to work effectively in the Open University courses. There is a critical mass and many of the groups quickly evolve a self-help capability, with the tutor/counsellor in a position to prevent misinterpretation or misdirection of effort.

Lundberg: Our experience is exactly the same as yours. About half the students taking the undergraduate course in human ecology are from outside the university, some of them with rather long professional experience. They have mixed well with the 'regular' undergraduates and certainly made important contributions to the course. The facilitating effect from the external students was a new experience to the teachers.

Waddington: In the School of the Man Made Future in Edinburgh quite a lot of people have come in from outside the university. They certainly liven up proceedings quite a lot.

Wilkins: We all seem to agree that we are faced with some fundamental difficulties. We have heard about the need for serious work and joining disciplines together, but presumably most of us would accept that we seek some fundamental innovation of approach. Professor Lundberg, you quoted what Chomsky[2] said about the universities possibly being centres for radical enquiry —which of course, except for the presence of some outstanding individuals, the universities never have been. You also referred to the fact that your Centre had connections with 'alternative' groups. Did these groups include political groups other than those represented by the government? To what extent can one usefully feed in not only the thinking but also the general attitude of all the radical and alternative groups? What use does the Club of Rome make of contacts of that nature? How can one feed these contacts into the universities? I agree it is most desirable that universities should try to break out of their institutional strait jackets and make contact with the community outside.

Lundberg: We have connections with 'alternative groups' as part of our contacts with the community outside the university. Like other countries we have groups of individuals trying out low-energy technology, subsistence economy and new types of social relationships. Established political forces tend to view such groups with suspicion and they cannot get any economic support. But it is important that these groups should get whatever advice they need and that their experiences should be evaluated. Within a fairly short time society may need large-scale experiments which will try out radically different technological, economic and social conditions. Meanwhile we can prepare ourselves with theoretical studies of how a low-energy society might function but it is certainly also important to incorporate whatever practical experiences are available.

References cited

[1] RAVETZ, J. R. (1971) *Scientific Knowledge and its Social Problems.* Oxford University Press, London

[2] CHOMSKY, N. (1969) The role of the university in a time of crisis, in *The Great Ideas Today*, Encyclopedia Britannica, Chicago, Ill. (Reprinted in *For Reasons of State*, 1970. American Book-Stratford Press, New York)

[3] CHOMSKY, N. (1971) *Problems of Knowledge and Freedom: The Russell Lectures*, Pantheon Books, New York

[4] MONOD, J. (1971) *Chance and Necessity*, Collins, Glasgow

[5] SACHAROV, A. (1968) *Progress, Coexistence, and Intellectual Freedom* [Translated by *New York Times*, New York]

[6] CELLARIUS, R. A. & PLATT, J. (1972) Councils of urgent studies. *Science* (*Wash. D.C.*) 177, 670–676

[7] ROYAL MINISTRY FOR FOREIGN AFFAIRS AND THE SECRETARIAT FOR FUTURE STUDIES (1974) *To Choose a Future*, Norstedt, Stockholm [Abridged English translation of *Att välja framtid*, SOU (official state report) 1972:59]

[8] STRAUS, R. (1973) Departments and disciplines: stasis and change. *Science* (*Wash. D.C.*) 182, 895–898

The future as a discipline and the future of the disciplines

ALEXANDER KING

International Federation of Institutes of Advanced Study, Paris

Abstract With the approach of the end of the millennium there has been a recent proliferation of studies of the future. This has been stimulated by the present rapid rate of change—political, economic, social and technological—which necessitates a prospective approach to policy planning. Mere extrapolation of sectoral trends is no longer sufficient in view of the importance of factors external to each sector, producing discontinuities. The situation is particularly difficult in technology, owing to the long lead time of research and development, which necessitates early decisions on projects which will be effective decades ahead and can no longer be left exclusively to the market forces.

There is a need on both national and international levels to encourage and make known the results of futures studies to the public and to decision makers, and for the encouragement of academic research, both on methodology and on particular issues and situations (including model-making). Many countries are considering how to do this. Within the university the location of such teaching and research, which is essentially transdisciplinary, is somewhat uncertain and has hitherto arisen in various departments as a result of individual enthusiasms.

Futures studies, as those on policy research and other transdisciplinary matters, are unlikely to constitute a discrete discipline. Indeed the growing number of such fields throws doubt on the continuing validity of static disciplines, and a more dynamic approach to the classification of knowledge is outlined.

In recent years there has been a rapid upsurge of interest in forecasting the trends in human affairs, of predicting future situations and of presenting scenarios of various possible or probable societies, desirable or undesirable, which may be pressed upon us, or towards which the authors of the studies would have us strive. Many of these are speculative—good or bad literature—and often deliberately provocative; some are patently false, while others are painstaking attempts to indicate the consequences of continuing with our present life styles and national policies, made in the hope that early warnings may result in corrective measures being taken in time.

Of course there is nothing new in this preoccupation with the future. Even the Delphic Oracle and the Old Testament prophets must have had ancient precedents. Our preoccupation reflects the distinguishing feature of *Homo sapiens*: that he is capable of thinking ahead, at least to some minor degree. What is new is the present recognition of the need to probe more systematically and rationally into the trends of present events, to foresee as far as possible the consequences of such trends, to see difficulties ahead, and to make a deliberate attempt to shape the future in accordance with evolving human needs.

As a result of this recognition, future-oriented activities and institutions which undertake these have recently proliferated, as have forecasting techniques and attempts to evolve a systematic and scientific approach to such studies. The present meeting is therefore to be welcomed as an attempt to place these new activities in an intellectual perspective and to see how far they are appropriate within the academic system and whether they are, in fact, the embryo of a new scientific discipline.

REASONS FOR THE NEW INTEREST IN THE FUTURE

The most elemental cause of the present interest in the future is the mystical significance of the approach to the end of a millennium and the reassessment of the human condition and destiny which this encourages. This is reinforced by the intuitive feelings of many, that change and impending change in the world is ominous and that we are at an important point of inflection in the evolution of society, if not at the brink of disruption. This is no mere *fin de siècle* flurry, but is, appropriately, an order of magnitude more serious. This situation has many similarities to that which existed during the decades preceding the end of the first Christian millennium when the end of the world was predicted. It gave rise to much uncertainty and restlessness, a sense of futility and unwillingness to take decisions, which quickly dissipated when the fateful day passed without disaster. It may well be that the year 2000 will likewise lead to calmer times, but preoccupation with the future is likely to persist.

This situation gave rise, a few years ago, to a rash of studies of the year 2000, some merely speculative but others useful as systematic assessments of present trends and taking account of various possible discontinuities.

A much more important reason for the present concern with futures studies arises from the rapid rate of change in the world, caused basically, perhaps, by technological change arising from scientific discovery, but manifested also in economic, political and social terms and through the rapid and uncertain modification of human values. In general, governments find it very difficult to look ahead in their legislation and to adjust policies in the face of external change.

The democratic system, with its average electoral cycle of less than four years, encourages an almost exclusive preoccupation with immediate issues, on the part of both governments and oppositions. This mattered little in earlier days of slower change, but today with the increasing importance of forces external to a nation and beyond its control, such as monetary difficulties, contagious inflation, scarcity and high costs of imported raw materials and energy, a period of five to seven years can see a fundamental transformation of the situation; hence the immediate issues on which a government was elected and which were of closest concern to the electorate can become quite marginal in relation to the somewhat longer-term developments.

Of course, governments have for many years attempted to project and to forecast. Medium-term forecasts are made, for example of economic development and growth, employment and demography, agricultural production, etc., and these can be important inputs in the formulation of national plans, where such exist. Such forecasts are, however, almost always strictly sectoral and pay little attention to cross-impacts from other sectors. Likewise national plans, whether dirigist or indicative, have up to now been strictly economic and have taken only marginal notice of social or technological development. Concern with the environment, the consequence of population increase and urban growth, recognition that economic growth is not an end in itself but the means to provide for social, educational and other development—these and many other factors in modern society are suggesting more and more the need for a new type of integrated and integrating planning which will require the development of reliable social indicators and many new types of forecasting and assessment of future trends.

These considerations suggest that futures studies cannot be developed and used in isolation, at least as far as their influence on policy-making and the public acceptance of change are concerned. They are to be seen as part of the approach to the problem of the management of complexity. In a world whose dimensions have been shrunk by science and invention, problems of scale compound with those of rapid change to generate a momentum and complexity which existing policies and institutions will find it hard to manage. Although strictly outside the scope of this meeting, the problems of complexity are so intimately linked to the need for futures research that it may be useful to enumerate a few of the elements of this complexity. These are:

— recognition in a starkly practical sense of the interdependence of the nations and of the vulnerability of energy and raw material supplies and price levels to political as well as market forces;
— recognition of the interdependence of both problems and solutions and

the need to foresee the interaction of solutions to sectoral problems with
those in other areas;
— the fact that world population is increasing very quickly and will
   double in just over thirty years;
— increase in the scale of world activity and hence of the demand for
   raw materials, energy, products and services, arising from both population increase and faster economic growth;
— rapid rate of change;
— generalization of expectations within the industrialized countries and
   between the rich and the poor countries of the world.

The situation has been likened by Dennis Meadows to that of a large ocean liner
which, owing to its momentum, requires many miles before it is able to change
course and hence needs early warnings from radar to avoid rocks ahead. It is,
of course, essential that the radar—or future forecasts—should be adequate and
it is doubtful that futures techniques have yet reached such a state of reliability.

CATEGORIES OF FUTURES STUDIES

The future is inherently unknowable and forecasts based on the projection
of present trends are rarely realized because of discontinuities, uncertainties
as to the time of levelling-off of exponential curves, and the inruption of external forces. Nevertheless much can be done. The central issue is whether the
world and its constituent nations can build in time a capacity and an initiative
with regard to future events and prepare contingency plans and policies to
meet them, rather than acting *post facto* when problems arise. It is a matter
of decreasing the degree of uncertainty with regard to the future rather than a
matter of crisis government. This new approach is not merely a matter of forecasting by the extrapolation of past and present trends which can easily collapse under the pressure of forces external to each nation. It is rather a matter
of exploring the unknown by probing where chinks appear, of analysing the
trends and potentialities of the present and of assessing the relative significance
of each trend, of examining choices and options and the probable consequences
of various combinations of these, of foreseeing incompatibilities, physical
road blocks and inter-goal conflicts, of constructing possible and desirable
microfutures. It will have to be a continuous process, kept under constant
review as events and deeper insights render modifications necessary. It is a concept of dynamic rather than of static planning.

Regarded in this light the prospective approach is an essential and inherent
part of the new policy science, and futures studies are an important part of
policy research.

The degree of uncertainty about forecasts of the future varies greatly from field to field. For example, technological forecasting, which was fashionable a few years ago, should be inherently possible since most technology arises from scientific discoveries which have already been made, but even here the uncertainties are very great.

Such futures studies as have already been accomplished vary greatly in method of approach and relevance. They can be categorized in many different ways, but it may be useful to suggest a few basic types and their characteristics.

— Firstly there is the purely *speculative approach*, generally literary rather than scientific, but at its best comprising many useful intuitive and imaginative elements; most of the utopias, Brave New Worlds, the 1984s, and much of science fiction fall into this category, which has little policy significance but which can greatly influence general thinking.

— Related to the above, but often more scientifically based, are *direct projections of existing situations* and trends, ranging from the not always irrational forecasts of Old Moore's Almanack to the reasoned scenarios of Herman Kahn.

— *Prophylactic futurology* projects and interrelates present trends to indicate the probable consequences of their continuation, not as prophesy but in order to draw public and political attention to future dangers so that deliberate changes may be introduced to ensure that the consequences are avoided and the curve of projection bent. The Forrester-Meadows limits to growth was of this type.[1] Technology assessment has a similar objective.

— *Prospective planning*, whether political, economic, technological or social, has important futures inputs as a necessity and is capable of using a wide diversity of techniques. It takes into account present trends and their interactions, includes the working out of the probable consequences of different possible decisions and the creation of alternative policies and strategies to meet the more likely contingencies.

— The *construction of utopias* or designing of desirable futures is a further approach which endeavours to suggest in detail general, sectoral or microfutures regarded as desirable, as goals towards which society should move and which may be taken as policy targets by society or its decision makers. Naturally such constructions are value-loaded and reflect essentially the values of their creators, who may, however, have been given their general specifications by particular political or ideological groups.

THE FUTURES APPROACH IN SCIENCE AND TECHNOLOGY

The time factor is particularly important in science and technology. The time scales of the world of science are widely different from those of the world of politics, a fundamental factor of national development which is insufficiently appreciated in political thinking and, indeed, in that of the economist, who habitually assumes that new scientific discovery and appropriate technological development are conjured up in response to economic forces. Much of the economists' hope of solving the longer-term problems depends on an implicit reliance on the 'technological fix'—without, however, giving sufficient importance to the time constraints.

Research and development are inherently long-term processes. From the first creation of a basic new concept in the mind of the scientist until its generalized application in the form of a new product or process or new type of institution takes upwards of thirty years. Of course there are innumerable smaller innovations which can be accomplished much more quickly, while major developments can be greatly speeded up by the massive efforts of crash programmes of the type which the United States used for getting men to the moon. But crash programmes are extremely expensive and are bound to remain the exception. In general, therefore, the research–development–production chain is very long and, for energy, for example, it threatens to be much longer than political exigencies will permit. Even when no fundamentally novel features are involved the process is slow. For example, in the French nuclear power programme—not a pacemaker in technological development—a quarter of a century elapsed between the first experimental pile going critical and the first nuclear power station going into service. When the rate of political, economic and social change is great, i.e. when the interval between successive, distinct sets of circumstances is shorter than the normal lead time of research and development, there is the fear that their results will come too late to have a fundamental economic and hence political impact. In periods of slower change, new technological developments did indeed evolve mainly in response to the forces of the market and helped to create the wealth and prosperity which we have enjoyed. In planned economies, likewise, technological developments are pursued mainly in support of a slowly evolving economic expansion.

These circumstances indicate the need to give special attention to futures studies in science and technology, and to relate such work to the political and economic process. It is a matter for partnership of a quite new kind between science, industry and government.

THE INSTITUTION OF FUTURES STUDIES

Viewed thus, from the point of view of the necessity of generating and refining futures research for the benefit of a nation or of the world, it is clear that such work will have to be developed in close cooperation with the user—the government, the international organizations or industrial enterprises—if they are to be fully effective. There is probably a need for two distinctive types of institution, the first an essentially policy-oriented unit close to the decision makers, which generates, stimulates and selects the necessary inputs of a prospective type and ensures that they are taken account of. The second type of institution is that for research, both of a long-term character, including the development of new techniques and the refinement of existing ones, and applied research which explores particular trends or constructs particular futures, micro or macro. The two types of institution would, ideally, be in symbiotic relationship and the futures policy units would no doubt stimulate research and, at times, have it undertaken in the futures research bodies by contract.

It may be useful to look at a few of the existing or projected institutional arrangements in this field. The pattern suggested above is, for example, being discussed at the moment in Canada where a conference of the interested parties has been called jointly by the Senate of Canada and the Economic Council; the proposal is to create (a) a national look-out centre on future trends and forecasts for the use of governments (federal and provincial), industry and the public, and (b) a futures research centre within the Economic Council to stimulate such research and act as the centre of a network of research activity in the universities and independent research institutions.

On the policy and applicational aspects, much is already being done by industry, where the trend of events which followed the petroleum crisis has given a new impulse to longer-term thinking and planning. Several large, progressive firms now have important units, generally working close to the president or managing director on long-term corporate policy, taking account of world political and economic trends, and looking for new opportunities and often, it should be added, for a new image. In some cases the director of research and development is given this role, which is an important move since it brings research planning much closer to overall corporate strategy than is normally the case.

On the governmental level, countries are taking a variety of measures. In the United States futures studies, like other activities, are approached in a pluralistic sense with little attempt to centralize or coordinate. Government departments have for many years been interested in such an approach, particularly with regard to defence strategy and technology, relying mainly on quasi-independent bodies such as the Rand and Mitre Corporations to undertake it by contract. Now however a number of major projects are in progress within the executive branch, for example in the Departments of Labor and of Commerce. There are said to be about eight separate governmental and non-governmental short-term forecasts of economic trends. A new body of some significance has been set up by the legislature to advise Congress on the physical, biological, environmental, social and political consequences of technological development. This Office of Technology Assessment has no counterpart as yet in other parliaments. Also in the United States, there are many non-profit bodies devoted to futures studies, such as the Institute for the Future in California, Forecasting International, and the Hudson Institute, while a large number of academic centres are devoted to such work, including the Center for Futures Studies at Portland, and the System Dynamics group at MIT and at Case Western Reserve University which houses the American end of the elaborate Mesarovic–Pestel World Model.[2] Significant also is the Commission for Critical Choices set up by Governor (now Vice-President) Rockefeller.

Another country with a plethora of futures activities is Japan, where the government's Economic Planning Agency is attempting to include social as well as economic factors and is working out social, inflation and welfare indicators. Large numbers of specific, regional and global studies are being carried out in government departments, private organizations such as the Japan Techno-Economics Society, and in the universities. The Netherlands also has a wide variety of forecasting and futures activities, ranging from the sophisticated work of the Central Planning Bureau, through the new and interesting Scientific Council for Government Policy, which is an experimental body responsible to the Cabinet as a whole and required to formulate long-term problems and policy directions for the country as a whole, to a number of interesting university studies and model building. Sweden likewise is taking a systematic approach. As mentioned by Professors Eldredge and Lundberg (this volume), the Prime Minister set up, in 1971, a commission to advise on this area of interest and to review needs and possibilities. As a result of its report 'To choose a future',[3] a Secretariat for Futures Studies has been set up in Sweden with strong financial backing from the government to promote research in the universities, to undertake technology assessment studies and to plan university courses on forecasting and futures. Similar activities are arising in many other countries.

The international organizations have been much slower in entering this field, although the Organization for Economic Cooperation and Development (OECD) has done a good deal of economic forecasting and is now engaged in looking at the long-term and medium-term supply-and-demand aspects of energy as well as at the concomitant technological and research needs. The United Nations was given a strong lead in this direction by U Thant before his retirement, and has recently set up, within UNITAR (United Nations Institute for Training and Research), its own commission for the future. The European Economic Commission has also entered the field of long-term assessment and forecasting and has set up its group, Europe plus Thirty, to advise on whether a comprehensive and continuing activity should be mounted.

Finally, an increasing number of private organizations on an international or national level, such as the Club of Rome, while not strictly futures study groups, are concerned with establishing a prospective approach. The Club of Rome was formed essentially through the conviction of its members that governmental and intergovernmental organizations with their archaic structures and weight of bureaucracy were too slow and too traditional to solve the complex, interactive problems of our quickly changing world and that a new impulse must be given. This has resulted in a significant stimulus to future-oriented research. Simultaneously and in informal relation to the Club of Rome two new international institutions have been created. The International Institute for Applied Systems Analysis in Vienna, with a competent international staff, should contribute greatly to the development of new techniques for probing the future and should be able to maintain high academic standards. The International Federation of Institutes of Advanced Study, with its twenty-three constituent institutes, each of which has great competence in its specialized field, is endeavouring to promote multidisciplinary contact between its member institutes and to organize common projects between them and other interested institutes and individual scientists. Its existing projects are all strongly future-orientated.

IS FUTURES RESEARCH A SUITABLE SUBJECT FOR ACADEMIA?

I shall not attempt in this brief paper to give a survey of the state of the art with regard to futures studies or to comment in detail on their validity and scientific level. It will be realized from what has already been said, however, that the subject has already penetrated deeply into the universities of certain countries and that the now recognized need for the results of such work is likely to attract more and more academic attention.

The answer to the question, therefore, seems to me to be very simple. If, as I believe is true, the universities are essential innovators in society through the development of new concepts and methods of thought, they can hardly avoid taking up the challenge of exploration of the future which is being forced upon us by the exigencies of our times, and which in many ways is a consequence of scientific discovery as well as of the technology which has been built upon it, stemming from earlier innovations of academia.

Certainly the quality of existing studies of the future varies greatly. Much of it is scientifically very weak, superficial and subjective, but not noticeably much more so than in many researches in the behavioural sciences which are already well embedded in the universities. Furthermore we are already seeing great advances in technique and sophistication and it is probably only in the universities and a few independent research institutions that the necessary interdisciplinary contact and deep competence in elements of the subject exist which will enable this process of refinement and development to progress on a sound intellectual basis.

This brings us to the point of discussing how such activities can find their place in the university system. Studies of the future are essentially multi-disciplinary or transdisciplinary. They have a need for a basic statistical and mathematical competence; they require a sound input from economics, sociology and psychology; at times they require the help of the computer; they have elements of cybernetics and systems analysis; they require deep political insights. It has been mentioned already that from the point of view of their application, futures studies can be regarded as a branch of policy research, itself a new, horizontal and multidisciplinary field. In fact the problem of futures research and the universities is part of the larger question of how university structures and attitudes can be modified to allow for an increasing extent of interdisciplinary contact and of multidisciplinary team formation. This need is widely recognized and receives a great deal of lip service, but in fact the results, especially in many of the older and more traditional universities, are far from convincing. Amongst other obstacles, career lines in a particular specialization are clear and good work leads to promotion; so time spent in multidisciplinary work is all too often regarded as a diversion from 'serious' research and teaching and detracts from career prospects. The result is often that, while a few devoted and adventurous people are willing to take such career risks, many brilliant people who might contribute greatly to the new horizontal fields are dissuaded from entering them. The fundamental need, then, is for innovation in the structure and attitudes of the universities if they, by the cultivation of the new, multidisciplinary fields, are to remain the chief innovators of society. This is a subject to which we shall return in the next section.

To my mind there are two essential requirements for the proper cultivation of futures thinking in the universities. Firstly there is a quite general need to encourage a more prospective approach in many subjects and faculties, in law and in education, in technology and in social studies. Too often it is assumed that tomorrow will be a slight modification of today and that tomorrow's teaching will be only marginally different from the present. In most subjects this is simply no longer true. The change to a more prospective approach is bound to be slow, but it will be forced into being by external events, public opinion and the demands of new cohorts of students. It could also be accelerated greatly in universities where there are lively centres for futures research which involve in their work colleagues from many departments and disciplines on an *ad hoc* basis.

The second and more difficult requirement is for the creation of centres that will undertake serious research on the future, developing methodology, bringing in all the necessary disciplines, and having intimate contact with the users of its work—decision makers in industry and politics. It is not possible to give any generalized opinion as to where in present university structures such a unit should be placed. This will be different in different cases and will often be determined by the vision and enthusiasm of individuals drawn to the field, from whatever department. At times the futures unit will be associated with policy research or international affairs; often already they are offshoots of an economics department; they may develop within science policy units—another multidisciplinary subject—or, if the impulse is essentially social, they may be under the dean of social sciences; again, they may well be found within new groups for systems studies, or arise from computer science. The location matters little, as does the diversity of titles which such units may invent. What is essential is that they be broadly based, genuinely multidisciplinary, and with relations throughout the relevant departments of the university.

ARE DISCIPLINES REALLY NECESSARY?

The present structures of education and of research, into which the new multidisciplinary subjects fit with difficulty, were historically determined by the classification of knowledge which crystallized in the middle of the last century when, especially through the gaining of new knowledge by experiment, specialization became inevitable and the scholar could no longer claim familiarity and authority across the whole field of learning. In the universities and elsewhere, science is still taught in terms of the disciplines laid down then—neat little boxes marked chemistry, physics, geology, botany, etc., which long appeared to be self-contained and practical, although the relationships between the disciplines were always appreciated. As the content of each of these boxes filled up, sub-classifications had to be devised, such as physical, organic and inorganic chemistry, which through specialization tended to become isolated from each other. Later, interface subjects such as biochemistry and geophysics began to appear and to find their importance, both intellectually and through their applications. In some cases the lines of demarcation became very diffuse. I still find it difficult to distinguish between physical chemistry and chemical physics, for example, and this tinge of sectarianism is still more marked in the social sciences where, for example, social anthropology, social psychology and sociology appear, at least from outside, to be distinguished more in the sense of orientation than of fundamental discipline.

With the expansion of research and the fine-structuring of specialization, still more complicated intersectional subjects began to appear in both pure and applied science, such as molecular biology or cybernetics and also fields essentially based on a particular methodology or set of techniques such as systems analysis. Finally, and more recently, less clearly defined fields of growth have been emerging, including futures research, policy research and other topics of a high degree of transdisciplinarity and no longer at the well-defined interfaces of a static two-dimensional or three-dimensional model. One such case with which I have recently had some concern is the study of brain and behaviour which lies at the point of convergence of a number of non-contiguous disciplines including molecular biology, neurophysiology, biochemistry, psychiatry, etc. Another such field is the intellectual background behind computer and information science, with its mix of mathematics, logic, information theory and linguistics.

With such new fields of investigation, the simple box classification of knowledge seems as irrelevant as the early Bohr models of the atom in an age of wave mechanics. Yet, as already stated, our university and research structures still operate on the early simplicist model which makes the exploration of the newer multidisciplinary fields difficult.

I therefore take the opportunity of this discussion of futures research as a discipline to raise the question of whether the time is now ripe for the classification of the sciences to be reassessed, with the structural and conceptual consequences which this would entail. The growing understanding of the linkages and interactions of the problems facing society, as well as of the linkages and interactions between the diverse fields of learning and approaches to the discovery of new knowledge, suggests the need to adopt a holistic and dynamic approach: in some sense a return to the reality of the unity of all knowledge. The newer interdisciplinary subjects such as that of our present concern should be regarded, perhaps, not as new and discrete disciplines but as foci of advancing knowledge, temporary subjects which can be consolidated only by contributions from many other fields and many techniques. They will later extend, by mergers with other approaches from equally transient points in the advancement of knowledge, to create new and probably equally temporary outposts on the frontiers of understanding, within which the forces of science will assemble for still deeper penetration into the unknown, including the unknown future. How can the institutions of research and learning be restructured in terms of the unity of knowledge and the dynamic nature of the evolution of science? Such restructuring is not merely a conceptual but a practical necessity.

Discussion

Valaskakis: The prophylactic approach that you are talking about, Dr King, is a useful one as long as it is not the only approach used. What it implies—and this is apparent in the first two reports to the Club of Rome[1,2]—is a sort of pathological model of society where we identify the bottlenecks and the negative aspects of society when the system actually breaks down. This pathological model is useful but in future Club of Rome activities (if not in the fourth or the fifth report then in subsequent reports to the Club of Rome) I would suggest that a positive reformulation of the world *problèmatique* should be attempted, where *opportunities* would be identified instead of bottlenecks. In other words what I am advocating is an eventual definition of *health* in society. This definition should precede the pathological findings. To achieve this I think a page could be borrowed from the French '*Prospective*' movement which distinguishes between two types of scenario. (The French 'Prospective' movement is concerned with the scientific investigation of the future and uses the scenario approach to define alternative contrasting futures.) One kind is the *projective* scenario which starts from the present situation and develops into the future. The other is a completely different type called the *horizon* scenario which starts with a future situation and returns to the present. If the return to the present is impossible, we still have a horizon scenario that is desirable but not feasible. The intellectual exercise at least provides us with a model of what we want and cannot have. What concerns me is that futures studies, almost everywhere, tend to be too overwhelmed by feasibility, and therefore too constrained by the present. What we end up studying, implicitly or explicitly—and I think this is true of the first and second reports to the Club of Rome[1,2]—is the 'future of the present' or in other words the future of the *status quo*, whether the *status quo* has lasted twenty years, fifty years or two hundred years. My plea then is for more *horizon* scenarios to reformulate problems and situations in a new light. The dominance of the projective scenario must be resisted.

King: I am in full agreement. The second Club of Rome report has already gone a little in that direction. Mesarovic and Pestel[2] are not considering the faults in the present system; they are providing scenarios, to indicate which alternative decision might represent the most desirable situation.

Waddington: Horizon scenarios, or normative scenarios, in which one tries to formulate the ends one wants to reach, really make better sense when certain value systems in the present can be identified which could define those required ends. But if one starts by being totally disconnected from the present, which has nothing to do with the projection, then I think one gets pretty unrealistic. If we connect ourselves, not to present circumstances but to some present value system, we may make a projection which has more realism.

Ziman: Dr King and Professor Lundberg quite rightly want to put inter-disciplinarity into the university, but the word 'discipline' suggests a serious scholarly approach—something that is not done in one's spare time. Of course such work is also done in people's spare time; but the term really implies a completeness of attention and professionalism that will produce valuable re-sults. Anything less is scarcely worth the effort. Our experience in science, overall, is that we must do things thoroughly and wholeheartedly: scientific problems are difficult and are not solved by good intentions.

Now why do people work at their disciplines? What makes them serious? There are really two reasons. One reason, in the context of the discipline, is that people are exercising their scholarship in public. They are putting something before their colleagues, who are going to be so critical that they have to be exact-ly right. This is the German scholarly tradition, and an excellent technique for getting first-class work. But I am quite sure that it is not the way you want fu-tures studies to go. That approach leads in the end to *academicism* directed towards the solution of artificial problems, within the paradigm of a particular group of scholars but lacking external reference. It is important to emphasize the other incentive towards getting it right, which is to have to solve a real problem. That is the *practical* reason for doing good work. For example, the radar development that was needed in the 1939–1945 war forced people to give of their best: they had to get it right for quite different reasons from schol-arly ones. I don't see how you can get the universities involved and active in futures studies unless that very strong practical aspect is given adequate weight. Without it these studies will inevitably degenerate into yet another manifesta-tion of scholasticism.

King: We do not need a lot of isolated scholasticism but we do need serious studies, for example on the elaboration of new methodologies for what I would call probing the future rather than forecasting it. Very few institutions outside the universities are capable of doing this. On the other hand the coupling of futures studies with real-life problems, with policy-making, decision-making and so on, is difficult to achieve, and possibly it cannot be done directly be-tween the average university, particularly those in the Latin countries, and the decision makers. It is not a black and white picture. We need both approaches.

Ziman: What would be the criteria of success, in a particular study, in a particular university, by a particular group or scholar?

Waddington: In operational research during the war we were modelling systems, and advising executives to issue certain orders on the basis of the model. Then we really had to find some facts very quickly, by observing what the results of those orders were. It was P. M. S. Blackett who really invented the whole operational research idea, and he emphasized that it had to be a short-term alternation, between model-making, and observation with empirical factual data. This is what we so far lack in futures study. The Club of Rome has no feedback on what actually happens when action is taken on the basis of its analysis, and it is difficult to see how the Club can get that feedback.

Ziman: In wartime operational research, you could take action—try something out, see what happened. We carried on with our model just long enough, or far enough ahead, to get something from which we could get a factual feedback.

Oldfield: My thinking at the outset is impeded by what I suppose is an elementary worry. When we look at the past, we see that all our research is ultimately academic, and the only thing we can alter directly is our perception of what happened. When we look at the future, study and research is in a fundamental sense non-academic, because we can in theory alter both perception and experience. This shift of mode, if I can call it that, often seems to be disguised, in writing and in speaking, by an illusion of the continuity and comparability of positive evaluation as we move from past to present to future. Has everybody else grown beyond this rather naive worry, and does it matter?

Waddington: I think this is one way of seeing the same problem. It is so difficult to get any factual feedback. In considering the future only fifty years ahead, we ought to be able to consider a gradual passage into the future, and we ought to be able to get some feedback from this. But it is difficult to see how to do it in many of these contexts.

Dror: There is an intellectual difference. Operational research is mainly oriented towards concrete decisions, while part of futures research is oriented towards what Sir Geoffrey Vickers calls 'educating the appreciative systems of the decision makers'.[4] So, broad educational effects should also be among the main targets of futures studies.

King: That is true. In the Club of Rome context our main approach is to talk to the decision makers and probe their concepts.

Platt: There is an area here which I think needs a new disciplinary base, a new theoretical base. That area is the nature of scientific inference when one is dealing with a complex ongoing flow system, where one cannot test to destruction—that is, one cannot cut off the child's protein if one wants to find the effects of protein on the brain. What we need is what I call 'green-thumb inference', the kind of inference that the woman taking care of her plants makes when she moves the plant into the sun. She does not make a physicist's measurements, by cutting off all the water, but instead she looks for a few little signals that show her whether there is too much sun or too little sun, or she puts a little water or plant food on it, and then watches for small indicators in the ongoing flow system.

In operations research, the anti-submarine warfare in World War II[5] was one of the best formal examples so far of this kind of ongoing process. We cannot stop the submarine chase that is going on, using the old methods, in order to test our theories about new methods. We have to continue with the old methods but make use of small fluctuations and small test operations if we want to infer the important variables underneath. I think we need to formalize this green-thumb inference method, or step-by-step bootstrap method of knowledge and control, if we are to understand or have any cybernetic guidance of society. The cybernetic ongoing understanding of the future is collecting as we go, and this cumulative process needs a formal theoretical analysis that has not been done yet.

Woodroofe: Is this really a new concept? Isn't economics based on observations of systems whose conditions the economists cannot control? Many so-called laws of economics have been postulated but lots of these laws have now been shown to be wrong. Conditions have changed.

Platt: That is why I think economics is a bad example of a way of acquiring futures-controlled knowledge. Economists have never learned from their failures.

Waddington: The balance sheet was useful in the past as a flow check-up but it is beginning to be inadequate, and anyway it only covers certain aspects of what happens.

Lundberg: In my opinion Dr King took a too pessimistic view with regard to the universities. We cannot destroy the present system with specialized disciplines, since they are needed in both teaching and research. But the universities may not be so inflexible as some of you seem to believe. We have to find ways of supporting forces within the university which can contribute to a renewal and this is better done with the carrot than with the stick. One of the problems is the present career structure. At present young research workers who move outside the central line of accepted disciplines are almost excluded from a future academic career. We must find ways of encouraging and supporting young research workers who want to devote themselves to the urgent problems of mankind. Financial support from special research councils devoted to future problems is one possibility.

Shane: Among the things that we rarely confront when we think about the roles of such organizations as the Club of Rome are some of the problems of multinational corporations. For example, until two or three years ago American oil companies were doing what the Arabs have been doing more recently— although without having it as widely known. When oil cost 16 cents a barrel, oil companies maintained the price at $1.75, and it cost American taxpayers nearly $5000 million in depletion allowances and about $3500 million in profits, sums that many would consider far too high. We also have the problem that many of the socioeconomically privileged in developing countries, the owners and rulers at the top of the pyramid, have more in common with the élite groups in other countries than they have with their own people. This has led to serious abuses. For instance, cash crops have been preferred in developing countries to food crops, with the present disastrous results in a period of famine. One cannot but wonder whether groups like the Club of Rome should endeavour to turn our universities into arenas for the debate of such problems rather than let them remain the cloisters for debate that many are now.

Waddington: We had better discuss this again later. This comes back to the question of should the universities teach their students something about these matters.

King: I was of course exaggerating in my remarks about university disciplines. I would not want to stop teaching of chemistry or pathology or any other discipline. But I think that fairly radical changes are required even to get the minimal necessary amount of transdisciplinary development.

References cited

1 MEADOWS, DONELLA H., MEADOWS, DENNIS L., RANDERS, JØRGEN & BEHRENS, WILLIAM W., III (1972) *The Limits to Growth*, Universe, New York; Earth Island, London
2 MESAROVIC, MIHAJLO & PESTEL, EDUARD (1974) *Mankind at the Turning Point*, Dutton/ Reader's Digest, New York; Hutchinson, London
3 ROYAL MINISTRY FOR FOREIGN AFFAIRS AND THE SECRETARIAT FOR FUTURE STUDIES (1974) *To Choose a Future*, Norstedt, Stockholm
4 VICKERS, SIR GEOFFREY (1965) *Art of Judgment*, Chapman & Hall, London
5 WADDINGTON, C. H. (1974) *Operational Research in World War II*, Elek, London

A dragon or a pussy cat? Two views of human knowledge

F. R. JEVONS

Department of Liberal Studies in Science, University of Manchester

Abstract Knowledge-handling institutions should be organized in a way that takes due account of the nature of knowledge. The basic question concerns the limits within which knowledge might change as societies change. Is it adaptable to our collective will? Or is it objective and impervious to human actions and wishes?

The writings of Popper and Kuhn help to throw some light on this question. With them as background, two current debates are examined. It is concluded that new knowledge systems will be alternatives within science rather than alternatives to science; and that technology is not completely socially determined but has a measure of autonomy.

It is important not to underrate the importance of the constraints set by what is externally 'given'. A dogmatic element in education seems to be an epistemological necessity. The implications for the organization and power structures of universities are not as conservative as they seem at first sight. 'Cliff effects' in the social distribution of expertise should be avoided.

I am not very ashamed to admit that I get very confused by those bits of the literature on the future which I have read. Quite apart from the undeniable possibility that literally anything *might* happen, there are such diverse views of where we *want* to go, and authors are not always careful to consider critically the basic aims of the societies they envisage.

Thus William Leiss[1] takes Bacon to task for implicitly equating scientific with social progress. Certainly I agree that the desirability of 'the effecting of all things possible' (Bacon[2]) is not self-evident. But Leiss's own criterion of social progress seems to be 'the abatement of social conflict', and although that sounds fine, it is not self-evident to me that it will automatically lead to, or is even compatible with, some other aims which also sound fine, such as the enlarging of consciousness, or human achievement in various other directions. The argument of *Report from Iron Mountain*[3] about the non-military functions of war and threat of war cannot be dismissed out of hand.

Then again, some people want technology to supply material goods and services in such copious abundance that we can use them with careless abandon and concentrate our efforts on higher things; while others, struck with the finiteness of the earth's resources, regard that attitude as like that of a man falling from the top of the Empire State Building and saying 'all right so far'. To David Dickson, in his book on *Alternative Technology*,[4] it seems to come as a matter for pained surprise that liberty and equality might not necessarily go hand in hand; whereas in practice, I usually see those two sitting on *opposite* sides of the negotiating table, and the formulas that finally emerge containing trade-offs between them.

It is against the background of such radical uncertainty about the direction of change that I want to consider the nature of that powerful agent of change, knowledge; and I do this with a very pragmatic purpose in mind. It seems important for knowledge-handling institutions to consider what kind of commodity it is they deal with, for on this depends the appropriate mode of operation and organizational style for them to adopt. Just as a cut-price grocery store is not likely to flourish if it adopts the same mode and style as a public electricity undertaking, so universities and other educational institutions are most likely to succeed if they structure themselves to take due account of the nature of the knowledge they handle. The theory of knowledge thus takes on a direct practical relevance; epistemology becomes too important to be left to philosophers.

LIMITS TO CHANGE IN KNOWLEDGE

Perhaps the most basic question to ask is: how far is knowledge adaptable to our collective will? Within what limits can it change as society changes? This is the question posed in picturesque terms by Feyerabend[5] in a passage from which I take the title of this article. Feyerabend says he prefers 'an enterprise whose human character can be seen by all... to one that looks "objective", and impervious to human actions and wishes. The sciences, after all, are our own creation...' Adopting this view, he says, 'changes science from a stern and demanding mistress into an attractive and yielding courtesan who tries to anticipate every wish of her lover. Of course, it is up to us to choose either a dragon or a pussy cat for our company. I do not think I need to explain my own preferences'.*

Pussy cat knowledge, in other words, is relativist: it is formed according to circumstances, which vary from place to place, and from time to time, and from

---

* In asserting that it is up to us, Feyerabend begs the question and, as I hope to show in this article, falls into his own trap.

society to society; it is not dictated by what is 'given' externally to human beings or societies. It is socially constructed, not imposed by outside authority. What an attractive view this seems! We are promised the kind of knowledge system we want. We are offered the opportunity to change it at will. Whatever kind of society we may in the future decide we want, we can have a knowledge system to fit it.

The modern relativist movement derives sustenance from the charismatic book by Kuhn on *The Structure of Scientific Revolutions*,[6] which in a mere thirteen years since it was first published in 1962 has become remarkably influential. Kuhn emphasizes that we cannot see uninterpreted facts of nature; we can only see nature through the spectacles of one paradigm or another.* Different paradigms or conceptual frameworks represent different commitments and, in the extreme interpretation, they are incommensurable, so that there are no standards by which we can say that one is better than another, except for standards based on our tastes and preferences.

I think this won't quite do. True, we can't know truth as such, or at least we can't be certain we know truth as such: all scientific knowledge is conjectural. But this does not mean that objective truth does not exist or that it has no bearing on our knowledge systems. Objective truth is the ideal we aim at, even though it is impossible to achieve, or at least impossible to be certain that it has been achieved. This view of truth is one of the deceptively simple, brilliant insights which can be retrieved from the exasperating thornbush of Popper's writings. Popper asks us to realize that 'all of us may and often do err, singly and collectively, but that this very idea of error and human fallibility involves another—the idea of objective truth: the standard which we may fall short of'.[9]

There is here a severe and salutary limitation on knowledge. Without having to fall back on a simplistically sharp distinction between facts and values, it offers a solution to the problem of the place of facts in a world of values, which seems a more pressing problem than that of the place of values in a world of facts.[10] Knowledge is seen not to be a *totally* human creation.† I take the scientific enterprise to be essentially the invention of regularities which more or less fit nature. Scientific knowledge is therefore bilaterally determined: the invention must be a human act but the fit depends also on what is 'given' externally to us in nature.

With this as background, let me now turn to somewhat less abstract matters

---

* For brief treatments of Kuhn and the Popper-Kuhn controversy, see Sklair[7] and Jevons.[8]
† I cannot therefore agree with Johnston,[11] whose reading of Kuhn enables him to see a 'bright gleam of hope' in the recognition that knowledge is 'a totally human product'. Cf. p. 59n†.

by tackling two questions which have cropped up in the literature recently. They are more closely related than may at first sight appear. One concerns the possibility of new and alternative knowledge systems; the other concerns the autonomy of technology.

ALTERNATIVE KNOWLEDGE SYSTEMS

It has been suggested that the urge to conquer and exploit nature extends itself to the urge to conquer and exploit man:[1] that the Baconian urge, if you like, inevitably turns into the Faustian. How far the link between the two kinds of exploitation is an essential one, and how far it is only a contingent combination, seems to me to be an open question: surely the wage slaves of industrial society are not more grossly exploited than were the domestic slaves of the ancient civilizations. But be that as it may, there are those who believe there is a connection and, being anxious to see an end to the domination of man by man, look for less domineering knowledge systems to go with less oppressive social patterns. Anti-science is once again quite fashionable. Blame for defects in modern societies should be attached, it is suggested, not to misuse of science but to the nature of the science itself.* Western science has, after all, been practised for a mere three or four centuries; perhaps mankind has not tried hard enough to test alternatives such as might be found, for instance, in Taoism or Zen.

I remain somewhat sceptical of these efforts. Those who complain of the domineering ways of the western scientific–technological mode are upset, I suspect, not so much by the fact of domination as by the crudity and messiness of the means of domination that have been used up to now. It is all very well to talk of living in harmony with nature instead of trying to dominate it, but do we really want that to extend to a policy of non-interference with the typhoid and cholera organisms? We should not confuse the wish for subtler and less obtrusive means of control with the suggestion that helplessness might be a virtue in itself. Persuasion may be a subtler means of control than command, but it is a means of control nevertheless.

The conquest of our physical environment does not inevitably lead to a better society, but better societies do surely depend on having power to control nature. The idea that technology is intrinsically bad is, I think, intrinsically absurd. What is bad is bad technology. *Absence* of technology would mean that we were evincing an incomprehending, blind helplessness in our material environment, and that cannot be better than wise use based on understanding.

Alternative knowledge systems will be evaluated according to the same ul-

---

* Calls for an 'African chemistry'[12] or a 'truly Indian science'[13] rest on analogous, though less extreme, assumptions.

timate criterion as scientific theories: do they work?* It is not a defence of science's current repertoire of theories and effects, which is indubitably imperfect and incomplete, to claim that science, regarded as the invention of regularities which fit nature, is a uniquely successful knowledge system. Its monopolistic position seems unchallengeable. Knowledge that works must be based on regularities, and regularities give power to control.† If some practice from African witchcraft turns out to work in alleviating disease—perhaps because, as Horton suggests,[15] it rests on analysis of social stresses instead of mechanical use of drugs—then it does not replace science but is incorporated into it. It becomes, not an alternative, but an addition to science. We have alternatives *within* science—for instance, different sources of energy and different ways of controlling insect pests—but new alternatives do not become alternatives *to* science as long as the current corpus of science does not become totally impermeable to novelty. And although science is assuredly not an entirely open-minded enterprise, neither are the paradigmatic blinkers completely effective in keeping out new viewpoints; not even the most ardent follower of Kuhn has been able to draw *that* interpretation out of history.

THE AUTONOMY OF TECHNOLOGY

It has recently become fashionable to insist that technology is not autonomous or neutral but that it is socially or politically determined. Thus Seymour Melman[16] criticises 'the myth of autonomous technology' and Dickson[4] makes a similar attack on 'the myth of the political neutrality of technology'.

Of course it is true that a society's technology to a substantial extent reflects its preferences and priorities. If, as Melman says,[16] more than half the research and development engineers and scientists of the United States functioned on behalf of defence, space and atomic energy agencies during the 1950s and 1960s, it is no wonder that American technology matches the needs of those agencies. But the match is never complete or perfect. If it were, technology would be the ideal slave: one that does exactly what his master (society) desires, and does nothing else at all. Such an ideal slave does not, unfortunately, exist. Melman says that each machine has built into it 'the particular requirement of whoever decides its characteristics and the uses it must serve'. That is so, but the characteristics are not *exhaustively* described by user specifications. Melman calls it

---

* There may be a wide variety of aims. If Zen works in producing certain states of consciousness, it can be regarded as a sophisticated behavioural technology. Moreover, theories need not work in the sense that a simple causal theory works; structure and process theories, for instance also 'work' in their own ways.[14]

† Not unlimited power, of course. Knowledge of the regularities of planetary motions does not enable us to control the motions.

'a distortion of understanding' to make technology 'appear as though independent of man's will'. But it is equally a distortion of understanding to deny that technology is *partly* independent of man's will.

The social determinist view of technology is a misleading half-truth because it fails to take due account of two things. First, it ignores those effects of technology which are either not foreseen or not desired or both. Such effects cannot be determined by any individual or group, except in some stretched sense. The effects of DDT on bird populations can hardly have been politically determined; nor, I imagine, was it part of the social function—whether manifest or latent—of the development of transistors to force pop music on those who dislike it.

Second, the social determinist view is based on inadequate appreciation of technology as a range of capabilities which goes beyond those which are actually used in any period of time.* One of the examples Dickson[4] uses to show the non-neutrality of technology is the telephone system. The system as we have it, he says, reflects the 'individualistic' nature of our society because it is designed for communication between two individuals rather than for group discussions. But to adapt the system for group use is easy: the technology is almost identical. The way we use the technology is of course determined by social preferences, but the range of capabilities is not.

Let me take another example: the stabilized world envisaged in *The Limits to Growth* by Meadows *et al.*[19] It is a world full of technology: stability was achieved in the computer runs only with a lot of resource recycling, pollution control and restoration of eroded and infertile soil. The argument in the book is not that technology is dispensable but that technology by itself is not enough. What kind of technology would be needed to help to stabilize the world? Many of the particular devices would doubtless differ from those now in use, but they would unavoidably rely on largely the same principles and components and skills. Much the same underlying know-how and hardware can serve both the god of growth and the fad for zero growth.

I conclude that technology does have a substantial measure of autonomy from the kind of society which uses it. In an important sense it is politically

---

* Ambiguities inevitably arise from different definitions of technology. Some definitions see it as a capability; for instance, Schon defines it as 'any tool or technique, any product or process, any physical equipment or method of doing or making, by which human capability is extended'.[17] Others see it as a process in action; for instance, Galbraith defines it as 'the systematic application of scientific or other organised knowledge to practical tasks'.[18] Both etymology and current usage favour the first type of meaning: etymology because *logos* means discourse, so that technology means knowledge about technique, not the act of applying it; and usage because we talk about technological capabilities—about technologies being available—irrespective of whether they are actually being used.

neutral and culture-independent. In so far as it is based on regularities in the physical world, in which we all have to live, it transcends social change. By its use of the most rigid inflexibilities of nature—those revealed by physical science—technology gives the greatest flexibility for social action.*

The fundamental issue is the degree of malleability or plasticity of knowledge. To take a totally social determinist view of technology would be 'relativist'; it would extend to the material world the implications of a relativist view of knowledge for the intellectual world.† I have argued that such a view of technology is misleading because technology is not determined entirely by society but has some life of its own, some properties which are not voluntarily put into it. We cannot pretend that it is created entirely according to our wishes; although we can try to change it in the long run, we must for the time being accept it for what it is.‡

COMING TO TERMS WITH THE DRAGONS

The common feature I have tried to draw out of the two issues—alternative knowledge systems and the autonomy of technology—is the importance, as a constraint on knowledge, of what is 'given' externally to us and stops us from moulding our knowledge systems to our taste.§ Knowledge, in other words, has a dragon element as well as a pussy cat element. Personally, I am not too unhappy about that conclusion. Unlike Feyerabend,[5] apparently, I am not too fond of cats, and I think dragons could be rather useful if we can get them on

* The separation between a capability and the decision to use it has another important consequence, which is obscured by failure to recognize the separation. Abuse-proof technology is a chimera. The appeal of sun and wind as energy sources is enhanced for Clarke[20] by the apparent difficulty of using them for military purposes: 'it is not easy to envisage what a solar bomb or a wind-powered missile would be like'. But Archimedes, according to the story, set fire to the enemy ships with burning mirrors. Man's inhumanity to man is not dependent on high technology; one can kill, maim and torture with the simplest technical means. However specifically a pitch-fork is designed to pitch hay, it can also be used to attack a neighbour; and ordinary workmen's tools will do to pull out toenails or to cut out tongues. This illustrates once again that technology is at the disposal of alternative political arrangements and value systems. It follows that technology is an inadequate moral scapegoat for the shortcomings of modern societies. As a converse of the fact that technology is partly independent of man's will, man's actions also remain partly independent of the technology he uses. Social choices about developing technology do not eliminate options for further choices about using it.
† Melman says 'only man, in fact, designs and shapes every particular technology'.[16] I cannot accept the 'only', for the same reason that I do not accept the 'totally' on p. 55n†.
‡ If you fail to recognize this, you must prefer Lysenko's genetics, which promises to develop new cereal varieties with preplanned characteristics in $2\frac{1}{2}$ years, to Vavilov's genetics, according to which it will take much longer.[21]
§ Even human creations, once they have been created, become part of the 'given'; short of complete collective amnesia, an item of knowledge is 'there' and cannot be wished away any more than can the Atlantic Ocean.

our side. The problem is how to make sure that they are on our side—remembering that, being to a degree autonomous, they will not automatically side with us, as they would if they were entirely creatures of our will.

Dragon-like knowledge to some extent dictates to us how it is to be handled. That is one of the things about it which is 'given' and independent of our wishes. The most important implication, as I see it, is that students are well advised to put up with a certain amount of dogmatism from their teachers because there is accumulated experience to learn from which will help to give expertise.

The notion of accumulated experience is contained in the epistemologies of both Popper and Kuhn, though in different forms and in each case in a somewhat backhanded way. In the Popperian scheme, although the supreme commandment is to be critical and to try to overthrow theories, it is nevertheless the case that the current corpus of knowledge is the result of a long process of evolution by trial-and-error and by learning from mistakes. The sub-title of Popper's book *Objective Knowledge* is 'an evolutionary approach'.[22] Modern knowledge contains the fruits of much hard-won experience, in the same way that modern living organisms embody the results of learning from a long series of evolutionary mistakes.

In Kuhn's view, although it is questionable whether the succession of paradigms is cumulative, the power to solve problems which an established paradigm gives is acquired by *accepting* the ground rules which the paradigm defines and the mode of approach which it dictates. 'A more efficient mode of scientific practice begins' says Kuhn, when a group of workers 'take the foundations of their field for granted'.[6] Education therefore must have something of the character of an initiation into problem-solving traditions. A dogmatic element in education seems to be an epistemological necessity. The epistemological price students have to pay is to recognize that their active participation cannot extend to the creation and criticism of all the theories and conceptual frameworks to be used.[23]

The consequences for university practice are that student-centredness has to be tempered with subject-centredness, and participatory learning–teaching styles with the recognition that there are some things about which teachers do on average know more than students. If we ask what it is about universities that makes us feel that, if they did not exist, we would have to invent them, the answer must surely include making the experience of the past available to the present for the sake of the future. The function of education, it is said, is to let the young learn from the mistakes of others instead of, more painfully, from their own; and that is just what Popper's evolutionary theory of knowledge amounts to, in much-enriched form.

There are implications also for power structures and patterns of control in universities. Sociologists of education are only half right when they say that what counts as valid educational knowledge is socially defined by those who hold power in the educational system—by the 'politics of the curriculum', in short.[24, 25] The reverse also holds: the appropriate distribution of power and social control reflects the nature of the knowledge being handled. Simple vice versa fantasies* about student control should therefore be resisted on epistemological grounds.

This sounds like a very conservative position. Is my appeal to accumulated experience just the time-honoured reactionary cry of those who resist innovation? Far from it, for two reasons. First, the argument is emphatically not an argument for no change. Rather, it concerns the type of change needed—which should be thought of, I suggest, as being a process of redirecting knowledge that already exists as much as it is a process of finding substitutes for it. Those are two very different matters; the strategy and tactics appropriate for redeployment are different to those required for replacement. Over-emphasis on replacement, which could be implied by calls for new knowledge systems, would reduce what is available for redeployment.

Second, I am not suggesting that all knowledge is of the dragon type. I have chosen here to emphasize the dragons,† but that does not entail forgetting about the pussy cats. There are aspects of knowledge where continual re-creation is as important as drawing on accumulated experience. Here the knowledge of the young compares favourably with that of their elders, and students can learn as much from each other as from their teachers; one of the best things a teacher can do is to adopt a fellow-student role and periodically to admit defeat in an argument.‡

For understandable reasons, this kind of educational experience is becoming more popular with students. Pussy cats have a more immediate appeal for many people than dragons. It would therefore be all too easy, in the expansion of educational provision, to leave things increasingly to the pussy cats. Society, it might be argued, does not need dragon-handlers in large numbers; a few engineers and technocrats are enough to keep the wheels turning, leaving

---

* The allusion is to the novel by Anstey[26] in which father and son swap roles.

† I have argued here for the dragon-like element in science and technology, where it is easiest to show, but there is such an element in most areas. For painting, Gombrich explicitly compares 'the rhythm of schema and correction' in the processes of perception and representation with Popper's philosophy of science.[27] Nevertheless, differences between subjects should not be obscured. The epistemological egalitarianism of Young[28] is ill-founded, as I have argued elsewhere.[23]

‡ He should also try unobtrusively to raise the level of discussion. The formation of value systems and the definition of social goals is not *only* a matter of taste and commitment beyond the reach of critical discussion. There are often inconsistencies and incompatibilities which can be exposed.

the rest of the population free to cultivate aesthetics or athletics or whatever takes their fancy.

Far be it from me to suggest that all students should be funnelled into the technocratic rat-race; but I would like to suggest that, unless we are careful, we might end up with an undesirable distribution of expertise through society. We should try to avoid what I would like to call 'cliff effects'—abrupt discontinuities in the level of expertise.* For experts isolated in their little islands of expertise it is all too easy to convince themselves and even others that choices are technologically dictated. It is not surprising if nuclear engineers regard the desirability of nuclear power stations as obvious. What should be options become disguised as imperatives, and that leads to the one-dimensionality that Marcuse[30] complains of.†

So I would like to see the contours of expertise widely spaced, and dragon-handling capacities diffused through society. I don't see how we can otherwise get the networks of overlapping competences necessary for pluralistic interests to be genuinely represented in the setting of social goals, and for expertise to be made or kept genuinely accountable to the wider public. For that reason, among others, I hope that the dragons will not be forgotten as education expands.

ACKNOWLEDGEMENTS

I owe much to stimulating discussions with Dr R. D. Johnston and other colleagues in the Department of Liberal Studies in Science.

Discussion

Black: There seems increasing reluctance to learn the factual basis of a subject, and we often forget that until we have this information we can't talk about it or make any useful progress. However, disciplines and subjects are man-made groupings, for the convenience of study, and if their existence creates intellectual blinkers they must have a marked effect on the ability of universities to accept innovation. From an epistemological point of view I think they may be basically irrelevant.

---

* An extreme discontinuity is that between the Morlocks and the Eloi in Wells' novel *The Time Machine*.[29]

† To accept the justification for this complaint is not to fall for Marcuse's confidence trick about 'true' and 'false' consciousness. All consciousnesses are influenced by social environment; it is difficult to see how one could judge what 'true' consciousness would result from the 'free development of human needs and faculties', because no consciousness uninfluenced by a social environment is available for questioning.

Eldredge: Professor Jevons, why don't you think that pure science leads technology? The results of pure science can be spun off in technologies but the 'engine' is pure science. $E=mc^2$!

Jevons: The notion of technology as just science which has been applied is much over-simplified. We have done a fair bit of work on this in Manchester. The metaphor that I think best represents the contribution made by science to technology is that science is not the mother of technology but nursemaid to it. It helps innovation to grow. It doesn't usually generate it, it is rarely the first impetus for industrial innovation, but it does help to overcome the difficulties that arise during the development of that innovation. When one tries to identify science inputs into industrial innovations, that is the kind of relationship that one finds.

Stewart: The progress of science and technology is an immensely complicated network in which pure science, applied science, development and exploitation each contribute to advance in the others. All parts of the system are essential.

Eldredge: Do you admit behavioural or societal technology as valid technologies, and if so what do you think of them?

Jevons: That seems too large a question to go into here.

Francis: How do you assess the comparatively recent tendency of people in the scientific community to become self-critical about the social dimensions of technology, Professor Jevons? This movement has achieved some significance in the United States. Barry Commoner, for example, has established a school of 'critical science', and he and people like him are closely linked with decisions of political and economic significance, such as the factors governing the introduction of supersonic transport. How much of this do you think is due to scientists waking up to the renewed possibility of being more directly involved in political processes? It is a dimension that even in our system of government in this country has been under-explored and under-exploited. In fact the scientist has traditionally been under-represented within the organs of government. The House of Commons Select Committee on Science and Technology has become the only open forum on questions of national science policy. Do you think that some movement in the UK will develop which is likely to correct that situation, even though these matters currently fall outside the framework of an orthodox training in science and engineering?

Dror: Before you answer that let me say something in the opposite direction to give you some more choice, Professor Jevons. Part of your dragon is in fact a paper dragon, but there may be a real or meta-dragon around. Most scientists are unable to handle policy questions because they are rather unsophisticated about policy matters. I would perhaps agree that the not too many scientists who are 'policy-sophisticated' don't play a sufficient role, but if the question is whether scientists as a whole are under-represented, I would say, rather, that they are sometimes over-influential. Many scientists are just not sufficiently in tune with the content, methods and climate of policy-making, and frequently they do more harm than good. So to move all of them into a different kind of symbiosis with knowledge and power requires, first of all, the re-education of scientists in policy-making. From this point of view I think that a lot of the scientists still need to meet the real dragon.

Jevons: I would half agree that scientists have been under-represented in policy-making but, bearing in mind your reservation about the different kinds of skills that are involved in the natural sciences, Dr Dror, I would re-emphasize the point I made at the end of my paper about the overlapping of areas of expertise. The 'dragon' kind of knowledge is by its nature more powerful than some other kinds of knowledge. It is knowledge that has proved its effectiveness in certain contexts and therefore carries certain kinds of power. These were emphasized in the 1960s when the science policy movement was at its height.

It almost seems sacrilege to say it in this company, but I sometimes wonder how much worse our current crisis is than crises that people have faced in the past. We heard earlier about the present 'crisis of crises'. As I look back in history, though, I am led to ask, when was the last period that did not have people who considered themselves to be going through a crisis?

Wilkins: In those previous situations, we weren't able to destroy practically all life.

Jevons: It would have needed more people to destroy nearly all the rest, certainly. Nuclear weapons have undoubtedly changed the situation drastically. But when has it been possible to take the future of mankind as guaranteed?

Woodroofe: In my experience, most scientists are not interested in policy areas. They are interested in their own specialization, and the cobbler wants to stick to his last.

Dror: I am not sure that we should always be sorry about this. Being a specialized scientist is often bad preparation for policy.

Valaskakis: You imply that technology is possibly a dragon because of the unanticipated consequences of technological decisions, Professor Jevons. I will take this argument further and imply that every human action has un-anticipated consequences. As the old Greek (or was it Chinese?) saying puts it, we should never call a man happy until he is dead, because all sorts of things may happen between now and his death to cancel previous evaluations. I am suggesting that in any kind of decision theory, in any kind of decision-making process, there is always a perpetual gamble. If you take this gamble too seriously you probably end up not making any decisions at all. An example may illustrate this idea: a friend of mine overslept one day and thereby missed a plane which was supposed to take him to an important business meeting. He subsequently felt very guilty and lazy until he found out the plane he was supposed to be on had crashed! This was an unanticipated consequence which righted what would hitherto have been a wrong move: oversleeping. What I am suggesting is that, if we accept the idea that whatever we do is a perpetual gamble, then why not forge ahead anyway? Of course we need a technology assessment, and prudence is a high virtue, but I am a little concerned about completely freezing technology because of its unanticipated consequences.

Jevons: I agree.

Valaskakis: So you agree that the dragon elements do not actually belong to technology alone but to almost any field of human endeavour, in different degrees of intensity?

Jevons: Yes, in the sense that in almost any field of human endeavour there are consequences which are unintended or unpredicted. The argument that technology has no autonomy seems to me to be very misleading because it suggests there are no consequences of technology other than those which are anticipated.

Valaskakis: What would your position be, for instance, if a wonder-drug was marketed to cure cancer if insufficient research had been done to assess its second and *n*-order consequences? Would you recommend forging ahead or would you recommend long and painful research for years? This is the sort of dilemma that a decision maker has to face every day. The dilemma in fact is as follows: if the wonder-drug is marketed, at best it will cure cancer; at worst it will both fail to cure cancer and at the same time generate unpleasant second-order consequences (as for instance in the thalidomide scandal where the drug caused the birth of deformed babies). If the wonder-drug is not used, a good twenty years may pass before the medical association or government declares it free of noxious second-order consequences. In the meantime many terminal patients who could have been saved have been left to die.

Jevons: There are already mechanisms for ensuring that a good deal of research is done on possible side-effects. But the dangers can never be reduced to zero.

Dror: This is not a scientific question but one about lottery values, a question about the evaluation of risks, or one value issue against another value issue.

Valaskakis: Risk can be mathematically computed. Uncertainty is a state of ignorance so great, in the technical sense, that no odds can be computed.

Dror: Whether you define the risks or not, choosing between alternative risks, including certainties, is a value issue.

Platt: I think Professor Jevons was saying that there are some subjects where teachers do know better than students. I am sure this is so, but you mustn't interpret teachers in this context as always being university professors or the ones at the front of the classroom. Increasingly, in a world of rapid change, we have found that it is the young assistant professor who knows the new biology and the old biologist who does not. Or it is the graduate student who does the top line research that informs the assistant professor. And frequently it is the first-year graduate student who has read the latest edition of the basic book who knows his subject better and hasn't mislearned or made the same mistakes that the older graduate student has.

In the last ten years, in the universities in the United States, it has been the students who insisted on environment and ecology courses, not the teachers. And it was the students who insisted on more black representation on the faculties, on more women's courses, and on a whole range of studies which had been neglected by the disciplinary professors. If I might go further, today a teenager knows more about how to repair a Suzuki than I do, and I need to go to him humbly as a student when I want to repair my motorbike. The eight-year-old girl may know more about hopscotch, and even the two- or three-year-old child may know more about laughter than I have forgotten, and I need to relearn it by sitting as a student beside that child.

In a healthy society, we all have our areas of expertise and we need to be mutually open to learning from each other. The old are learning from the young, and part of the meaning of the revolt today against the disciplinary professors is that the rest of society has its own expertise, its own values and its own knowledge which must be mixed in.

Jevons: You have given some splendid examples of overlapping fields of competence.

Ziman: I want to be a dragon's advocate here and breathe a little bit of fire and smoke over some futurology. The future only exists as a mental construct, an intellectual extrapolation of the present. This extrapolation is made uncertain by unpredicted or unpredictable events and these uncertainties multiply uncontrollably as time goes on, until the future becomes vague beyond comprehension. Even if, in some sphere of activity, we had a 'calculus of extrapolation' it could not model the whole future of the human race. The best calculus can model only one small aspect of the future and, therefore, can only make a prediction subject to the assumption that adjacent and related aspects do not change.

Yet we know that every aspect of life—natural, technical and social—has its characteristic 'transformation time', which I have tried to set out in this table of characteristic transformation times. For example, if you don't have food

Table 1 (Ziman)
Characteristic transformation times of various aspects of human affairs.

	"Natural"	Technical	Social
1 minute	Respiration	Accident Fire Traffic jam	Nuclear War Murder
1 hour		Cooking	Riot Theft
	Cell Division	Flight	Repose Meeting
	Digestion		
1 day	Storm		
	Flood Illness	Food Garbage Voyage	Battle Revolution Foreign Exchange Conference
1 month	Starvation	Manufacture	War
	Epidemic		Stock Exchange
	Gestation		Commodity Market
1 year	Crop	clothes	Political Power
	Infancy Bird Mammal	Apparatus Car	Employment Education
10 years	Childhood Generation Human	Machine Factory Railway Furniture	Economic Growth Marriage Corporation Party
100 years	Tree Population Forest	House Canal Road City	National Development
1000 years	Landscape	Irrigation system Tomb	Dynasty Church Language Culture
	Climate		
10,000 years	↓ Species		

for a month, you starve; you are *transformed*, in that length of time. A modern war takes from a few days to a month to resolve itself, so the situation has changed in that interval. A nuclear war takes a few minutes, so they say. The Stock Exchange changes over a period of months to the extent that one loses the feel for a 'trend'. The values suggested here are sheer guesswork, and we could argue about all sorts of details; but I think that most of them are within a factor of 10, one way or the other, of what anyone would write down about the characteristic time scale of actual events—the way we see the world, the rate at which things do change.

Mathematically speaking, it is impossible to make a reliable extrapolation for any *particular* aspect of the future over a time that is much longer than the transformation times of the *other* aspects to which it is connected. I am not saying here that you couldn't try to do it and make plausible-looking predictions. You might have a perfectly good calculus for discussing how the Stock Exchange is going to behave over a long time, in terms of Stock Exchange forces. But you are bound to bring into that calculus other features in the diagram—political decisions, changes of government, commodity prices, and various other economic and social factors—which would be beyond the predictive scope of the calculus. The unpredictable events or changes in these other aspects would introduce uncontrollable uncertainty into the attempt at extrapolation. You might think that you have a perfectly sound formula for the factors that you are explicitly predicting, but the statistical fluctuations in 'external' elements connected with your chosen aspect are going to force it into uncertainty. In the absence of a complete Laplacian prediction machine this is the fundamental limitation to all attempts at studying the future. The fire and smoke of the dragon are not to be sneezed at; these are the realities that one learns as a 'hard scientist' in the prediction game.

Dror: What are the possibilities for changing some of the longer time cycles through the social applications of modern technology, such as genetic engineering or climatological changes? Isn't it one of the problems that technology will change some of the nature-given time cycles?

Ziman: I am talking about a different problem. I am not talking about possible interactions between various 'aspects' or 'factors'; whatever we may achieve by conscious effort those events are eventually going to be dominated by other events beyond our control. If the climate cycle is changed by human intervention in, say, atmospheric circulation, does that mean that the sunspot cycle can be changed?

Dror: A 2 per cent change may be critical for human survival but not significant in the cosmic scale. We must put a subjective time interval into the calibration of times, as a focusing or prismatic device for seeing how a policy perspective differs from the point of view of some pure scientific interest.

Ziman: The technology for climate control will assume, for example, some sort of political stability for the whole of the earth, to maintain the enormous devices that would be needed to make it work over long periods. This is one of the great problems about nuclear power. As we look at history, we learn that a dynasty or a power system, a type of society, may only last a few hundred years.

Dror: That is more than enough for present policy purposes.

Ziman: Yes, but that is the limit. When you say you are going to predict something, and drive it through, you are going to have to overcome what might be called the inherent climatological correlation time, whether it is fifty or one hundred or five hundred years, by technical power and prediction. I insist that that is a purely intellectual construct, because there is inherent in your argument an assumption about stability in other factors which is not justified by any of the evidence that we have at the moment.

Platt: This is why *limit* calculations, as in *The Limits to Growth*,[19] can be so important. They may be absurd in terms of a small-scale structure, or extrapolation from the present; but if you see what you believe to be physical or biological limits, these give an overall shape, an overall size, to the bottle within which the other reactions and changes must take place. It is important to know where those limits are.

Shane: In 1973 I published a study of trends amongst futurists.[31] In the early 1960s much of the thinking that was being done was done on a linear basis. By the middle 1960s, the future had begun to be thought of as a fan-shaped phenomenon, with a number of alternative, probabilistic futures of the kind that we now anticipate. By the late 1960s students of the future had reached a point where they accepted the concept of cross-impact: the concept that what was going on in one field (e.g. holography or mood-influencing drugs) would, in the long run, have a substantial impact on, say, the methodology and the content of instruction in secondary schools. These trends are cumulative, of course: linear projections were not discarded. They all became tools for futures research. At present the emphasis, it seems to me, is on value decisions which have to do with how we cope with the different alternative futures that loom before us. Most futurists, in the United States at least, have become extremely chary of making any projections of the kinds that Kahn and Wiener made in the late 1960s,[32] because they have been inaccurate so many times.

Eldredge: You seem to think that the bottle of the universe has already been built, Dr Platt, but the bottle might conceivably be rebuilt if we interfered, at a sophisticated level, with reality. You also say that these things happen in time-sequences. If anybody happens to believe, as I do, that there may be a useful societal and behavioural technology, then that would change the whole framework of how decisions are made and speeded up. As a very soft scientist, I think you are mistaken in assuming that the bottle of natural things is completely fixed. I think we can 'mess about' with almost everything in the universe.

Platt: Let me give you an example of what I meant. American television sets are now turned on for six hours a day on the average—but if the human race lasts for a thousand or a million years people will not watch television, or any other representation of an external world, for sixty hours a day because there are limits—there aren't that many hours in the day. Similarly with such things as exploration of the globe—in the last forty years people have gone to the top of the highest mountain, the bottom of the deepest ocean, and lived at the North and South Pole with hot and cold running water and helicopter service. Today, satellites go around the globe every two hours, photographing things down to the size of a football. This means that the exploration of the globe is finished. We have come to the end of that particular bottle.

Eldredge: Who is left at the bottom of the great Atlantic trench? Do we know all about that?

Platt: No, but it is very different from the age in which Burton spent three years searching for the source of the Nile with a hundred porters and then didn't find it. The speed of light has limits, the earth has limits, sunlight has limits, life has limits; and it is useful to know approximately where these limits are before we reach them. The kinds of optimists who always say 'But we will invent new things beyond the limits!' are like people in a bus heading towards a cliff who do not try to turn the steering wheel but instead discuss how some day they can invent buses with wings. It may be true that they could do this, but it shows a lack of perception of the real-time, real-world operational limits.

References

[1] LEISS, W. (1974) Utopia and technology: reflections on the conquest of nature, in *Man-Made Futures* (Cross, N., Elliott, D. & Roy, R., eds.) pp. 20–30, Hutchinson Educational, London

[2] BACON, F. (1627) *New Atlantis.* Reprinted in Johnston, A. (ed.) (1965) *Francis Bacon,* pp. 161–181, Batsford, London

[3] LEWIN, L. C. (introduced by) (1968) *Report from Iron Mountain on the Possibility and Desirability of Peace,* Penguin Books, Harmondsworth

[4] DICKSON, D. (1974) *Alternative Technology and the Politics of Technical Change,* pp. 146, 178, 183, Fontana/Collins, Glasgow

[5] FEYERABEND, P. K. (1970) Consolations for the specialist, in *Criticism and the Growth of Knowledge* (Lakatos, I. & Musgrave, A., eds.) pp. 197–230, Cambridge University Press, London

[6] KUHN, T. S. (1970) *The Structure of Scientific Revolutions,* 2nd edition, p.178, Chicago University Press, Chicago

[7] SKLAIR, L. (1973) *Organised Knowledge,* Hart-Davis, MacGibbon, London

[8] JEVONS, F. R. (1973) *Science Observed: Science as a Social and Intellectual Activity,* Allen & Unwin, London

[9] POPPER, K. R. (1965) *Conjectures and Refutations,* 2nd edition, p.16, Routledge and Kegan Paul, London

10 TISELIUS, A. & NILSSON, S. (eds.) (1971) *The Place of Value in a World of Facts (Nobel Symposium 14)*, Halsted Press/Wiley, Chichester
11 JOHNSTON, R. D. (1974) On scientific knowledge. *Times Higher Education Supplement*, 26 July, London
12 JEVONS, F. R. (1972) Chemistry in Africa. *Nature (London)*, *236*, 92
13 REDDY, A. K. N. (1974) Is Indian science truly Indian? *Science Today*, pp. 13–24, January
14 ELIAS, N. (1974) The sciences: towards a theory, in *Social Processes of Scientific Development* (Whitley, R., ed.), pp. 21–42, Routledge & Kegan Paul, London
15 HORTON, R. (1971) African traditional thought and Western science, in *Knowledge and Control* (Young, M. F. D., ed.), pp. 208–266, Collier-Macmillan, London
16 MELMAN, S. (1974) The myth of autonomous technology, in *Man-Made Futures* (Cross, N., Elliott, D. & Roy, R., eds.), pp. 56–61, Heinemann Educational, London
17 SCHON, D. (1967) *Technology and Change*, p. 1, Pergamon Press, Oxford
18 GALBRAITH, J. K. (1969) *The New Industrial State*, p. 23, Penguin Books, Harmondsworth
19 MEADOWS, D. H., MEADOWS, D. L., RANDERS, J. & BEHRENS, W. W., III (1972) *The Limits to Growth*, Earth Island, London
20 CLARKE, R. (1974) Alternative technology, in *Man-Made Futures* (Cross, N., Elliott, D. & Roy, R., eds.), pp. 333–339, Hutchinson Educational, London
21 MEDVEDEV, Z. (1969) *The Rise and Fall of T. D. Lysenko*, translated by Lerner, I. M., p. 19, Columbia University Press, New York
22 POPPER, K. R. (1972) *Objective Knowledge: an Evolutionary Approach*, Clarendon Press, Oxford
23 JEVONS, F. R. (1975) But some kinds of knowledge are more equal than others. *Studies in Science Education 2* (in the press)
24 YOUNG, M. F. D. (1971) An approach to the study of curricula as socially organised knowledge, in *Knowledge and Control* (Young, M. F. D., ed.), pp. 19–46, Collier-Macmillan, London
25 BERNSTEIN, B. (1971) On the classification and framing of educational knowledge, in *Knowledge and Control* (Young, M. F. D., ed.), pp. 47–69, Collier-Macmillan, London
26 ANSTEY, F. (pseudonym of Guthrie, T. A.) (1882) *Vice Versa*, Smith and Elder, London
27 GOMBRICH, E. (1960) *Art and Illusion*, p. 271, Phaidon Press, London
28 YOUNG, M. F. D. (1974) Notes for a sociology of science education. *Studies in Science Education 1*, 51–60
29 WELLS, H. G. (1895) *The Time Machine*, Heinemann, London
30 MARCUSE, H. (1968) *One Dimensional Man*, Sphere Books, London
31 SHANE, H. G. (1973) *The Educational Significance of the Future*, Phi Delta Kappa, Bloomington, Indiana
32 KAHN, H. & WIENER, A. J. (1967) *The Year 2000: A Framework for Speculation for the Next Thirty Three Years*, Macmillan, New York

Social decision prerequisite to educational change, 1975–1985

HAROLD G. SHANE

School of Education, Indiana University, Bloomington

Abstract   It is a common premise on the part of persons who are less than thoughtful that schools should provide leadership as humankind moves from the present to the future. This paper takes the position that the schools have not performed, and in all probability never can perform, any yeasty leadership function in social change.

If, like a highly polished speculum, schools can merely reflect the society in which they have their being, then certain social decisions are prerequisite to any new basic educational change. The success with which social change occurs depends on the image or images of the future which a given human sub-set accepts and the way this group chooses to approach the future.

Points developed include: (1) some premises which may be helpful in contemplating the future, (2) probable developments of the next decade which are likely to have a bearing on cultural change, and (3) a roster of important decisions which must be made if schools are to have clear guidelines as they seek to serve the society that supports them.

The paper concludes with speculations on the probable nature of educationally portentous decisions that are emerging, and with a timetable for educational change between 1975 and 1985.

During 1972–1973 I had the privilege of studying certain aspects of the status and current directions of futures research (sometimes called policies research) in the United States.* The project, funded by the US Office of Education (USOE), was based on 82 personal interviews in more than twenty futures study centres such as Rand, the Hudson Institute, and the USOE Educational Policy Research Centers at the Stanford and Syracuse Research Institutes.

During these months of inquiry, and in the past year of study with specialists

---

* The futures research study was reported to the U.S. Commissioner of Education in mimeographed form early in 1973, then rewritten and published as *The Educational Significance of the Future*.[1]

in a number of disciplines* it has become apparent that education has a critical, important role to play during the closing decades of the present century. By 'education' I mean to include the many sources of instruction to which traditional 'schooling' is rapidly losing its monopoly: the mass media, federally supported programmes such as the Job Corps, self-instructional materials, 'teaching packages', and the like.

Even as I became more and more deeply aware of the importance of education during the 'crisis of transition' and the 'crisis of crises'[2] through which the world has been passing, I became increasingly aware of the fact that faith in the power of education *per se* to solve many of humankind's problems was not only naive but a potentially dangerous misconception.

THE PARADOX OF WEAKNESS AND STRENGTH IN EDUCATION

Education has never been an effective ingredient in changing society. For example, while there were many significant developments in the culture during the 1960s in the US, they were neither stimulated nor initiated by the schools and education-related agencies. It was pressure from blacks in the US that led to the development of black studies, for instance, and it was demands from students goaded to the point of rioting that led to curriculum change and to the 'greater relevance' now presumably found in the curricula of secondary and higher education. It was *not* pioneering by educational leaders that led to the drive for improved women's rights. Pollution, resource depletion, and the tragic wars in which our age specializes were assailed for the most part in scholarly and political arenas that were remote from the classroom, and usually by people who were not professional educators.

While the schools, like a highly burnished speculum, tend to *mirror* rather than to *initiate* social change, they are nonetheless important elements in the processes of cultural change that are underway. How does one explain this paradox of education's combined weakness and strength: weakness as a change agent and strength as an agency for reinforcing change?

For one thing, it is the men and women exposed to the mass media and educated in the public and in the independent schools of the developed world who have, since 1900, removed ten-year-olds from our coal mines, revolutionized worldwide concepts of human rights and human dignity, broken genetic codes, experimented with behaviour modification, smashed the atom, and devised 'Green

* My work during 1973 was funded predominantly by the Danforth Foundation in St Louis, Missouri. This organization provided substantial support, including money for three 1974 symposia that I planned. Participants included Kenneth Boulding, Lester R. Brown, Theodore Gordon, John Platt, Robert Heilbroner, Willard Wirtz, Jonas Salk, and William Irwin Thompson.

Revolutions' (cf. deRopp[3]). To phrase it succinctly, the schools and other educational media might be likened to intellectual launching pads for the careers and contributions of men and women whose ideas and whose influence would one day change the earth. Through the established processes of education they transmitted both the cultural heritage and a large measure of substantive content.*

Second, since we recycle our school population every twelve to fifteen years, education—broadly conceived—is an indispensable means of introducing children and youth to emergent social decisions and to their role in the world of the future. Third, education effectively can be used to attack certain specific social and environmental problems ranging from illiteracy to the need to borrow from rather than to consume the world's resource pools. Finally, education often can help the learner to develop a talent for identifying and implementing or discarding new alternatives in the light of their consequences. It is contributions such as these that probably will continue in the future to motivate us to give support to schools which, in the US, consume more tax money at present than anything except expenditure for armaments and for the cost of past wars.

SOCIAL DECISIONS PREREQUISITE TO EDUCATIONAL CHANGE

While education, including traditional concepts of schooling, is an enormous potential asset as our society moves into the emerging futures that lie ahead of us, its full value cannot be realized until certain antecedent decisions are made by society.†

More explicitly, in the contemporary crisis of transition, education very much needs to regain its wonted sense of direction. This, I think, can be acquired only from a societal matrix which has once again developed a body of accepted values that can serve as a gyroscope whirling to keep the society on the course it has laid out for itself. As noted earlier, the effectiveness of our educational agencies will reflect—admittedly with some distortions—the social setting of either a healthy or a sick society. They can supplement, implement and reinforce change, but they cannot create it.

We can only hope that the decisions that society makes, either purposefully or by default, will be moral ones. By 'moral' I mean choices that are *just* and

* There are those who argue that the schools are deteriorating because, judging by some indicators, median achievement scores have declined. I would contend that *youth of top ability* continue to perform as well or better than a generation ago. However, lower median scores, in an era of universal compulsory education, tend to draw attention away from the *range* of performance which continues to reflect the work of a number of first-rate young scholars.
† Throughout this paper, unless otherwise noted, the term *society* refers to the US. While I believe that all or most of my generalizations apply to other developed nations, it would be difficult for me to defend the transferability of these generalizations.

equitable. I will not look too carefully at this hope, even though I am convinced that present threats to the biosphere will serve to heighten our consciousness and help us to find the wit and wisdom, the character and compassion, needed to move us from our present evolutionary stage as creatures who are 'the missing link between animals and human beings' as Loren Eisley once phrased it.

Whether our social decisions ultimately prove to be equitable ones is a matter for speculation beyond the scope of this brief paper. Let me turn instead to some of the actual problems and issues which confront humankind. The decisions they demand promise to extend our intellectual stature by several cubits in the quest for viable solutions.

The problems which I have singled out as being particularly in need of attack were not selected arbitrarily on the capricious basis of subjective judgement. They were compiled—as already noted—from the 82 conversations with futurists that I recorded in 1972–1973 (Ref. 1, pp. 42–49). These problems were confirmed and some additional ones imperilling the human prospect were identified in 1973 and 1974 through four projects for which I obtained funding.*

So much for background information. Let us now look at a roster of important decisions that need to be made if education is to regain the sense of direction it has lost since 1950. These include:

(1) Decisions regarding our future use of technology: continuation of present exploitative policies versus more prudent evolution or even sophisticated devolution (dynamic contraction) of present practices.

(2) Conclusions regarding the prudent use and sharing of transnational resources such as air and water and regarding the equitable sharing of national products such as wheat, soybeans, oil, tin, lead, coal, copper, and so forth.

(3) Choices regarding the use of electrical, chemical, and psychological behaviour modification techniques—a grievous problem which is further complicated by the question of whether we have the wisdom that should be exercised as a prerequisite to decisions about the raising or lowering of levels of such qualities or behaviours as aggressiveness, violence, memory, docility, or withdrawal.

(4) Selection of policies that can restore and maintain in the future the

* The Association for Supervision and Curriculum Development funded a small by-invitation conference in Washington, D.C. during August, 1973 for purposes of identifying problems of the near future and the decisions they required. Among the 14 participants were Alvin Toffler, John Platt, Lester R. Brown, Elise Boulding, Arthur Okun, and Thomas Green. The Danforth Foundation in 1974 (see p. 74 *n*) funded conferences in St Louis in January and February of approximately 300 persons each and also sponsored in October a three-day Washington D.C. dialogue treating the moral aspects of imminent social decisions.

integrity of our economic–industrial and political–military systems.

(5) Decisions regarding what we consider the 'good life' to be in a world becoming less and less able to have wrenched from it the raw materials that are needed to maintain the life styles developed in the West since 1900.

(6) Conclusions regarding the use of finite and dwindling financial resources* to provide for the needs and wants of wide-ranging human sub-sets: the old, the very young, the poor, the advanced student, occupational groups, ethnic and religious minorities, youth, dependent children, the handicapped, and so on.

(7) Choices as to whether the gap between the 'have-nots' and the 'haves' can and should be decreased and, if so, by what variety of means.†

(8) Selection of policies and practices which can minimize some of the shortcomings of mass media and maximize their value—especially the value of television—without resorting to imposed controls, including censorship.

(9) Decisions regarding what the developed world is willing to give up (if anything), and in what order, so that a more equitable distribution of food and other resources can be ensured for the world's poor.

(10) Choice of what honourable compromises shall be made in the processes of reaching decisions such as the nine exemplars listed above. Patently, many diverse opinions will need to be reconciled as such compromises are reached.

The importance to education, and more explicitly to schooling, of the decisions facing society can scarcely be underestimated. The content of instruction and the attitudes that education presumably should strive to foster are at present the objects of uncertainty and disagreement, at least in the US. This is a relatively recent development. For most of the past two hundred years American educational institutions have shown great viability. As Tyler wrote recently,[5] '...during these two centuries the illiterate learned to read, immigrants from many diverse cultures were assimilated in an increasingly pluralistic society, and social mobility and gains in individual economic status have been phenomenal since 1875. The labour force has been educated for both a technological and a post-industrial society. Furthermore, socialization of students in the spirit of the

* From the early years of the Kennedy Administration (1962) to the last full year of the Nixon Administration (1973) Medicare, housing and student subsidies, federal welfare costs, etc., grew from a few billion to over $41 000 million (cf. Glazer[4]).
† As reported in the *Washington Post*, August 8, 1974, the idea of a ceiling on all earnings has been seriously proposed in Sweden by Professor Gunnar Adler-Karlsson.

"new education" (as advocated by John Dewey, William H. Kilpatrick, George S. Counts and others of their persuasion) has not inhibited the development of either individuality or of unique talents.'

The educational achievements to which Tyler refers, however, were made possible by an era of certainty. The Englishman or American of 1910 or 1915— and in all social classes—*knew* what was 'right' and 'wrong', what was black and what was white. There were few if any of today's infinite shadings of grey to impede decisive action. Education helped to preserve yesterday's behavioural maps even after it began to be recognized that these maps no longer matched the changing terrain of 1930 or 1960.

Patently, the schools and other educational agencies now go begging for the want of a society that has developed new certainties that are congruent with new and still-emergent survival patterns for the planet as a whole.

PROBABLE DEVELOPMENTS OF THE NEXT DECADE WITH A BEARING ON EDUCATION

It is always comfortable to speculate with respect to what Stuart Chase labelled 'the most probable world',[6] since no one has completely reliable information about the future. That which has yet to occur can't be organized for study—we can only select and project possible developments that our enquiries suggest will take place, keep a tight rein on our prejudices, and perhaps avoid creating self-fulfilling or self-defeating prophecies. Therefore the paragraphs below attempt to avoid presenting propaganda for the sort of world which personal bias might motivate me to describe. There seems to be no way, however, completely to control my selection of the scholars on whose ideas I have drawn.* I seem to remember best the ideas of thinkers whose reasoning I find to be most stimulating.

First, if we are to have a workable and individually satisfying society in the future, it seems almost certain that a maturing humanity will need to be appreciably more self-disciplined than the one which developed in the US between 1950 and 1975. What does greater self-discipline imply for education? While I do not see us returning to an arid, didactic, rote-memory type of education, the elementary school seems likely to place more stress on basic skills in an 'open' setting.

At the secondary level, programmes seem likely to become less permissive, to emphasize greater self-discipline and self-direction, and to provide more

---

* While not a comprehensive guide, the references suggest the range of writers whose views I found stimulating.

'action-learning' and 'service learning' in the world of work. There probably will, in a more disciplining educational environment, be more exits from and re-entries to secondary and postsecondary schooling. Content doubtless will be modified further to stress consideration of the biosphere. That is, in a school of engineering one may learn not only *how* to build a commercial airstrip, but *whether* the proposed site is ecologically a sound one.

A *second* development that probably can be anticipated, as Seaborg has suggested, is that in the developed world we will begin rather soon to think in terms of being *users* rather than *consumers* of basic resources.[7] All educational agencies, and the mass media in particular, will be placed on their mettle to put this concept across if Professor Seaborg's idea proves to be one whose time has come.

A *third* possibility—a likelihood, rather—is that we are in the twilight phase of extravagant, self-indulgent living. Tomorrow's society may well prove to be a post-affluent as well as a post-industrial one! How well we learn to be 'users' rather than 'consumers' will be a challenge to education—a challenge to carry us quickly from the twilight of conspicuous consumption into a new day in which, in Gabor's apt phrases, we will achieve '...a mature society, stable in numbers and in material production, in ecological equilibrium with the resources of the earth'.[8]

Space permits mention of no more than a *fourth* opportunity for education, although a dozen could be listed. This is the probability that the intellectual and technological capacity of humans will, respectively, improve and increase. Laboratory research reviewed by psychologist Krech[9] indicates that we may be on the threshold of learning a great deal about behaviour modification as well as about its concomitant problems! Extension of technological skills and accomplishments and their almost inevitable increase in sophistication need no documentation.

How educational agencies actually will interpret and respond to probabilistic futures such as the four sketched above it is difficult to say. But two points—perhaps rather obvious ones—can be made with considerable confidence: (1) The clarity and forcefulness with which pressing social decisions are made and implemented by adequate funding surely will weaken or strengthen our educational agencies accordingly; and (2) as a tested vehicle for fostering the views supported by their supporting society, the schools and other instructional media remain one of our best bases for attacking basic problems and for creating a suitable psychological climate for promoting wise choices among alternatives by persons of all ages: the very young, youth, mature students, and senior learners.

FIVE PREMISES FOR THE PRUDENT GUIDANCE OF FUTURE EDUCATIONAL CHANGE

Once society has made up its mind about the future for which it is willing to strive, educators and citizens have the interesting task of deciding what posture to assume as they confront the coming decade. The following advice with a bearing on educational change is offered:

(1) Recognize that the future is analogous to an edifice of infinite size: its structure takes form one brick or block at a time, but its general architecture must be planned in advance, just as lunar landings in the past decade took years to consummate. Good education is built day by day, but also must have a constantly expanded horizon.

(2) Be prepared to be surprised. An unanticipated system break of some kind is forever around the corner. Keep educational agencies flexible.

(3) Keep in mind that the future is not what it once was thought to be: it has been 'contaminated' by our spectacular success in, say, lengthening life spans, improving material comforts, speeding up transportation and communication (although the *means* of communication have outraced *intelligibility*), and in mediating the environment. Our very success has betrayed our 1950 or 1960 visions of what 1980 or 1990 would bring.

(4) Avoid populating the future with projections of today's accepted guidelines for conduct; they will almost certainly be inadequate as we work to bring about the educational change which tomorrow will require.

(5) Remember that facts can be the enemy of truth. Much of what we believed in the past—even in the hard sciences, and certainly in the soft ones—has been discredited or modified. Today's 'facts' may well be yesterday's fables when tomorrow comes.

The social decisions of which our schools and related instruction agencies stand in need should be made as quickly as possible. Among other reasons, it is essential that these decisions be reached to relieve the pressures of present uncertainties.

If we in education are fortunate enough to achieve from society a renewed sense of purpose and direction, we can hope to move through three stages of educational evolution in the years immediately ahead. I would speculate that from 1975 to 1980 we will find ourselves in *Stage I*, an interval which I shall call the 'preintervention period'. Here our route is clear: we need to begin to understand 'what we must do'* but curricular and instructional intervention will be difficult to achieve overnight because of the inertia of large educational agencies.

Stage II might be thought of as an 'alternative approach' interval, one which I speculate could extend from, say, 1980 to 1990. During this decade the ideas generated in Stage I could be methodically phased into the workings of the educational community. Our route is less clear, but the opportunity for change is greater because of the lead time provided by Stage I.

After 1990 or 1995, we should be crossing the threshold of *Stage III* which is one of 'crucial uncertainty'. *Uncertain* because it is difficult to envision world dynamics fifteen or more years hence; *crucial* because humankind has relatively few years to put itself in order. And by Stage III we should begin to know whether or not the sequence of social decisions→educational change→goal achievement has begun to improve our chances for attaining better techno-futures, sociofutures, biofutures, and human futures for the people on our planet.

Discussion

Waddington: Our discussion is about what the universities can or should do about the problems of the future, rather than about whose estimate of the probabilities of the future is best. Professor Shane has given us a splendid summary of the major problem areas which are very much in everybody's mind at present. He mentioned that there are several ways of approaching each problem area, with nobody's answers likely to be 100 per cent correct. This of course is what biological life in general is about. Success in evolution depends on ability to deal with the unexpected. The problems facing man today are already thoroughly in the minds of many students, and it is quite time that the universities started doing something about them.

Ziman: Professor Shane's list of decisions that need to be made is a splendid list of standard and familiar liberal aspirations, reforms, programmes, worries, extrapolations, etc., of our time. But I would be very worried if teaching about the future or about its possibilities were left just to those rather bland categories. The future may be much harsher than Professor Shane implied, and people need to be armed by their education to meet graver eventualities than those we have been talking about. Nuclear war is one of the harsh possibilities which were not mentioned. This seems to be the terrible problem of our time but strangely it is not one of the things people teach about.

* I refer to the education dimension implicit in John Platt's article.[2]

Waddington: It is discussed in my futures textbook.[10]

Ziman: It is one of the central problems for peace research. Then there is revolution. Revolution is not just about the social contract between haves and the have-nots. What Professor Shane refers to as 'The poor and so on' may be what it looks like in the US, but it doesn't look like that in Africa or Brazil. The possibility that the whole social structure of the world may be rearranged by these forces has to be taken into account. We should not necessarily support such forces but we should try and see what they are about. Yet they are not on that list either. Another problem, a more difficult one to talk about, is the possibility, not merely of the corruption of the politicians but of their psycho-pathologies—the Amins of this world. Some of us here calculated that one per cent of the human race at any one time has always lived under a political monster. This is part of the human condition and it is one of the possibilities. Not to teach that seems to me again a failure to arm people for the future.

Valaskakis: Once again I would like to point to the very real danger that exists when we are too constrained by the present. Professor Shane mentioned that universities can, or should be, a mirror of society. I think the danger lies in the universities being *rear-view* mirrors of society. I see the ideal function of the university both as a *distant early warning system* for the future, and as a mirror or rear-view mirror of society. And for this I would like again to make a plea that we should have more normative forecasting and horizon scenarios. I have a suspicion that some of your suggestions in the list may be mutually incompatible, Professor Shane. I would take the fifth item, the definition of the good life, as my starting point for defining all the others. The others seem to me very much a reflection of present problems and present perceptions, in the same way that Charlton Heston is now seen by us as both the definitive Ben Hur and the definitive Omega Man. If we moved from projective forecasting to horizon forecasting we would achieve a salutary divorce from the present. The most useful forecasting so far has been done, in the opinion of many, by science fiction authors: they have separated themselves from their present, and have created scenarios of the future, and they have not been bogged down by present circumstances, present viewpoints, present paradigms.

Waddington: Universities of course have several different functions. Undoubtedly the early warning system is one important function. Universities also have to handle young people, aged from 18 to 21 or so. The items in general surveys such as Professor Shane has given us are all around us, in the atmosphere as it were; but it will take students some time to put all these things together if they are left to themselves, and if they are all under pressure to get a degree in some specialist subject. Once they have caught up with where thought is at present, we can start thinking about helping them to look into the future. But we must not forget the down-to-earth function of bringing them up to date with current thinking.

Jevons: Professor Shane and Professor Platt have both referred to students as the originators of women's studies, black studies, and so on. Sociologists say that innovations tend to arise not from the middle of the hierarchy of seniority but from the top or the bottom. Does that apply to innovations in universities? Professor Shane, as a professional educationalist, have you any evidence about the sources of innovation in education?

Shane: Until the 1960s much leadership input tended to come from persons at the top, from established educational thinkers. But from the 1960s onwards there was much more pressure from students in the drive for women's liberation and the various 'student liberation movements'. It was pressure from these groups, ethnic groups, and the like that brought about many changes in the content of instruction on our campuses in the US.

Waddington: Have women's liberation and the student movements really contributed anything new to the world's wisdom, or to professional education? Did women's lib. add to our understanding of how society works, and of women's position in it?

Shane: My own insights were appreciably deepened in the 1960s with regard to the under-the-skin feelings of an appreciable number of blacks, women, undergraduates and so on. I was insensitive at first, say, to women's rejection of male-oriented language. I tended, for example, to think of *man*kind rather than *human*kind, simply because it was the usage I learned in childhood. It was many years too, before I realized the nature of the inner seethings in the hearts of many blacks. But we were able to communicate more effectively by the late 1960s. The passing years have heightened my consciousness of the inner feelings of other people.

Waddington: I think the question is partly local.

Platt: I think we are facing not a gradualist future, but a decade of disasters. Nuclear escalation is a probability with the superpowers. At a lower level, Professor Shane did mention nuclear terrorism. It is highly likely that within the next few years there will be a Hiroshima-type bomb on Tel Aviv, or New York City, which is somewhat easier to get into and has a larger Jewish population than Tel Aviv. Economic disaster is possible. Maoist revolutions may happen in South Asia, in Africa, in South America—not that they are necessarily disasters for the rest of the world. They may in fact be considerable gains, somewhat like the Chinese gains in bootstrapping people off the bottom of poverty. But the response to such revolutions by the CIA and by Russian world politics could trigger some of the larger nuclear disasters.

I could go down a considerable list of such potential disasters in the next decade. I think it will be very different from the last decade or two, where in a certain sense the alarms and developments in the high information society, becoming aware of its large problems, have been relatively peaceful. Today we have moved into the international arena with this high information and with these new global problems, and we have all the problems that come with multiple actors in non-zero-sum game theory, problems of conflict, cooperation, game-playing and so on, where large numbers of administrations are forced increasingly into situations that no one wants yet everybody gets into. I think we are in a pre-revolutionary situation in which it is essentially impossible to predict the year 2000—just as it would have been almost impossible in 1775 to predict the year 1800, with the French and American democratic experiments still ahead. Even seventy years ago, in 1905, with the Russian revolution ahead, with one-fifth of the human race going communist, the destruction of all the aristocracies and kings of Europe, the flapper era, and so on, it would have been impossible to predict the year 1930. The future will depend, in a quite unexpected step-function way, it seems to me, on accidents of constructive leadership or accidents of assassination or accidents of collision of two crises at a crucial moment, with somewhat unpredictable public and international responses. The possibility of forecasting the year 2000, and the kind of global structure we shall have at that time, depends on the way in which we make use of these crises, and the way in which we do our homework now to prepare to make use of them. The alternatives are very hard to predict, but I think that in this kind of quantum-jump situation, all extrapolations, Delphi forecasts, or gradualist or incrementalist forecasts, are almost certain to be wrong.

Perry: Does the fundamental dilemma for the universities spring from the enormous growth of communication at all levels in the world? What the universities may have to decide is whether they go on teaching about futurology to an intellectual élite who will then make their mark as leaders in the world, or whether they should try to turn their attention to a much larger segment of the population. In other words, should they reach down to a lower level and to larger numbers? The response of leaders is eventually going to be determined by what they judge their followers will accept. Maybe that is where the universities ought to be directing their efforts rather than towards pure scholarship in such studies.

Waddington: Don't you think the universities will have to do a bit of both? They should reach much further down to the general public, but I hope this can be done without losing altogether the forward-looking role that we have also been talking about, which is possibly not confined to the élite but is likely to have more impact on the élite. The combination of mass appeal and high-grade scholarship is the difficult but essential task of universities.

Perry: I was pointing out the difference but I was not suggesting that the scholarship should disappear.

Woodroofe: The universities have the role of looking forward, warning the rest of the community of the dangers ahead, and influencing the decisions that the top people in the community are making. I suspect that they should teach first about the present. My contact with university students, and indeed with some university staff, suggests that they don't understand the present. They do not seem properly equipped to understand what they read in a good newspaper. Many of them do not know the basics of economics, the way industry and commerce work, or the way government works. Before we start teaching the future let us have a good base by understanding the present.

Waddington: But wouldn't you agree that what is happening is always a lot of processes? There is no such thing as the present. Whitehead defined the present as the fringe of memory tinged with anticipation.[11] We can't in fact teach the present without teaching either a bit of the past or a bit of the future, or a bit of both.

Woodroofe: Absolutely. I wouldn't mind if we were teaching ten years behind the times or even longer, but I don't think that we are up to date as far as that.

Kumar: I wonder whether other people are having the same problems about this discussion as I am? The main reason for us getting together is to talk about what kind of contribution the universities can make, in a teaching capacity, to thinking about the future. But the other main thread that keeps coming through is, how do we actually think about the future? What do we as a group think about the various problems and methodologies? I can see that there is a certain overlap here but I find it difficult to concentrate my mind on both simultaneously. As a kind of practising futurologist I have one way of thinking about the sort of problems that Professor Shane listed; and as somebody involved in university teaching I have another way of thinking about how I can put over a way of thinking about the future to undergraduates. It is not an enormously great problem to think about how undergraduate courses about the future might be put on in universities. I teach a course called 'The sociology of industrial societies', large parts of which are concerned with the processes of social change, and one can deal with things as far ahead as one wants to. I know other people are doing this in the sciences. Whether one wants to put these studies together in some sort of school, or have a degree in futures studies, seems to me to be a bureaucratic problem. It may be just a matter of different bureaucratic rigidities at different universities which determines how difficult it is to persuade faculties to allow these courses. I would like some guidance about what kind of discussion you would like us to have about the teaching element in putting on futures studies. What kind of problem and evidence ought we to be talking about? I find that thinking about what the future is going to be is a different kind of mental exercise from thinking about arranging such courses.

Waddington: One question is: are we properly educating our students if we give a somewhat future-oriented course on the sociology of industrialization to those few students at a university who are taking that type of degree, while we give nothing that is future-oriented to those who are doing standard biology or chemistry? As you say, Dr Kumar, it is a bureaucratic question whether we can have courses on futures studies, or have to be content to allow the future to be brought in by any lecturer who happens to be interested in these matters as they concern his specialty. That is the essential question I think we are discussing. Personally I don't think it is adequate to leave individual lecturers to bring in some future-oriented matters only if they feel like it. On the other hand, I don't think we want to have a total degree course in futures studies and nothing but futures studies. My view is that at an elementary university level—and I have chosen the second year for my experimental course—we should have a superficial broad course, mentioning all aspects of the future, for practically all students. Then some of them will go into specialties like industrialization, where they will get a lot more of it. Some of them will study languages and get much less of it, and so on.

Eldredge: It seems to me that we are also discussing the total function of the university in society. I think there are three main audiences for the universities. First there are the students, who are a captive audience. Second, there are the decision makers. Futures studies may play the role of an intelligence officer serving his commander. There are many commanders, or decision makers, in society and the university has a major function in dealing with those decision makers, trying to loosen them up. Finally, in a democratic society, there is a third audience—the people: nobody dares to do anything unless the people, however defined, are at least told what is going on. I think that the Open University attitude of open, popular, advanced education is an absolute necessity. In my own work in urban studies, where we move on to urban planning, we now tend to think in terms of 'alternative horizon scenarios' because in 'multigroup' or 'mosaic' societies one must offer different sorts of possible futures. One of the most difficult is to develop realistic alternative future scenarios.

References cited

[1] SHANE, HAROLD G. (1973) *The Educational Significance of the Future*, Phi Delta Kappa, Bloomington, Indiana
[2] PLATT, JOHN (1969) What we must do. *Science (Wash. D. C.) 166*, 1115–1121
[3] deROPP, ROBERT E. (1972) *The New Prometheans*, Dell, New York
[4] GLAZER, NATHAN (1972) The Great Society never was a casualty of the war, *Saturday Review*, December, pp. 49–52
[5] TYLER, RALPH W. (1975) Can American Schools meet the demands they now face? *Viewpoints: Bulletin of the School of Education, Indiana University, 51*, 2
[6] CHASE, STUART (1968) *The Most Probable World*, Harper & Row, Evanston, Illinois
[7] SEABORG, GLENN (1974) The recycle society of tomorrow. *The Futurist, 8*, 108–112, 114–115
[8] GABOR, DENNIS (1972) *The Mature Society*, Praeger, New York
[9] KRECH, DAVID (1969) Psychoneurobiochemeducation, *Phi Delta Kappan 50*, 375, March
[10] WADDINGTON, C. H. (1975) *The Sources of the Man Made Future*, Cape/Paladin, London
[11] WHITEHEAD, ALFRED N. (1926) *Science and the Modern World*, Macmillan, New York

Additional reading

BECKERMAN, WILFRED (1974) *Two Cheers for the Affluent Society: a Spirited Defense of Economic Growth*, St. Martin's Press, New York
BOULDING, KENNETH E. (1964) *The Meaning of the 20th Century*, Harper Colophon Books, New York
BROWN, LESTER (1974) *In the Human Interest*, Norton, New York
COLEMAN, JAMES S. *et al.* (1974) *Youth: Transition to Adulthood*, University of Chicago Press, Chicago
DICKSON, PAUL (1971) *Think Tanks*, Atheneum, New York
EHRLICH, PAUL R. & EHRLICH, ANNE H. (1974) *The End of Affluence*, Ballantine Books, New York
FREEMAN, S. DAVID (1974) *Energy: the New Era*, Vintage, New York
HEILBRONER, ROBERT (1974) *An Inquiry into the Human Prospect*, Norton, New York
HOSTROP, RICHARD W. (ed.) (1973) *Foundations of Futurology in Education*, ETC Publications, Homewood, Illinois
KAHN, HERMAN & WIENER, ANTHONY J. (1967) *The Year 2000: a Framework for Speculation for the next Thirty-three Years*, Macmillan, New York
KAHN, HERMAN & BRUCE-BRIGGS, B. (1972) *Things to Come: Thinking of the Seventies and Eighties*, Macmillan, New York
KOSTELANETZ, RICHARD (ed.) (1972) *Social Speculations*, Morrow, New York
MESAROVIC, MIHAJLO & PESTEL, EDUARD (1974) *Mankind at the Turning Point*, Dutton/ Reader's Digest, New York; Hutchinson, London
SALK, JONAS (1972) *Man Unfolding*, Harper & Row, New York
SALK, JONAS (1973) *Survival of the Wisest*, Harper & Row, New York
SCHUMACHER, E. F. (1973) *Small is Beautiful: Economics as if People Mattered*, Harper & Row, New York
THOMPSON, WILLIAM IRWIN (1974) *Passages about Earth*, Harper & Row, New York
TOFFLER, ALVIN *et al.* (1967) 'Toward the year 2000: work in progress', *Daedalus*, summer
TOFFLER, ALVIN (1970) *Future Shock*, Random House, New York
TOFFLER, ALVIN *et al.* (1974) *Learning for Tomorrow*, Random House, New York

From academic hothouse to professional dugout: a mean free path

JOHN M. FRANCIS

Heriot-Watt University, and Society, Religion & Technology Project, Church of Scotland Home Board, Edinburgh

Abstract   This paper deals with the task of assessing new technologies and with the definition of key subject areas for multidisciplinary research within universities. In the United Kingdom, for example, the universities could develop an invaluable network for monitoring land use, food production and energy supply at a regional level. The opportunity to contribute to an overall planning framework which effectively integrates social, economic and environmental factors would be an important longer-term objective. To illustrate this point, the paper refers to the escalating effects of major industrial developments in Scotland resulting from the exploitation of North Sea oil and gas resources. It is suggested that the regional analysis of critical resource potential in land, food and energy would provide a core of relevance for futures studies in the universities and also establish a focal point for departmental interests within each university.

At the start of my paper I make no apology for the fact that my views are a product of my own peculiar path of experience. This can best be illustrated as follows:

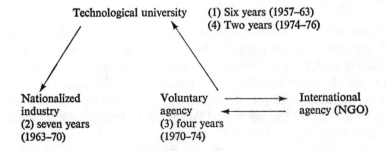

Technological university   (1) Six years (1957–63)
                                     (4) Two years (1974–76)

Nationalized industry (2) seven years (1963–70)

Voluntary agency (3) four years (1970–74)

International agency (NGO)

Despite our particular form of enlightenment in the West, this is not a well-trodden path. In my case, having returned to base, I am more than ever inclined to believe the old adage—'the more things change, the more they are the same'.

The purpose of my paper is not to register frustration but rather to signal one or two opportunities that I believe are there for the taking among those who can project an integrated view of the future.

In brief, I should like to deal with the task of assessing new technologies, with the definition of key areas for multidisciplinary activity and with the nucleation steps that must be taken in the very near future to provide a planning framework at a regional level which is more appropriate to the age in which we live. The latter part of the paper will obviously bear heavily on my own interpretation of what is happening in Scotland largely as a result of developments related to the exploitation of North Sea oil and gas resources. This problem is one of resource management on a relatively large scale and over a time scale that does not allow the future to be discounted lightly in terms of social and environmental factors. If ever there was a positive need for integrated planning of industrial development embodying new content and new directions, there is ample evidence that this need exists in Scotland under the pressure of recent events. The failure of the academic community to make an effective connection with these problems—apart from highly individual contributions at public inquiries and the like—suggests a degree of improvization and an almost characteristic lack of anticipation. The value of an early warning system in key subject areas, such as land use, food production and energy supply, that could be provided by certain universities on a regional basis and as part of a national network should not be underestimated. In the first instance, this would provide a core of relevance for futures studies and a focal point for departmental interests within each university.

THE ASSESSMENT TASK

General case

In recent years, a supposedly new discipline referred to as 'technology assessment' has been emerging from the shadows. The idea has achieved a certain credibility in the USA with the establishment of an Office of Technology Assessment within the Congress, although the greatest stimulus must have been the statutory requirement to prepare formal environmental impact statements in line with the National Environmental Policy Act.[1] The approach is founded on the straightforward principle that technology includes interacting social and physical components. The combination of physical technologies (the hardware) and the social technologies, embracing organizational and managerial skills, represents a complicated interface that cannot easily be determined. The primary role of the technology assessors is to explore this interface by:

(1) defining the assessment task;
(2) describing relevant technologies;
(3) developing state-of-society assumptions;
(4) identifying impact areas;
(5) making preliminary impact analysis;
(6) identifying possible action options;
(7) completing impact analysis.

In this methodology, the physical technologies are assumed to be causal factors and therefore the logical starting point for assessments.[2] It is also assumed that, starting with the physical technologies, it is possible to trace through the consequences of these technologies for both the social technologies and for society at large. The objective is to identify those points where changes in either the physical technologies or the social technologies would result in significantly different results to those that might otherwise be achieved. Several multidisciplinary teams that have taken this road have ended up with the belief that no method or theory exists which will adequately explain the ability of our society to develop complex technologies.[3] While that problem is not directly relevant to this short paper, some elements of the final analysis must contribute also to the functional task of technology assessment. It is necessary to be specific, and I shall choose the example of a multidisciplinary research team brought together inside a university in the United States to conduct an assessment of Outer Continental Shelf Development.[3] The team consisted of a marine biologist, a lawyer, a physicist, two political scientists and three engineers. The project was funded by the National Science Foundation's RANN programme (Research Applied to National Needs) and it ran for the period from September 1971 to March 1973. The initial task was to prepare a detailed description of offshore operations and accordingly three subsystems were defined:

(A) Exploration.
(B) Drilling and production.
(C) Pipelines, storage and transport.

It was then possible during the data-collection phase of the systems analysis to identify the critical pieces of hardware (the physical technologies)—such as wellhead safety devices—and the social technologies (rules, regulations, procedures and the responsible statutory agencies). The goal was to develop a matrix which would give some indication of how the physical and social technologies interact. It was possible to reach certain conclusions fairly quickly as a result of this procedure:

(1) Physical technology systems in use in the late 1980s would be substan-

tially the same as those in use today. (This does not indicate that the technology is unchanging but that the changes are expected to be evolutionary in character and will take place on a component-by-component basis.)

(2) Information is limited to publicly available sources and the currently stated views of the domestic industry and contractors involved directly in offshore oil and gas operations.

(3) Lack of information leads straight to the difficulty of determining which of the impacts are costs and which are benefits, as well as to the problem of giving these factors specific weightings.

The realization that in this instance the physical technologies were not driving the system caused the team to turn their provisional methodology around and to concentrate on major modifications required in rules, regulations, procedure, etc. It was concluded that correction of all detectable weaknesses in the physical technologies was well within present state-of-the-art capabilities, and that improved regulatory procedures would induce the application of the best available physical technologies. In turn, this would stimulate new research and development activities to make a creative contribution over the next fifteen years. In a comparatively short space of time, this team had made an effective, if incomplete, synthesis of this important area of technology, had focused on the otherwise fragmented appreciation of the problems, and had worked their way out of a job. While this can serve as an illustration of the advantages of a flexible team approach working outwards from a university base, it is a critical part of my argument that in the UK there is an immediate need to deploy some of our university resources in this direction. I shall come back to the specific opportunities later in the paper.

The particular case

During the past four years, I have had the privilege of directing a project sponsored by the Church of Scotland on 'Society, Religion and Technology', which has certainly taken me in some unexpected directions. Since I was appointed to this post in 1970, directly from a research and development background in the nuclear power industry, it will not surprise the members of this seminar that I was soon very much involved in the continuing struggle to understand the problems of population and pollution, peace and poverty, in the period leading up to the UN Conference on the Human Environment held in Stockholm in 1972. Principally through the agency of the World Council of Churches, but also because the project was based in Scotland, I organized and took part in a multitude of study groups, workshops and public meetings at every conceivable level. While this may have been a fairly typical experience for many scientists of my generation, it did persuade me not to go on pursuing these issues at such a high level of generalization. It was necessary to find an appropriate middle path that would allow an element of professional competence to survive alongside these broader concerns. I simply found that a total disengagement from the intensely pragmatic world of the physical technologies was not possible in my case. The chain of circumstances which led me into a 'problem-centred' approach was similar to that encountered by the team already mentioned, but unfortunately without the nicely-balanced constituency of a project team and the ancillary resources. In mid-1972 the problems facing Scotland were immediate and obvious. An entirely new industry was being born, geared to the increasing scale and pace of offshore oil and gas exploration in the northern sector of the North Sea. The planning response was slow and uncoordinated; public sector investment in roads, housing and general community services was heavily time-lagged—not able to match the incoming wave of industrial development projects which swept the country. The conventional wisdom on resource management and integrated environmental planning failed to make a connection with events on the ground. Decisions taken at local authority level were based on rapidly redrafted development plans, and these decisions were subsequently endorsed by Ministers at the Scottish Office. It was happening, it was important, but it was outside the commonly regarded axis for development in Scotland (namely the central belt). It was time to build up a more general appreciation of the significance of these events and to try and place them in a more realistic social and environmental context. Historians will, I feel sure, come to regard that period as a watershed for Scottish industrial development in this century, but it found the country quite unprepared and largely ignorant of the political and economic significance. For the Church of Scotland project, it was not only a vital opportunity to begin some initial stocktaking of the prospects for the offshore and onshore industry but a challenge to make some connection with the ongoing debate concerning the major factors of population growth, resource depletion and environmental hazards. The procedure was improvised and the final report undoubtedly contained many imperfections, but the response to the publication indicated that it did fulfil a clearly felt need on the outside of the industry.[4] Since then, a series of studies have been conducted at a community level and at a regional level; the investment in manpower has been surprisingly small but the analysis that has been generated will, I hope, be of lasting benefit in many situations throughout Scotland. This method of working does however place a large emphasis on the continuity of personnel directing the programme and on a wide network of contacts at many levels throughout the government machine, industry and local authorities. It demands a good deal of application and a certain amount of footwork. In a highly dynamic political and economic situation the outcome is always uncertain, but the discipline of exploring the future choices is certainly never dull.

Many consultancy and planning organizations have now elected to operate in this mode. It has become almost a prerequisite of local planning procedures that a general analysis of the social and environmental impact should be prepared on the occasion of a major development proposal. In some areas, the groups possess no local knowledge and have to begin their task with a sweep of facts and figures relating to the area in question. While this is now an accepted part of the planner's skill in formulating strategic and tactical choices, there has been a very limited diffusion of this technique into other areas of decision-making.

ENERGY AS A KEY AREA

The case against centralization

It should not be necessary to dwell on the connection between events in Scotland and the problems of national energy policy. The task of 'embedding' the energy system in relation to

- the atmosphere
- the hydrosphere
- the ecosphere
- the sociosphere

underline the enormity of the challenge when taken forward at an analytical level. Fortunately, there is at least one organization in existence that is prepared to encounter this task, even if only as a global dilemma. I recently visited the International Institute of Applied Systems Analysis (IIASA) in Laxenburg, outside Vienna, and met Wolf Häfele, the Deputy Director, who gave me a breakdown of their mode of operation. It is his synthesis of the task ahead that I have to quote to you as the mainspring for my own argument:[5]

'It is necessary to identify and understand all system problems that are inherent in the various options for large scale energy supply. This will be a continuing task and will probably never be completed as energy systems expand further and further. The task is not a matter of algorithm. It is a matter of technological and social substance. Scenario writings and life-style descriptions will probably be among the tools for accomplishing this task. It will be in particular important to identify the various interweavings that become important with the increasing size of energy production. This requires to some extent discipline oriented work but only to the extent that it is necessary for the identification of discipline oriented questions. From then on it is the task of the various scientific disciplines to pursue the questions so identified in connection with the systems analysis'.

This is the technique that has resulted in the first-class appraisal of the US energy situation published by the Ford Foundation Energy Policy Project based in Washington, D.C.[6] Although this operation was probably more generously funded than the previously quoted example of the team based at the University of Oklahoma, it is the style of project management that stands out in this instance. Members of the Ford Foundation team were able to move from and return to the Federal Administration at the end of a two-year term. Indeed some members of the team were in a position to contribute to the Federal Energy Administration Project Independence Blueprint that was published in November 1974.[7] I wish to stress that this is another example of an elaborate multidisciplinary effort that succeeded because of the essential flexibility and consolidated vision of the individuals concerned. Within the UK, it appears that there has been some hesitation on the necessity for such an effort. However, a recent report on Energy Research from the Advisory Board for the Research Councils[8] does register an interest in establishing and supporting multidisciplinary research groups that will undertake exploratory studies: 'Such assessments will have to take account not only of the scientific and technological aspects of the various energy options, but also of economic and sociological features such as the organisation and financing of existing energy-producing industries, fuel marketing strategies and the vulnerability of modern society to energy shortages, however caused'.

This suggestion is a suitable counterweight to the Department of Energy formulation of a large-scale computerized model, which simulates the management and growth of the UK fuel economy at the present time. It has been claimed that this is the most important single energy-planning tool available in the UK, but in view of the highly centralized nature of the technique and its relevance to policy-making, it seems unlikely that many of the results will be widely disseminated. There is an urgent need for independent reappraisal of the UK energy system, but in view of the difficulty of this task, it can probably best be managed on a regional basis. While the Department of Energy model can possibly be interfaced with future models to be developed by the IIASA in arriving at a global synthesis, there is a positive need for energy planning at a regional level in the UK where the planning constraints, including the availability of land, water and manpower resources, are already critical locational parameters far beyond the description of even the most sophisticated model. Independence and precision at this level can therefore be placed at a premium, while the advantages of connecting the energy sub-system with other sub-systems, including agriculture, transport and building industries, also at this level, should be very apparent.

Regional studies

It is at this point that the universities should come into their own as regional centres of excellence, with not only a declared concern for perfecting the standards of undergraduate and postgraduate education, but an equally clearly defined contribution to the social and economic planning processes out of which the future springs. Unlike most other agencies, the universities have a standing complement of professionals who combine effectively in the teaching role, but remain otherwise a largely uncoordinated body of people and ideas. There would seem to be a substantial case for establishing multidisciplinary teams in each university to give regional emphasis to critical areas of assessment—food, energy, housing, transport are the obvious examples. Where there are two universities in reasonably close proximity, then a division of labour according to the available baseline of competence in subject area would obviously have to take place. Alternatively, each university could elect to concentrate exclusively on one or two subject areas of specific interest to the surrounding community.

If this is a pious hope, then by way of contrast I should like to know how it is going to be possible to nucleate 'futures' studies in universities if the more spontaneous forms of interdepartmental cooperation are not available. It may be that my views are far too pragmatic to be taken seriously in such a meeting as this. Either that or my plea to connect with the realities of the planning process, which I see as the inertial devices of the next twenty to thirty years, comes too late for it to make any real difference. I do not hold to such an obviously pessimistic view, but I am apprehensive that as most people inside and outside the universities lower their time horizons so that they can weather the coming economic storm, the relevance of the future as an academic discipline may look increasingly remote.

There is a tangible connection that can be made under some of the headings that I have already mentioned. I should personally prefer to see it happen that way.

Discussion

Waddington: This is a fine introduction to the question of the relevance of research. You are obviously putting forward something considerably broader and more thorough than what has already been done, for instance, by the Department of Urban and Regional Planning attached to the School of Architecture in Edinburgh. Could you say a bit more about how your idea differs from earlier surveys, like the Middlesborough Survey and Plan in the 1930s, on which my wife worked, where the region was surveyed before the plan was made?

Francis: The statutory requirements for planning procedures necessitate modifications on the basis of a short-term analysis, although longer-term projections are frequently attempted. In contrast I am suggesting that, for example, the pattern of energy use within a region needs to be known in some detail so that we can understand how energy is being used in that community and how to anticipate the actual requirements with a much higher degree of precision. It seems to me that this analytical task is an ongoing task. It isn't something that can be done in five or six months so that a development plan can be adapted for a region; it is basically a consolidation of all kinds of resource data at a regional level, representing a pool on which the planners could draw. I believe it would be far better than the improvised superimposition of planning strategies which tends to occur in many parts of the country at present. I am simply suggesting that this requires a large technical and analytical component which is currently lacking, and consequently the planners don't have access to the kind of information that they need. It is quite useless to talk about a 'systems' approach to planning until this situation is remedied.

Eldredge: At the Harvard Business School the instructional method is to analyse one case study after another and let the students draw what they can from these data. Some good reliable futures investigations could come out of a series of case studies which could be either regional or sectoral, or perhaps both. It is a marvellous teaching device, as well as providing research results, because students can play an active part in the surveys. Students often say they don't want to talk about the future but want to *do* the future. They prefer what is now called experiential learning. Case studies can be used first as an active teaching device and then could be generalized at some future date, so that we not only don't have to reinvent the wheel but—as Professor Dror has said—we don't have to reinvent the broken wheel; this would be a step forward.

Dror: I think one should go a little further and not base the idea of futures studies on technology assessment alone, which itself needs a broader base in social futures, international futures and so forth.

The subject matter of this symposium is the future as an academic discipline. This goes far beyond teaching and certainly far beyond undergraduate teaching. One of the main purposes of an academic discipline is to provide knowledge; and, I think, we should emphasize that futures knowledge which is useful for policy-making may be even more needed now than futures teaching among undergraduate students.

Another main function of the universities is to prepare professional people for their callings, and again I would regard the absence of policy professionals able to deal with complex problems as an even more serious and acute problem than inadequate understanding of the future among citizens at large. This doesn't mean that I regard the role of teaching undergraduates as unimportant but I would not regard it necessarily as the most important role, and certainly not as the only function, of the universities.

We may be able to agree more or less on a list of important problems affecting society, like the one Professor Shane presented, but I have great difficulty in seeing a real connection between those lists which are intellectual thinking exercises and the present real agendas of most governments. In other words, putting present decisions and futures perspectives into gear is very difficult. Many people seem to assume that there will somehow be a *deus ex machina* quantum jump. But the social decision-making machinery needed for dealing with these types of problems does not exist either nationally or internationally.

This means that we need new bridges. I would say we need a double bridge: one between knowledge and power, and one between the present and the future. One way of looking at some of the functions of universities is to look at their possible role in providing those bridges. I have spent most of my life at universities and, being rather interested in this matter, I have found much more useful work going on at Rand Corporation-type think tanks than at universities. Some universities do some useful things and some think tanks do a lot of nonsense things, but in general universities have a lot to learn from the structure of think tanks if they are to adopt the bridging function.

I am trying to study the policy-making system in Great Britain. Although interesting attempts at improvement have been made—such as the Central Policy Review Staff Programme Analysis and Review, the special advisers, the work of Political and Economic Planning (PEP), and so forth—there is no policy research organization equipped to handle 'macro-social diagnosis'. This is something that universities should develop by trying to do it themselves, by training policy professionals and by encouraging the establishment of think tanks. In this way the academic discipline of futures studies, if it is intellectually feasible, may fill a real social need.

Waddington: It must be not only intellectually feasible but also administratively feasible.

Shane: Some years ago John Fischer published an article which was most prescient.[9] He suggested, for example, that architects should be taught not only their technical and professional skills but also to question whether, from an ecological point of view, an airport *should* be built in Chicago, when biospheric–ecological problems might ensue. Of course, this leaves unanswered the question of *whose* viewpoints shall be accepted as to what is 'sound' or 'desirable' from an ecological point of view. Conflicting opinion in the academic arena as to whose ideas should be reflected could lead to a lively conflict.

Francis: Many of the problems that I described in my paper were not anticipated and yet they have recently occurred within a concentrated time scale. The problems were not anticipated because it was almost impossible to predict the offshore oil and gas potential in the North Sea without going and drilling to establish the scale of the reserves. Under these circumstances, the planners could relax back into the position that they didn't have to anticipate a particular sequence of events because it wasn't their problem at that moment—there was only a limited frame of reference, there was no contingency plan, there was no alternative strategy. Nearly all of the regional growth-points were in the wrong place when it came to administering the industrial development pattern that emerged with the build-up of offshore production. To that extent we do need to have a base-line study going on at many levels. Land use is a fundamental consideration in determining settlement patterns and almost inevitably too many easy assumptions are incorporated concerning community needs and the need of individuals on that point, particularly when it comes to multiple land-use functions in certain critical development areas. There are many problems in this country of that kind. We really don't know the real asset value of a particular land area until it is already committed and subsequently sterilized. To that extent there has been a total deficiency in strategic planning at a national level. The Central Policy Review Staff, for example, which is working on energy conservation at present, throws all the balls in the air and simply makes blanket recommendations, with no real idea of what the actual contribution can be at the regional level. There is no machinery for making connection with the broad policy decisions or for the actual meshing of these decisions at a particular regional level. Energy requirements over the country as a whole are really quite disparate. Any general energy policy that is smeared over the whole country has an almost unanticipated effect when interpreted by local authority planners and similar concerns. A general policy can create all kinds of problems and for that reason I am very suspicious of any exclusive reliance on central policy machinery.

Black: You said that when the oil development came, it caught everybody napping. I am not a futurologist so I don't have to pretend that I know what the future is going to contain, but it certainly contains change, and change at an increasing rate. Professor Waddington has pointed out many times that, biologically, the success of evolution is to be found in its ability to cope with the unpredictable, and I would suggest that this is true of social evolution too. So what we should be developing in our students is the intellectual ability to cope with change. The old linear thinking whereby we go one step at a time along a fairly defined road is probably no longer adequate, as Professor Waddington has also pointed out today. Increasingly I see general undergraduate education—not specialist education—as developing the ability to cope with the unpredictable. Of course what happened in Scotland was unpredicted, and all the growth points were in the wrong place, but this is what happens in life.

Waddington: Are you saying that the university already provides this ability, or that it should provide it?

Black: I am saying that it *should* be providing the ability. At the moment it does not, and one reason why people get out of date is that they have been educated in a limited way.

Dror: Is this more a question of intellectual or of emotional training?

Black: Both; they can't be separated. I believe that we have been letting our undergraduates down by not giving them the emotional as well as the intellectual basis they need for coping with rapidly increasing change.

Waddington: I don't believe that when he was at Imperial College John Francis was indoctrinated with the notion that he was likely to change his profession radically, from being a professional nuclear power engineer to being whatever he may call himself now.

Perry: That makes me think of what I was trying to do when I taught pharmacology, where the rate of change is more rapid than in almost any other discipline in the medical schools. Although I tried hard to tell the students that they would have to face up to change, there was little I could tell them about how to prepare themselves for it. Change could not be foreseen because one never knew what the chemists were going to come up with. Apart from some general principles in the way of looking at evidence and judging it, what one is really trying to do is to introduce something right outside the subject, that is a state of mind prepared to receive change. I don't know if one department can do that alone. That is a naive remark but it does seem to me that it is quite important to realize this.

Waddington: I think there is going to be an even more fundamental effect. It really signals the end of our classical idea that education goes on until people have a degree at the age of 21 and then stops. At the Open University students can take a course at any stage in their lives.

Stewart: The report of the Advisory Board for the Research Councils[8] to which John Francis referred was really issued to show what research related to energy the Research Councils were funding in the UK and to indicate possibilities for the future. Universities have two principal contributions to make, one in teaching and the other in research, partly in regional problems and partly in general ones. The constraints on universities in building up interdisciplinary teams and breaking down barriers between departments are considerable. These, perhaps, can best be overcome by interdisciplinary teams being built up within a university with outside support. The system of dual support for universities could achieve this in the UK. The Research Councils can fund people who form a unit or a group of some sort within a university, and that group can draw in people from various departments of the university who become interested in the problems the group is dealing with. Sir Ernest Woodroofe made the point that if a research function is to operate together with a teaching function to undergraduates in such fields, a few permanent people are needed, plus a set of people who come in and out of the system. Could one not derive a system where, with a small permanent group, *ad hoc* groups could come in for a time and study particular problems of the day, energy being one such problem?

Waddington: Who should take the initiative in forming such groups? Many universities have quite a lot of people who could form an effective group if they were brought together. Sometimes one person likes organizing things, so he whips up his pals, who work out an interdisciplinary group which may be successful. Quite often an outside planning body, like one of the Research Councils, may know that there is a general problem and would be only too willing to fund an interdisciplinary group. Does the Council have to wait until somebody comes and asks for that? For example, from about the mid-1960s it became obvious to biologists that the world was soon going to run short of animal foodstuffs, and that the oil-seed cake and so on, which we used for feeding cattle in the UK, was going to be eaten in the countries where it is grown. It was clear that Britain ought to rethink its livestock industry. But there was no one in British research or in the science policy set-up to whom this could be said. The problem doesn't really belong to the Agricultural Research Council, which basically deals with British agriculture and not with conditions abroad. So what happened? The British livestock industry went over from feeding its cattle at least partly on home-grown grass to feeding them on home-grown or imported barley and other imported foodstuffs. This turning away from home-grown to imported foodstuffs developed just when everybody who raised their eyes to the world at large saw that imported foodstuffs were going to get scarcer and more expensive. This is what we are caught with now.

The point is that there was no central body looking at the world outside. That would be the most elementary futurology on the world scale rather than on a local scale. And, if there had been such a body, does the British administrative machinery provide any way in which a central forecasting body could stimulate the types of scientific research within the universities that it knows ought to be there?

Stewart: Some of the Research Councils prod the universities into doing work which the Council considers desirable but which is not reasonably covered at present. I think this practice is growing, particularly in the present financial climate. It is important that people in universities and elsewhere should also prod the research councils for money and draw the problems to the attention of the Research Councils. Both responsive and positive approaches are necessary.

Dror: Experience in other countries indicates the need for some redundancies in such institutions. A whole network of bodies is needed, with different perspectives and different loyalties. Some should be nearer and some further from the main policy makers.

Lundberg: Dr Francis, when you called for increased interdisciplinary contacts within the universities you stated that the departments combined effectively in teaching but not otherwise. Actually they usually don't combine even in teaching! It is our experience in Göteborg that interdisciplinary teaching is a good way of establishing contact. Undergraduate or graduate courses like those proposed by Professor Waddington may thus have the secondary effect of creating an interdisciplinary platform for research and external activation.

Waddington: Nearly all our organizations are vertical, either in hierarchies or undivided disciplines. We are bad at horizontal cross-connections. There is inadequate theorizing about such structures, and I think there is a lot to be done in systems-thinking about organizations with both horizontal and vertical links.

Francis: I agree with what Sir Frederick Stewart said about groups as points of nucleation. I also agree that the university has to put its house in order as far as revitalizing its own constituency is concerned. On a subject such as energy there are many contributing groups outside universities who are looking for a meeting point, which doesn't seem to exist. For the past two years I have been a member of the Oil Development Council for Scotland, and there is no way of making contact with the government machine other than by contacting each part of the energy system independently. There is no coordinating link at the regional level.

King: There is something of a paradox in your approach, Dr Francis. You were stressing the need for regional and local consideration of futures and of trends. I think you are right here, and this is true in many ways other than in futures studies. It is certainly true for participatory democracy and decision-making at local levels. But at the same time we have to indulge a lot more in global thinking. One of the problems is how to marry these two apparently contrary needs. For governments the importance of external factors is increasingly great. Recently a man who had been the Head of State of a small, highly industrialized, rich country told me that he had abandoned political life because it was no longer any fun: there was no room for manoeuvre at all and everything was determined from outside by what happened in the United States or in the Arab countries. This may be an extreme case but the influence of external forces is great in relation to contagious inflation, to the monetary system, the balance of payments, and to many other things. The force of these external factors is not yet reflected in the general trend of political thinking.

Waddington: The number of people in the world now who expect they will ever have autocratic power to decide things for themselves is small. I think your friend is suffering from a trend that began long ago in most countries. I am sure Sir Ernest Woodroofe would say that even Unilever has not total freedom to do whatever it pleases all the time.

King: In what we have said about horizontality within universities we are talking a little as if universities were monolithic structures and were roughly of the same pattern everywhere. But we are talking of a certain type of Anglo-Saxon university. In France, a survey of social science research in universities showed recently that there is practically none. Nearly all the social science research in France is done in independent institutes because the university system has been too rigid to accept it, or to find ways of financing it. Different countries have different approaches, and there is a good deal to be learnt from some of these as case studies. In our Anglo-Saxon system the flexibility is marvellous in some ways; on the other hand we haven't explored all the possibilities. In Japan, for example, there is a well-established way of starting serious research for a new subject. The universities get together and form temporary or permanent organizations—they may have institutes or they may not—which act on behalf of the university system as a whole. So instead of fractional work starting in many places, national institutes are created, each for simplicity under the management of a particular university, so that neither management nor resources are fractionated. That institute is able to give doctorates on behalf of the whole system to people from other universities.

Waddington: That is similar to what we have done in this country in relation to nuclear power.

King: That is for certain very expensive equipment, but the Japanese system is used more flexibly and in other ways.

Another experiment is the approach taken by the University of Manitoba, where a Vice-President for Multidisciplinary Studies has been appointed, whose job is to stimulate these studies. He formed institutes which existed only on paper. For instance, one project was on a very practical subject—the total water resources of the prairie provinces of Canada. On the Board of this institute, the Vice-President would probably act as Chairman. The chemistry department, the agricultural people, the law people and so on would join, and all aspects of the subject would be looked at. A programme in common is created and then elements of the programme are undertaken by different parts of the university, with the interdisciplinary discussion in this paper institute. There is even the possibility of giving contracts to other universities inside or outside the country for elements of the work for which the university lacks the skills. We ought to explore, in this country and in others, a large number of alternative approaches.

Waddington: In the University of Edinburgh we have to some extent explored this type of institute by what we call 'Schools'. The School of the Built Environment brought together architects, town planners, civil engineers, lawyers and so on. And there is a School of Epistemology; it was going to be called the School of Experimental Epistemology but nobody could swallow that! These Schools have been quite active in bringing together different interests. They have not yet achieved really large-scale activities, but I think this is due partly to financial stringency, and partly to the lack of research programmes capable of attracting outside funds on a big enough scale. But they are a beginning.

Ashby: Dr Francis said that it is the universities which have failed in Scotland. Universities in Britain have to be regarded as a constellation of anarchies; they are virtually acephalic—that is, without a head. Therefore to approach a university as a corporation and to expect it to do things as a corporate body is not to my mind a practical political solution to the problems you have been raising. However, we do have in this university system a remarkable tradition of *laissez-faire* liberalism for the individuals inside it. What you must ask, Dr Francis, is not that the universities as corporate bodies should take an interest in the oil problem in Scotland, because I think this would be an inefficient way of doing it, but that certain groups of experts in the universities should do so.

I entirely agree that interdisciplinary groups are needed. Alvin Weinberg has been trying to press for these in America for some time. Generally the nucleation force for these groups has been either research councils, or foundations like Ford or Nuffield, or even local stimuli, such as the Sabrina project in Bristol. This project is trying to do for the Severn the sort of thing that you have been talking about for Scotland, although they haven't so far made great progress.

In our experience the difficulty about institutes which exist on paper and not as physical entities inside universities, has been that unless they are well financed —which again means that an outside body is helping to support them—they have to borrow people from departments of biology, history and so on. These people are always being drawn back to their departments; they feel they had better keep their roots there. So 'paper institutes' can't get the full loyalty they need.

I agree that if we are to instil in universities an appreciation of future problems, the case-history method of bringing undergraduates and staff into planning studies is one way to do it. But we must remember that all attempts at forecasting on the microscale have so far been extraordinarily disappointing. If it is true that the present is going to produce the future, then it is the past that has produced the present. The manpower prediction committees that served (or mis-served) the British government for years made deplorable mistakes over comparatively simple predictions such as the production of medical doctors: they only had to look at the age distribution of practitioners to work that out; and yet they got it all wrong. Planning, although necessary, is something which can only be used as a base. If we are to teach planning for the future in universities the key thing we have to get into the minds of the young is something that the staff of the university can't themselves supply. And that is how to build bridges between planning and political decision. If I had to devise a course of futurology in universities I would be cautious about predicting the future because the past is littered with failures in prediction. But I would be enthusiastic about telling the young how to cross the bridge from planning to political action. It is possible to do this: the bridges are in fact being crossed all the time. But this would mean bringing into the universities, on secondment, the people who are making the decisions, and battering them with questions, about (for instance) how a Royal Commission report gets turned into legislation.

Woodroofe: I suspect that in that particular line a good deal of experience is available already, particularly in America. In order to plan in business, people have to make assumptions, define objectives, assign priorities and then decide how to achieve those objectives. The assumptions are really where one tries to predict the future. What is the purchasing power going to be? What are the social changes if women go out to work? Some assumptions are on a long time scale—if you are growing palm oil trees you need about twenty-five years—but most are on a five-year scale. After working this way for a long enough time one is able to monitor the results against the assumptions, so one is learning all the time. This learning process on a microscale, particularly in the short term, probably would provide a lot of experience if it could be tapped. To the best of my knowledge it has not been tapped much by universities.

Ashby: Would you second a very bright young man of 35 from your firm to the universities to explain the processes?

Woodroofe: Fortunately I am retired and don't have to answer that question! Maybe we don't need to second people so much as get them to work together. From time to time Unilever seconds people to universities, but what has happened much more is that some of our scientists have been appointed as part-time professors or associate professors in universities, delivering a certain number of lectures, and responsible for a number of research students. I think this is the way to do it.

References cited

[1] COUNCIL ON ENVIRONMENTAL QUALITY (1973) Guidelines: preparation of environmental impact statements. *Federal Register, 38* (No. 147), Part II, August 1

[2] JONES, MARTIN V. (1971) *Project Summary: a Technology Assessment Methodology*, p. 7. The Mitre Corporation, Washington, D. C.

[3] KASH, DON E., WHITE, IRVINE L. *et al.* (1973) *Energy under the Oceans: a Technology Assessment of Outer Continental Shelf Oil and Gas Operations*, University of Oklahoma Press, Norman, Oklahoma

[4] FRANCIS, JOHN & SWAN, NORMAN (1973) *Scotland in Turmoil: a Social and Environmental Assessment of the Impact of North Sea Oil and Gas on Communities in the North of Scotland*, St. Andrew Press, Edinburgh

[5] HÄFELE, WOLF (1974) Energy systems. *IAEA Bulletin, 16* (No.1/2)

[6] FORD FOUNDATION ENERGY POLICY PROJECT (1974) *A Time to Choose: America's Energy Future*, Ballinger, Cambridge, Mass.

[7] FEDERAL ENERGY ADMINISTRATION (1974) *Project Independence Report*, FEA, Washington, D.C.

[8] ADVISORY BOARD FOR THE RESEARCH COUNCILS (1974) *Energy Research: the Research Council's Contribution*, p. 11, Science Research Council, London

[9] FISCHER, JOHN (1971) Survival U is alive and burgeoning in Green Bay, Wisconsin. *Harper's Magazine 242*, 20, February

Sclerotic structures and the future of academic organization

J. N. BLACK

Bedford College, University of London

Abstract Universities have developed strong organizational structures that act to inhibit change. Reshuffles of the academic mix can be achieved, though the problems of dealing with redundant departments have not yet been solved and are exacerbated in periods of financial stringency. It is doubtful whether really major changes can be accommodated in existing structures. If universities are to respond to innovations of the magnitude implied in some of the titles of the papers at this meeting, some or all of the following problems will have to be solved: restrictive practices based on departmental autonomy; resistance to change in individual teachers arising from excessive tenure and an implacable 'hands-off' attitude to 'my own work'; wasteful duplication of effort between universities by which less central subjects are taught in small, barely viable units in many places. Resolution of some of these difficulties will involve careful examination of a number of academic sacred cows and is unlikely to be achieved without increased central direction.

Much of the discussion at this meeting has been concerned with the type and style of teaching in universities in the next few decades. Most of us accept that there will be a need for many changes in the type of courses offered, though we may not agree on what they should be. I propose to deal with a different theme —the impediments in the way of introducing innovations into university structures—in the hope that if we can identify the problems in advance some of them at least can be 'short-circuited' in the event.

By structures I mean the basic units of organization into which a university is divided. These commonly incorporate a central Administration; Faculties (broad subject groupings); Schools (narrower subject groupings); Departments (usually taken to be the essential teaching and research grouping); Units (either within departments or outside and across departmental boundaries). It would probably not be usual to find Faculties, Schools and Departments all coexisting; two would normally suffice to provide a structure with academic cohesion but without the additional administrative effort and delays of a further tier in the organizational hierarchy. Nevertheless we can all, I suspect, point to complex groupings introduced more for personal or 'political' than for academic reasons.

I propose to deal basically with the department as the central organizational structure which would be called upon to take the brunt of any changes. From the title of this paper it may be assumed that I am predisposed to the view that academic structures have become rigid, thus preventing free flow of 'bits' of 'information' (however described) through the interdepartmental (or faculty or school) barriers.

This is not to say that universities do not adapt (or have not adapted) to change. To suggest this would be monstrously unjust, and I may refer to Perkin's recent article for an analysis of such adaptation.[1] As Perkin points out, universities have had to deal with students with new and disturbing motives, and there can be no reason for assuming that the trend away from uncritical acceptance of traditional course structures will diminish. I think the trend is more likely to intensify, not so much in demands for relevance, as the shallowness and ambiguity of such a concept becomes more apparent, or by a rejection of logical argument as the basis of intellectual activity, as the tide of social emotionalism retreats, but rather towards a separation of general from specialized education, with the latter becoming increasingly a postgraduate concern.

Similarly, universities have made major strides in altering the balance between staff and students in decision-making fora. It may well be that the concessions towards greater participation have had two results not always apparent to those taking part. First, they have led to a greatly increased work-load for the administration and, since the processes of consultation are time-consuming and open to manipulation of almost Byzantine opportunism, greater power in the hands of the permanent structure. Secondly, I suspect—but cannot prove—that greater participation is a potent factor for the maintenance of the *status quo*; contrary to expectation, it may be easier for an energetic and single-minded operator in a formal hierarchical structure to bring about far-reaching innovations than it is for an army of angry young men in a system of participatory democracy.

It is also true that universities have gone a long way in introducing new courses in response to changing requirements, notably in subject areas which straddle existing disciplines. I do not seek to diminish their significance by saying that these are fundamentally new ways of assembling the academic jigsaw, and sometimes give the impression of being made to work in spite of, rather than because of, accepted structural conventions.

The changes universities may face can roughly be grouped as follows:

(a) New subject matter within a discipline;
(b) New disciplines;
(c) New combinations of disciplines;
(d) New teaching methods;
(e) New links at inter-tertiary level.

To deal quickly with the last two points, it is noteworthy that the only large-scale innovation in British universities for many years has been the setting up of the Open University. As an innovation this has to be compared with the introduction of non-collegiate 'civic' universities in England (for which models existed in Scotland) or the development of federal structures in Wales or London. The possibility of links with polytechnics and teacher-training colleges, thought by many to be one of the most likely as well as the most desirable of the developments in higher education, is now being tested, but there seem to be major underlying problems of regrouping.

NEW SUBJECT MATTER IN EXISTING DISCIPLINES

The pace of development, particularly in the sciences and social sciences, is such that teachers may quickly become out of date, needing to vary their subject coverage as they get older (at an age when to do so becomes harder). The outstanding difficulties for universities in meeting the demands of changing subject matter are twofold. First, the contractual right of tenure—often from the age of 25 or 30 to retirement—denies universities the ability to replace staff as academic considerations would suggest. Reliance upon tenure may sometimes lead the individual to sit back and fail to keep up with his subject, though I do not know whether this would be cured by, say, a system of five-year appointments. More publications might well mean worse, but we all know colleagues whose papers are delayed for incorporation into a monograph, then withheld for a book which itself is eventually earmarked for his retirement and is ultimately condemned to oblivion, along with the author and his reputation.

The second difficulty is one of retraining. Lord Annan has suggested that anyone wishing to remain all his life in an academic career will have to be prepared to retrain at intervals, but I doubt the efficacy of this: first, the older a man, the more scholarly 'capital' he has accumulated and the more resistant to retraining he will be; his status depends on the opinion of his colleagues in the same subject, and to begin again dissipates that status. Secondly, we are touching here on one of the most important factors involved in resistance to change in universities—the divided loyalties of a university teacher, first to the institution in which he serves and second to his discipline. (Lord Ashby's 'Thank Offering to Britain Fund' Lecture of 1969 contains an elegant dissection of this attitude.[2]) When someone says 'I teach philosophy at the University of Mummerset' what he usually implies is that he is a professional philosopher who happens to teach at the University of Mummerset, not that he is first and foremost a university teacher whose subject happens to be philosophy. Of course not, you will say; his subject is the thing he really cares about, and he is never given any instruction in teaching, it being tacitly assumed that a good scholar can automatically communicate his subject. (Any student can give the lie to this and it is odd how quickly one's experience as a student is forgotten when one becomes a scholar–teacher oneself.) From this stems the importance of 'my own work', and the corpus of published work which constitutes the basis of professional status. The tradition of investment in personal intellectual capital, however important as a vehicle for scholarship, certainly brings with it resistance to change.

Besides, do we really want retraining on a vast scale? I have a feeling that those teachers who should be retrained may turn out to be those whose contribution to academic life is small in their present subject and likely to be even smaller in the next, and that those who would respond best to the challenge of retraining are also those who can be least spared from their own subject. The extent of change must surely be limited; apart from the slow build-up over the years of a repertoire of techniques in a given subject, there are 'casts of mind' which, I would think, severely limit individual flexibility. I say nothing of that sacred cow, academic freedom, which encourages an academic in the view that he can do whatever work he wants to do regardless of the needs of his institution or the community at large. May I paraphrase—'Academic Freedom—how many crimes are committed in thy name?'

NEW DISCIPLINES

A comparison of a university calendar of today with one of fifty or even twenty-five years ago reveals the emergence of departments representing subjects that seem to be quite new. Over a long period of time one can discern patterns of construction and demolition, old names being replaced by new ones, departments splitting and lumping in an attempt to reflect the changing state of knowledge. Straight changes in name do not concern us (e.g. in my own college, 'Natural Philosophy' changed to 'Physics' in 1872, while in my last university the change had still not happened a century later), and many changes of name do not really introduce anything new (witness variations on the theme of

English, English language and English literature). More important are subjects which are not so much new as bits of old ones achieving independent status—as, for instance, genetics, which has emerged from other biological departments as a subject in its own right. Such changes are easy to bring about, since the 'core' of the subject and the teaching and other staff are available, and as a subject becomes differentiated the hold of the parent department weakens, so that all that is necessary is a recognition of departmental status reflected in suitable accommodation. Both subject and staff are then safely within their own ring fence.

The problem of dealing with emerging and declining subjects is not difficult to solve at a time of expansion in university finance. A new department can be set up through normal planning by the allocation of enough posts and facilities from 'development' funding. It is possible to short-circuit a run-down department by setting up a parallel department, differently named, which can gradually take over, so that existing staff can be allowed to drift on until overcome by retirement. In periods of financial stringency, however, it becomes almost impossible to justify funds for such exercises—indeed, pressure grows for departments (particularly those not currently favoured by students) to merge and pool their resources. We can then expect a 'closing of the ranks' as each department, fearing that a new post somewhere else may mean the loss of one of its own, tacitly agrees not to pursue competitive policies. There is, too, a size below which a department ceases to be viable. If it cannot be closed down or absorbed, it can, however, be reduced to a care and maintenance basis, thus countering the argument that if it were to be closed it would be hard to re-establish it if there were to be a recrudescence of demand.

The history of forestry teaching in this country illustrates this. In 1960, there were departments at four universities teaching much the same course. An anticipated decline of employment prospects led to changes; one department developed a strong interest in wood science and technology; one changed to forest biology, a unit in a larger programme of biological teaching. One changed to natural resources, teaching forestry along with a number of 'new' subjects, such as wild-life management, against a background of general ecology. The fourth remained basically unchanged. It is doubtful how many of these developments in what is, after all, a minor subject could have been achieved in anything but the period of post-Robbins expansion. Today these departments would probably have been left to wither on the vine.

The problem of changing departmental roles is not so much one of creating new or alternative departments, but of deciding what to do with the old ones. It may be possible to run them down quickly, if the age structure of the staff is favourable, or to disperse the staff to other departments, or to agree a programme of early retirement (although the machinery for this has yet to be agreed and it will never be cheap), but counterarguments based on such premises as possible return of student interest and the maintenance of valuable intellectual diversity, reinforced by considerations of tenure and tradition, are not easy to refute. It may be that resistance to change is greater in large organizations, as is often said, but the close personal links in smaller ones result in all proposals being considered in an emotional way that highlights the problems of the individuals.

NEW COMBINATIONS OF DISCIPLINES

Probably most changes now facing universities come into the category of new combinations of disciplines, and in times of financial constraint there are likely to be pleas, particularly from departments finding it difficult to recruit students, for an increase in the number of joint degrees offered. Certainly there are many more 'unit' type courses available than hitherto, and some of the new universities have constructed their main curricula around courses of this type. If these new general courses are introduced against a background of strong departments, with well-marked territories, a number of problems are likely to arise.

(1) In contradistinction to single honours students, students on joint courses etc. do not 'belong' and have no 'home' in any department, a situation which plays into the hands of the disaffected. (See Lord Annan's report on the troubles of Essex University.[3])

(2) Departments are jealous of the standards of entry of their students, and, unless students are admitted to the Faculty (or School), are apt to set entry qualifications incompatible with free choice of course.

(3) Similarly the construction of unit degrees may be complicated by excessive demands for prerequisite courses. There is considerable and justified pressure against composing a degree from a wide range of subjects without some intellectual 'backbone' to support them, but this requirement need not prevent wide choice.

(4) Strong territoriality in departments can increase overlap between courses, and unnecessary duplication. It is hard to separate departmental from personal factors in such situations, but at the root is the strong feeling of departmental identity and autonomy. Unnecessary overlap is one of the most wasteful uses of academic resources, and is not always easy to identify, let alone correct.

(5) If it can be accepted that good teaching should be illuminated by

cogent and appropriate research, a major difficulty seems to be the paucity of interdisciplinary research. Emphasis on specialization only accessible to the initiated does not provide a pattern which the 'joint' student finds easy to emulate.

(6) Another problem is that of degree standards, for it is often difficult to obtain agreement between departments on classification—even at the pass/fail borderline. The situation is made more difficult by the heterogeneity of the experience brought to a class by students whose course background is different.

So far I have been dealing with departments, and have emphasized the extent to which reorganization is confounded by departmental demarcation. Teaching across faculty boundaries is harder to achieve, not only because of timetabling problems, but because teachers on each side tend to assume a familiarity with basic principles and outlooks which does not necessarily exist. It has been most successful where objectives are limited, e.g. German or Russian for scientists, economics for engineers, etc. Courses of general cultural interest should, one would think, be everywhere available, but it is not easy to tempt students to them unless they carry credit in the examination system. Nor are they popular with those who are asked to teach them.

If it is true that traditional organizations are almost too rigid to accommodate the modest changes required today, it is unlikely that major developments which universities may face in the future will be achieved without rupture. I refer not so much to the intellectual problems of the transmission of experience, the sensing of value judgements and the basis of rationality, but to the way these are manifested in teaching programmes. What will have to be done to ease the introduction of major innovations?

I suspect that there may be two areas of interference with what we have come to regard as necessary props of university and academic autonomy. Firstly, the contractual rights of tenure of individuals, with a possible change in the balance between scholarship and teaching in favour of the latter. Secondly, an end to the scandal of duplication of subject matter between universities—not, of course, in the major academic disciplines but in those where mini-departments are maintained in many places for a relatively small number of students. Today even a federal university like London finds its hands tied when it tries to 'rationalize' departmental structure across the constituent colleges, and the time must surely come when this nettle is grasped, even if it means direction from the centre or the appointment of teachers not to an individual university but to a central pool. One can imagine the hue and cry which would greet this proposal, but it is the only way in which I can see major regroupings coming about without unacceptable and wasteful financial overprovision. The autonomy and independence of universities currently sheltered by the existence of the University Grants Committee is already probably further eroded than many academics suspect by such matters as national negotiations on salaries and conditions of work for all grades of staff, and by the 'earmarking' method in the quinquennial system (a system which is of doubtful relevance anyway in the present financial climate). Few of us, probably, would welcome increased bureaucratic intervention in university matters, but if we find that the changes required of us are of such magnitude that we cannot meet them within existing structures, it is hard to see how our paymasters can be prevented from calling the tune. I do not like the implications of this conclusion, still less do I wish to make recommendations in this direction; rather, I feel that it is inevitable.

Perhaps the greatest difficulty in accepting really radical innovations in teaching programmes will prove to be the task of altering the feeling, widespread within the universities (if declining outside them), that universities have a privileged place in society which protects them from the rough blast of economic blizzards. I have been saddened by the number of times when, in recent months, attempts to instil some measure of financial prudence in the face of inflation and cutbacks have been met by demands to spend to the hilt, and beyond, on the grounds that university spending is not to be questioned, and will always be met by a grateful government. This, despite all the quotations one can muster from the University Grants Committee and the Committee of Vice-Chancellors and Principals. Universities must shed the comfortable illusion that they have a special privileged position in society, and face the fact that like other public enterprises they have to account for their use of public funds, not so much in the book-keeping sense required of us by the Auditor-General, but in relation to the size of the public purse, and their contribution to society. The 'mystique' of the university, and the privileged position of both staff and students have to go—or have to be swept away. If this mystique is seen to stand in the way of desirable innovation the risk is that the universities will be swept away, too, in a babies and bathwater syndrome perhaps to be replaced by institutions of more appropriate structure.

Discussion

Platt: Universities are among the most durable human institutions. They have lasted longer than any others except religions. A number of universities in Europe have lasted through many changes of government and dynasties, and in the US Harvard University has lasted through three systems of government. I don't think they will be wiped out.

Black: The rate of change is getting quicker.

Perry: The Open University has been called the only innovation in the UK but there is a paradox of which you may not be aware. First, the Open University could not have begun in the UK unless it had been started as a new and independent institution on its own. I don't think it would have evolved out of existing institutions. Secondly, we haven't discovered, in the Open University, how to institutionalize innovation; we are liable to become just as sclerotic in a different form. We are caught on the horns of that dilemma.

Regarding unit or modular systems, we require almost nothing in the way of entry qualifications and we leave it to the good sense of students to make up their own coherent package of courses. It works in the sense that they refuse to take a rag-bag of assorted credits, as many people thought they would. They tend to choose sensible patterns. But I think this is only true of our kind of student who is an adult with experience of life and highly motivated in a particular direction. I suspect that it would not be true of 18-year-olds straight out of school.

Jevons: I wonder how far the paucity of research recognized as interdisciplinary is due to the apparently transient nature of interdisciplinarity. Interdisciplinarity is a self-transcending process: as soon as it becomes successful it ceases to be called interdisciplinary because it has become labelled as a new discipline. Take as an example my own former discipline of biochemistry. The name is a verbal fossil which tells us that it originated as an interdisciplinary study, but few people nowadays think of it as interdisciplinary.

Ashby: I think Dr Black's diagnosis is absolutely correct. Unfortunately he may have diagnosed something like Huntington's chorea for which there is no cure. One is comforted by the fact that the British universities, at any rate in the eighteenth century, were in a state that was even worse, yet they recovered. No one has adequately analysed the causes of that recovery. It certainly was not due to a succession of Royal Commissions or interventions from outside— these did occur but all they did was to push at doors which were already open. It was probably largely the influence of Germany on the new universities (London and Manchester); and Oxford and Cambridge revived under the threat that Manchester might become a better place than they were!

Eldredge: We are treating this at the level of the university as an institution, but there is another level—that of personal development. I have been in an interdisciplinary field (urban studies) for over twenty-five years. There is transference of skills in such activity—one doesn't lose one's academic capital by going into something different with mutual cross-fertilization. Loss of academic skill does not occur when one begins to transfer around. Dr Platt, for example, has moved from one field to another in his work. I was a sociologist of revolution and then I became a planner to see how to eliminate vicious revolution. There are all sorts of ways of shifting back and forth as an individual inside the system in the US, which is, as noted earlier, a disorganized system offering more freedom to the individual than the rather tighter systems of England or Sweden.

Waddington: The administrative structure tends to be treated as a cross-country racecourse by the really enterprising person. Most innovations get done by people who find some way to work the system, which they accept as a challenge which is interesting to meet.

Lundberg: In most countries the cost of basic academic research is only 10–20 per cent of the total expenditure for research and development. Have the British universities asked themselves how sclerotic they are relative to other research agencies? The sectoral research agencies are politically directed and generally seeking solutions to short-term problems. In the end they may turn out to be much more inflexible than the universities which have always benefited from changes generated by internal forces.

Waddington: That is a good point. The question of flexibility needs to be considered in relation to the question of scale. In universities things may look difficult to shift, but they are not of the scale of Oak Ridge or even Harwell, or laboratories of that kind, which have outlived their immediate purpose. It is difficult to know what to do with those places, though there has been some limited success with finding new roles for them.

Valaskakis: University reform is important but I am not sure that the tenure system should be severely challenged or removed. The relationship between job-security and poor performance is by no means established. In fact a good case can be made for universalized tenure outside the university system. The Japanese work on the tenure system within industry, and as we know they seem to be very competitive. To keep people on their toes we may have to have a built-in system of incentives and promotions completely separate from tenure. The permanence of employment need not be challenged.

Black: I am not suggesting that we should take away all tenure. It is a necessary part of the commitment to scholarship, though it may need to be modified. Other difficulties arise when administrative responsibilities are linked to tenured positions. In this situation, change can be blocked and the interests of other staff may be prejudiced. That is where I part company with it. Another point: does the Open University accept the faculty/department type of structure for its staff?

Perry: We don't have departments as spending units but as research and recruitment units. I think they are a necessary part of a permanent structure.

Woodroofe: The Japanese system of tenure in industry is breaking down. In the past, many Japanese companies solved the problem by having specific departments, often called general affairs departments, to which they transferred people who were getting in the way.

Waddington: It is probably true that the universities have been neglectful in providing acceptable wastepaper boxes for people who have lost their usefulness where they are.

Ashby: Tenure is a terribly difficult problem. One compromise might be to grant tenure at a 'basic' level in the academic profession after a probationary period, but to promote people above this basic level only for periods of, say, five years. Thus a professorship would be reviewed every five years, and the holder at the end of such a period might well go back to being a lecturer again. That would have a healthy effect on ourselves and our colleagues!

Black: I think this is right. It may even be necessary to appoint academics not to one particular university but to some body representing the academic profession as a whole, so that they can if necessary be moved, and subjects can be grouped. Perhaps what we also need in this country is a University of the Chiltern Hundreds—a lovely old house, lawns, a library, and very deep armchairs!

Eldredge: In America we make failing academics into administrators.

King: We also make successful academics into administrators, unfortunately.

Lundberg: In Sweden only full professors and associate professors have tenure. This makes it very difficult for a young scientist to move outside the accepted border of his discipline. The absence of tenure may be a strong barrier to innovation.

Shane: While I do not disagree with Dr Black, I think that in the US we have reached a point at which we cannot improve the future of the universities just by removing today's problems. There must be more basic changes. Our universities need to become different kinds of institutions. I doubt, for instance, that we should continue to drift towards a universalized baccalaureate degree in the US—at least as higher education is now constituted. I favour a variant of the Open University concept for the US—a form of post-secondary education based on the concept of continuing life-long education. In the future, I hope we can cut the red tape and apply the concept of the Open University in lieu of the 'open admissions' policies now in vogue. We need to satisfy the aspirations of some of the people who quite rightly feel that they have not had fair secondary school opportunities. We need, therefore, to contemplate opening the university to motivated, able, persons and letting them study in our schools even when they lack formal qualifications. Let me give a personal example. My sister was a high-school drop-out—married at 16, divorced at 20. But being a determined, able woman—one who never needed to be liberated—she persuaded the Dean at an eastern US university to admit her to the journalism programme. By the time she was 30 she was an accredited White House correspondent, a member of the *Newsweek* staff, and a member of the staff of the *Baltimore Sun*. In our new emergent university structures we need to find imaginative ways of satisfying the aspirations and needs of enormous numbers of people like my sister in ability, confidence and stamina.

Waddington: Dr Black has drawn attention to the asymmetry in this process. We are loosening up enormously over the age of students and the qualifications we demand of them. We are trying to set up life-long entry and re-entry, with freedom to go in and out of the university all through life. But the life-long tenured appointments on the staff side make the system asymmetrical. Maybe it should be like that. To abolish tenure now, without some substitute, would bring innovation to a halt; no one could afford to do it. If you have tenure, your bread and butter are assured.

Platt: Twenty years ago there was a British book called *Redbrick University* which I thought hit the nail on the head in terms of the sclerotic structures of those days. It discussed the incentives for continued intellectual productivity in different schools. There was a chapter on 'The Professor and His Rose Garden', as I remember it, which I did not find in the American edition. The point was that as soon as a person became a full professor, with tenure, he turned his energies to trying to grow the best roses in the community, partly because he was at the top, then, with no reason to work any more. I would like to suggest that there may be a difference in the positive rewards and incentives which the American full professor still has, to keep his research going full blast, and the rewards the British professor goes on receiving. The American professor may still do research so that he will get to move to Harvard or to California. He may still try to become the president of a national professional society, even though he has never been chairman of the department or Dean of the Faculty. I can think of at least half a dozen academic and prestige rewards of various sorts for continuing research and scholarship in the US, which in a certain sense are not there for his British counterpart because departments are dominated by the professor at the top of the pyramid, whose other rewards are connected to his rank rather than his work. It seems to me that it is safe for a system to offer tenure, as a valuable protection for academic freedoms and for experimentation, only if we also have the other methods of reinforcement for those with tenure at the top—methods which stimulate continuing ongoing research.

Shane: If an American professor is troublesome enough to the administration he is virtually sure to be promoted to being a Dean.

Platt: He can resist that! The flat-topped departments in which there are many professors who are more or less equal (like the Chemistry Department at Oxford in the 1950s) are much more of an encouragement to graduate students. Where there are many specialties, many different points of view, the student may usually escape from one professor to another or find another channel at another university. The single-professor type of pyramidal hierarchy is the source of the sclerotic character in most British and European universities as much as anything else and, I believe, far more damaging than tenure itself.

Waddington: There is something in that. On the other hand, I think it is easier to move, in the US, from partial professorship to chairmanship of a company or something, not by doing research yourself but by organizing a large team of Ph.D. students to do it for you. This can be done in Britain, but with more difficulty. I think that is the other side of what you said.

Perry: Size is a factor too. The average number of staff in British departments is still in single figures.

References cited

[1] PERKIN, H. J. (1974) Adaptation to change by British universities. *Universities' Quarterly,* *28* (4), 390–403
[2] ASHBY, SIR ERIC [now Lord Ashby of Brandon] (1969) The academic profession. Fourth annual lecture under the Thank Offering to Britain Fund. *Proceedings of the British Academy 55,* 163–176
[3] ANNAN, NÖEL GILROY, baron (1974) *The Report of the Annan Enquiry,* pp. 29–30, Essex University

Eclectics: elements of a transdisciplinary methodology for futures studies

KIMON VALASKAKIS

GAMMA, Université de Montréal/McGill University, and Département des Sciences Economiques, Université de Montréal

Abstract Futures studies involve two families of issues: those relating to *forecasting* as such, and those relating to the effective *understanding* of complex reality which in fact is a precondition for forecasting. Other than straightforward mathematical techniques such as extrapolation and envelope curves, more subtle forecasting methods such as scenarios, Delphis and cross-impact matrices depend for their success on an understanding of the present. Eclectics is an attempt to model the present in a transdisciplinary fashion. The starting-point is an extended philosophical notion of *scarcity*, the analysis of which leads to certain basic theorems of choice. These theorems are then made to apply to what we call *quaternary* commodities—that is, abstract commodities not usually treated in economics, such as 'nationalism', 'achievement', 'prestige', 'freedom from stress', 'justice' and 'influence'. The approach involves the definition of *content* from fields such as psychology, sociology, anthropology, political science and the choice of *method* from economics (which is seen here as identical to the theory of choice). The advantage of eclectics is that it provides for rigorous treatment of 'non-economic' variables (and therefore humanizes the economist) while at the same time exporting choice theory to other social scientists (thereby formalizing what have hitherto been imprecise techniques).

The business of attempting to treat the future as an 'academic discipline', i.e. as an activity where the rules and rigour of the scientific method can be applied, leads to two families of issues. The first is concerned with forecasting techniques as such, and we now have an array of mathematical, non-mathematical and quasi-mathematical techniques to choose from. The second is the actual base from which the forecasting will be done, i.e. an image we have of the present, of the past, or of the future. The tempting fallacy would be to entirely separate these two issues. This could lead to results not only incomplete but actually misleading. As Herman Kahn has eloquently put it, in one of his famous one-liners: 'There are two serious errors in forecasting. The first is to assume that a rate of growth is constant. The second is to assume that it will change'.

In point of fact, we can assume nothing. Rates of growth may or may not change, extrapolation is often absurd and yet rejection of extrapolation may turn out to be unnecessarily timid. Whether we construct scenarios or use contextual mapping, Delphi or cross-impact techniques, we must, in each case, first attempt a thorough understanding of the 'base'. This is what some futurists and historians have called *synchronic* analysis. Once the synchronic dimension is well understood the *diachronic* or time-dependent dynamic analysis can be brought in. This paper will focus on the analysis of the base and its potential for forecasting. The problems and opportunities of diachronic analysis have been treated elsewhere.[1]

As far as understanding of the base is concerned, it has been the fashion in recent years to consider interdisciplinary studies as a necessary method for the investigation of complex reality. In Gamma we wholeheartedly agree with this view but would like to take the 'faddish' elements out of it and define the approach as precisely as possible. To do this we have to distinguish between the following:

> *A mono-disciplinary approach* is very sectoral and partial. It implies a study involving only one discipline. Such an approach we find very unsatisfactory for the celebrated reason (first given by Kenneth Boulding) that although universities are administratively divided into departments, nature is not. The universe has no 'economic department' working separately from its 'physics' department. To assume otherwise is to court irrelevance.

> *A multidisciplinary* approach involves parallel inputs from different fields in apposition to each other and unintegrated. This is of very little use since the vital interdependences are not identified.

> *An 'undisciplined'* approach although well-meaning leads nowhere. The starting and finishing points are that 'everything depends on everything'. The temptation here is to conclude pessimistically that there are 'imponderables' in human behaviour not subject to analysis, thereby ending the tale without further ado.

> *A cross-disciplinary* approach involves the marriage of two or three disciplines by the establishment of methodological 'bridges'. Examples of such marriages are: political economy, biochemistry, social psychology, astrophysics. They are a distinct step forward, relative to any of the preceding, yet fall short of a completely unified scientific method.

> *An interdisciplinary* approach is an 'intellectual commune' so to speak, in which many disciplines cross-interact. In principle a generalization of

the cross-disciplinary approach, it is the penultimate step before the transdisciplinary approach.

A transdisciplinary approach really calls for the unification of science where all existing disciplines are integrated into a super-discipline. It is difficult, yet, we feel, an ultimately attainable goal.

In our perception a 'discipline' is really a generalized theory akin to a 'language'. It will be noted that the etymological origin of 'theory' is the Greek *Theoros*, i.e. a spectator. A theory is a way of looking at things, neither true nor false, but either more useful or less useful. Different spectators have different perceptions of the same spectacle. As in a sports event such as a football game, some vantage points are better than others. The 'better' depends on the purpose. If we are interested in watching passing plays rather than goal scoring, a seat near centre field might be better than one near the goals, and vice versa.

A theory is couched in certain words and concepts which when numerous enough elevate it to the rank of 'discipline'. Hence economics is a 'language' of thought that possesses, like all languages, a vocabulary and rules of syntax. The same is true of each and every discipline. The vocabulary of economics includes perhaps five hundred technical concepts; political science, anthropology, psychology, etc., each contain as many if not more; and biology and medicine probably head all the lists with many tens of thousands of technical words in their vocabularies.

The 'rules of syntax' are different to some degree, since some disciplines pride themselves on possessing a particular methodology made-to-measure for the problems encountered within that discipline. Thus an anthropologist will rely extensively on field work, the experimental psychologist on controlled experiments, the historian on analysis of rare documents and the economist on model-building. We now arrive at the statement of the crucial problem of transdisciplinarity: *To achieve transdisciplinarity we must utilize both a common vocabulary and common 'rules of syntax' (i.e. a common methodology)*.

THE FORMAL DESCRIPTION OF 'ECLECTICS' OR 'MEGA-ECONOMICS'

A systemic (as opposed to an administrative) classification of disciplines involved in the study of human behaviour yields five basic hard-core social sciences. In alphabetical order we have:

Anthropology. Presumably the science of culture, anthropology with its many subdivisions overflows into and overlaps with other related fields.

Economics. Presumably the science of scarcity. Up till now the scarcity at the basis of economic theory has always been interpreted as material scarcity. In this study, I shall attempt to show otherwise.

Political Science. Presumably the analysis of power, its ramification, its subdivisions, its organization and manifestation. Obvious overflows can be seen with every other behavioural science.

Psychology. Presumably the investigation of the nervous system. From its obvious biological connection psychology also intrudes into economics, sociology and anthropology and, in some schools of thought, is part of philosophy.

Sociology. Presumably the science of groups and social interaction. Very close to anthropology, it is nevertheless considered distinct by sociologists and, in Auguste Comte's initial conception, is the all-inclusive behavioural science.

History and geography are, in this systemic view, not separate activities but dimensions of the preceding disciplines. Hence we can have historical anthropology, economic history and geography, political history and geography, etc. History introduces a time-dimension to the analysis and geography a space-dimension.

The harder sciences are also related to the behavioural sciences. There is a biological foundation to all behaviour. Biology in turn depends upon *chemical* conditioning and chemistry ultimately depends on the laws of *physics.*

A potential unity of science exists, then, not only as far as form is concerned but also content. If the various linkages between the separate fields of investigation are mapped out and precisely identified, we may achieve interdisciplinarity.

Eclectics is a transdisciplinary approach which features the adoption of the methodology of economics in combination with the terminology of all behavioural sciences. (We hesitated between the two terms eclectics and 'mega-economics'. Our original choice was 'mega-economics' since the approach we will be describing can be viewed as an extension of the subject-matter of economics. We now prefer 'eclectics', which is to signify the combination of the economic theory of choice with non-economic variables derived from psychology, political science and sociology.)

(a) The starting point: an all-encompassing view of scarcity

In traditional economics, scarcity is an objective situation where material resources are insufficient to satisfy unlimited wants. In most standard economic texts, it is the famous trade-off between 'guns and butter' which illustrates the inevitability of choice under conditions of scarcity. However, with the development of economic thought and especially the increasing mathematization of economic theory, the problem of choice was seen to be independent both of *material* resources and *objective* scarcity. In contemporary form, the theorems of choice (which constitute the central part of what is now known as microeconomic analysis and used to be known as 'principles of economics') are purely formal propositions equally applicable to all trade-off situations. Thus the same body of analytical thought can be used to study 'guns versus butter', 'Gross National Product versus Quality of Life' and even 'virtue versus power', 'love versus selfishness'—indeed almost any of the famous dilemmas of philosophy.

In the mind of the proverbial 'man in the street', economics is 'business', and rightly so, for the mainstream of the economics profession still deals with shoes, ships and sealing wax. The eighteenth century Physiocrats viewed agriculture as the only 'true' productive activity. Marx claimed that 'materialism' was the mainspring of history, meaning by materialism the pursuit of primary (extractive) and secondary (industrial) commodities.[2] To this day services are not accounted for in the GNP of the Eastern European socialist countries, under the pretext that tertiary activities are 'unproductive'.[3]

In eclectics we replace these restrictive interpretations by positing the following. Scarcity is a subjective situation that exists in the mind of the consumer. It can relate to the insufficiency of either material or non-material commodities. If we suppose that N stands for subjective needs (whether natural or artificial, real or imagined) and C stands for commodities or resources, then three situations are possible:

(1) $N < C$ (opulence)
(2) $N = C$ (equilibrium)
(3) $N > C$ (scarcity)

The third situation gives rise to choice. The other two do not. It is our contention that the third situation is the cause of most social problems. I shall defend this apparently bold statement later.

(b) The next step: identification of the set of 'quaternary' commodities

The perception of scarcity forcing a choice between guns and butter, or 'wine and cloth', is comparatively easy. Much less so is the perception of scarcities in 'leisure', 'time', 'the quality of life', 'tradition', etc. To deal with such problems we introduce a new set of commodities to be entitled *quaternary commodities*.

Let us suppose that there is some final goal which directs human behaviour.

If human behaviour is purposive then that is tautologically true. If not, we must assume that behaviour is mechanistic, i.e. explainable by the laws of physics rather than the cybernetic laws of information. The overwhelming evidence seems to be in favour of the purposive interpretation (even if some purposes are unconscious) and therefore I shall not belabour this point.

Let us call the final goal of behaviour in humans, 'felicity' (or happiness, satisfaction, pleasure, utility, quality of life, or whatever cliché one prefers). There is, then, a felicity function, at the level of each individual, which would explain this individual's behaviour. It may be the case that some people like Roquefort cheese, others not, etc. The preference functions are individual and we assume consistent.*

Let us now claim that a felicity function can be expressed as follows:

$$F_A = f(p, s, t, q)$$

where F_A is the total felicity (f) or happiness of A, p is the set of primary commodities (those extracted from the soil, the sea, the forest or the crust of the earth), s the set of secondary commodities (transformed commodities involving labour and capital), t the set of tertiary commodities (services), and q the set of quaternary commodities defined in the next paragraph. What the felicity function says is that happiness for A depends on his consumption of various types of commodities in certain doses.†

A quaternary commodity can now be defined as an entity which (*i*) is capable of producing felicity in one person, (*ii*) is scarce, (*iii*) is abstract, (*iv*) is not at present marketed.

Characteristic (*i*) ensures that the entity is indeed a commodity in that it can produce satisfaction. Characteristic (*ii*) ensures that it is not a free good which would then make choice unnecessary. Characteristic (*iii*) ensures that the commodity is neither a primary nor a secondary one. Finally characteristic (*iv*) ensures that it is not a service because services are indeed abstract commodities which are marketed. Only non-marketed commodities can be called quaternary.‡

It is important to note that, in our model, felicity and commodities have their symmetrical opposites. Infelicity is 'disutility', dissatisfaction, unhappiness or illfare, and discommodities are entities producing infelicity in any one person.

---

* More about consistency, transitivity and conscious or unconscious motives later.
† The division of economic activity into primary, secondary and tertiary sectors is attributed to Colin Clark in his *Conditions of Economic Progress*.[4]
‡ Although the 'quaternary' idea has been used in regional economics and planning it is very superficially related to what we are discussing here. The quaternary sector in regional economics deals with high-technology services.

The identification of certain quaternary commodities may involve a roundabout process of *minimizing a discommodity*.

How are we to identify quaternary commodities? First we must bear in mind that quaternary commodities are not necessarily 'good' or 'bad'. In fact we propose a threefold division:

(*i*) Symbiotic quaternary commodities: those whose consumption by A increases not only A's but B's felicity.

(*ii*) Neutral quaternary commodities: those whose consumption by A does not affect B's felicity.

(*iii*) Parasitic quaternary commodities: those whose consumption by A actually decreases B's felicity.

Second, we propose that the actual discovery of quaternary commodities be left to the relevant specialists. Since, in the systemic view of behavioural science there are four specialists other than economists, namely psychologists, political scientists, sociologists and anthropologists, we can classify quaternary commodities as 'psychological', 'political' and 'sociocultural'. All abstract commodities directly satisfying needs arising from the operation of the nervous system can constitute the subset of psychological commodities. Political commodities are those motivated by the need for power and its derivatives. Finally, sociocultural commodities are those that are identified by the sociologist and anthropologist around the notion of the 'group' and 'culture' (the information shared by the group).

There is an interesting symmetry to note here which makes eclectics possible. Psychologists, sociologists and anthropologists have a tendency to refer to desires and wants by identifying them with a prefix 'n', denoting need. They speak of n-affiliation, n-aggression, n-recognition, n-status, etc. Translated into the language of eclectics, n-recognition is a discommodity denoting a state of infelicity for the individual concerned where there is an unsatisfied desire for whatever constitutes recognition. The commodity which will satisfy the desire will be prefixed by a 'c' (for commodity). We will then have perhaps c-prestige satisfying n-recognition, c-power satisfying n-aggression, c-religion satisfying n-rectitude, c-legal justice satisfying n-equity, etc.

(c) The final formal step: developing theorems of choice to deal with quaternary commodities

To recapitulate my argument so far, I present two tables. Table 1 summarizes the subject matter of eclectics: *choice applied to abstract as well as materialistic situations*. Table 2 introduces the key concepts of eclectics in the form of a

TABLE 1
The subject matter of eclectics

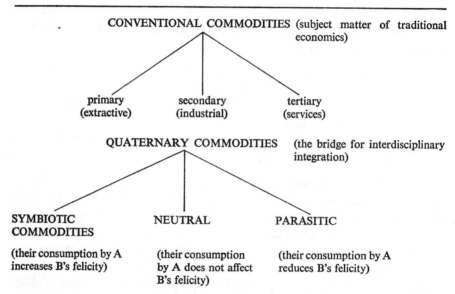

CONVENTIONAL COMMODITIES (subject matter of traditional economics)

primary (extractive)   secondary (industrial)   tertiary (services)

QUATERNARY COMMODITIES   (the bridge for interdisciplinary integration)

SYMBIOTIC COMMODITIES   NEUTRAL   PARASITIC

(their consumption by A increases B's felicity) | (their consumption by A does not affect B's felicity) | (their consumption by A reduces B's felicity)

Definition of eclectics: The combination of the methodology of economics and the concepts of all social sciences to arrive at a general theory of behaviour around the concept of choice.

glossary of terms. Having identified the quaternary commodities and their underlying needs, we then formally represent this in decision theorems with references to a felicity function.

It might well be asked: why is this approach which includes decision theorems more useful than other multidisciplinary approaches? The answer is that it allows (*a*) economists to make use of variables that they usually omit by either politely calling them 'non-economic' or impolitely calling them irrational, and (*b*) other social scientists to think in 'economic', i.e. cost–benefit, scarce, 'can't have your cake and eat it too' terms. The most important conflicts that arise today are of the 'good versus good' rather than the 'good versus bad' variety. It is easy to deal with the latter and most difficult to deal with the former. If we take the trade-off between say c-culture (through restrictive economic policies) and c-GNP growth (through free trade, liberal policies, etc.) the narrow economist will unconsciously assign a zero-value to the non-economic goal, nationalism, and call it irrational, and an infinite value to economic growth. The socio-anthropologist will assign an infinite value to c-culture and a low value to 'materialist' growth. The eclectic approach avoids these two

TABLE 2

Partial glossary of terms to be used in eclectics

Scarcity=a subjective state which exists whenever a person's (or group's) needs exceed the resources at his command. If N is needs and C stands for commodities or resources, then logically we have

      (1) $N > C$
      (2) $N = C$
or (3) $N < C$

      Needs may be real or artificial. They exist in the mind of the consumer. (1) denotes scarcity, (2) denotes equilibrium, (3) denotes abundance.

Choice=decision process made in allocating scarce resources (i.e. commodities) to satisfy needs. Choice implies scarcity. If there is no scarcity there is no need for choice.

Felicity These two words can be used interchangeably to refer to happiness, satisfaction,
or Utility: pleasure, or whatever it is, a given individual wishes to maximize. Although there is no formal difference between the two words, utility connotes usefulness and this is not what we have in mind. Therefore in most cases felicity will be used.

Disutility The opposite of utility or felicity. Refers to pain, dissatisfaction, displeasure
or Infelicity: or more generally whatever it is that we want the least of.

Commodities: Entities that have the potential of creating felicity in at least one person. They may be concrete or abstract, visible or invisible, private or public.

Discommodities: Entities that have the potential of creating infelicity in at least one person. They may be concrete or abstract, visible or invisible, private or public.

Infelicity cost: The cost in terms of dissatisfaction (or displeasure or infelicity) of choosing one alternative. Infelicity cost includes real cost and opportunity cost.

Real cost: The measure of cost in terms of some material or directly quantifiable thing, i.e. measuring the cost of painting the house in terms of the cost of materials plus the cost of labour.

Opportunity cost: The measure of cost in terms of the felicity of opportunities foregone. For example, I paint the house for three hours and use $10 worth of paint. My opportunity cost is the movie I missed plus whatever I could have alternatively bought with my $10.

---

excesses. Through decision-making techniques like indifference maps, cost–benefit or cost-effectiveness calculi, minimax–maximax game modelling, etc. the *problèmatique* will be accurately represented and an enlightened choice made.*

    Economics has an array of highly sophisticated concepts, laws, techniques and models for choice and decisions. The unfortunate thing is that these powerful

---

* It would be beyond the scope of this paper for me to describe each of these techniques. They will be the subject of a forthcoming book.

tools have been used for trivial problems of everyday life when they could also be used for the really interesting problems of society. In a nutshell, then, eclectics involves convincing both economists and their colleagues of the value of identifying '*quaternary commodities*'.

The emphasis is on 'quaternary' when talking to economists because they already know all about commodities. The emphasis must be on 'commodities' when talking to the other social scientists because they are already aware of the 'quaternary' aspect but tend to forget that all choices, under scarcity, involve costs.

POTENTIAL APPLICATIONS OF ECLECTICS IN FUTURES STUDIES

(a) A guide for the understanding (and therefore prediction) of human behaviour

As was noted earlier, we tend to dismiss what we do not understand as irrelevant, imponderable or irrational. If one adopts the systems view of an ordered universe (cosmos rather than chaos), the irrationality in other people's behaviour is a measure of our ignorance of their underlying motives. There is method in almost every madness. If we were to understand this method we would be able to 'explain' behaviour. Behaviour will be adequately explained when we can accurately predict future behaviour: hence the connection with futures studies.

A common mistake which leads to obviously incorrect predictions is not taking sufficiently into account the relativity of beliefs, ideals and preferences. Consider an example reported by Herman Kahn of two categories of people working the night-shift at a post-office in California. The first category includes hippies, getting the high overtime rates for a few weeks in order to live the rest of the year on the commune. Their demand for money may be about $2000 a year or whatever it costs to live for that period of time on a commune. To earn it they may work overtime for six weeks and then leave. The second category includes lower middle-class people newly arrived in the affluent society. They work overtime to supplement their $10 000-a-year regular jobs and to be able to buy the colour television set which they need to live up to their desired image of themselves. Through quaternary commodity analysis their desires would have been identified and their behaviour explained.

Another example is concerned with people's consumption of c-leisure. Leisure is an allocation of time and although often confused with idleness in fact may involve a greater calorie expenditure than 'work'. In Table 3 I suggest that c-leisure is the commodity that satisfies n-freedom from labour stress. It is assumed that 'labour' which is work solely performed to obtain an

TABLE 3
An illustrative list of quaternary commodities

Type of quaternary commodity	Discommodity or need	Commodity	Identification primarily reponsibility of
Symbiotic (Felicity of **B** increased by **A**'s consumption of these commodities)	n-communication	c-language	Psychologist, sociologist, anthropologist, linguist, cybernetician, etc.
	n-affiliation	c-solidarity	Sociologist, etc.
	n-affection	c-love	Psychologist, philosopher, anthropologist, sociologist, etc.
Neutral (Felicity of **B** unaffected by **A**'s consumption of these commodities	n-freedom from labour stress	c-leisure	Psychologist, sociologist
	n-freedom from boredom	c-excitement	Psychologist, anthropologist
Parasitic (Felicity of **B** decreased by **A**'s consumption of these commodities)	n-aggression/control	c-power/ influence	Psychologist, political scientist, sociologist, biologist
	n-recognition	c-prestige/ status	Anthropologist, sociologist

income involves some infelicity. This infelicity may take the form of stress. C-leisure may replace this stress with either idleness or felicity-bringing work. The professional tennis-player may play the piano for relaxation. The professional pianist may play tennis for the same relaxation. There is nothing intrinsic in either piano-playing or tennis which stresses or relaxes an individual. It is all a question of subjective perceptions which will appear on a felicity map.

Table 3 presents an illustrative list of quaternary commodities that emphasizes the symmetry between the need and the commodity. The first group of *symbiotic* commodities includes the need for communication, for affiliation and for affection, and possible corresponding commodities of language, solidarity and love. The very identification is at this stage an amateur job, since it is the author, *qua* general citizen, identifying these commodities on the basis of readings. The proper identification must of course be done by psychologists, sociologists and others. It is apparent that in each case we have a symbiotic situation, since language, solidarity and love are cooperative activities.

Neutral commodities are those whose consumption by A does not affect the felicity level of anyone else. Leisure and excitement could possibly fall into this group.

In the parasitic category, commodities such as power and influence on the one hand or prestige/status on the other are obviously zero-sum and competitive. A's influence over B's behaviour (i.e. A's ability to determine or change B's decisions) may reduce B's influence on his own behaviour. Similarly if a person desires to have the longest car in his neighbourhood for prestige reasons he is preventing someone else from having the longest car.

(b) A step towards the construction of meaningful welfare indicators

All societal forecasting is hampered by the problem of indicators of societal performance. The familiar GNP measure is really an index of the production of primary and secondary commodities in the communist countries and primary, secondary and tertiary commodities in the capitalist countries. This economic accounting is seriously deficient today. Some proposed recent measures like the Tobin–Nordhaus–Samuelson NEW (net economic welfare) measure merely add to the GNP the cost of antipollution industries and non-renewable resource depletion. It is marginally better than the GNP index. Finally, the recent trend towards social indicators, although a laudable initiative, to be sure, falls far short of the ideal. The plethora of social indicators now current (newspaper per thousand inhabitants, number of surgeries per thousand, psychiatric treatment per thousand, etc.), only reveals their basic flaw: *it is by no means sure what in fact they are indicating.* There is no underlying theory of behaviour, just a mass of statistics.

Quaternary commodities constitute an attempt at identifying elements of a theory of behaviour. Although the endeavour is by no means easy, quantification of these commodities is possible.

Quantification itself, it should be noted, may be done with three separate degrees of precision.

At the first degree, two entities are identified as magnitudes and compared, using adjectives such as 'greater than', 'equal', or 'smaller than'.

At the second degree, two or more entities may be compared and rank-ordered—1st, 2nd, 3rd, etc. This is *ordinal* quantification.

Finally, at the highest degree of quantification, entities are given precise *cardinal* numbers—1, 2, 3 etc.

Although full quantification is only complete at the third level, much information can be obtained by use of one of the other two. Some quaternary commodities are reasonably well-suited to quantification, others much less so.

Some attempts have been made to quantify c-power,[5,6] c-achievement,[7] c-leisure, c-justice, etc. These attempts have often been only partially successful but we feel that the reason for this is incomplete information about the nature of the commodity itself.

Economic theory itself has thrived using ordinal quantification. The key elements of economic theory are usually not fully quantified. Instead concepts such as 'opportunity-cost' have been used very successfully. Opportunity-cost is the measure of the cost of choosing alternative X by computing the anticipated disutility or infelicity of giving up the best other alternative that could have been obtained had X not been chosen. If we apply this to quaternary commodities, the cost of c-nationalism (non-membership for Britain in the EEC, anti-American policies in Canada, anti-Ottawa policies in Quebec) can be a slowing of economic growth—a directly quantifiable index. The idea that 'opportunities foregone' can be a measure of the cost of choosing is, in my view, a most fertile way of approaching complex societal problems.

(c) A guide for long-range planning

Long-range planning involves a decision procedure where goals have to be ordered. A favourite technique for ordering goals in a systems approach is a hierarchy or relevance-tree. I have had the opportunity of utilizing such a technique coupled with the introduction of quaternary commodities in a long-range planning exercise in Africa, entrusted to the University of Montreal. A research centre of the latter institution was asked to prepare long-term orientation for the Republic of Niger. Our chosen starting point was an identification of high-order goals by the Niger government. These goals were implicit and, after some prodding, it was found that the Niger government wished the nation to achieve: 'a high material standard of living with national unity and independence within an interdependent world'.

All policies were to be chosen by reference to this supreme goal. It soon became obvious that there was not one supreme goal but three, and that they were incompatible. The material standard of living goal was easily rewritten as a desire for rapid economic growth. The second goal of national unity was identified after careful analysis as meaning *regional balance and high spatial integration* of the Niger economy. This was particularly important since different tribes inhabited each region of Niger. Centrifugal forces were also working in favour of separatism.

The third goal of 'independence within interdependence' really referred to Niger's desire for a loosening of ties with its two major and overwhelming economic partners, Nigeria and France. Nigeria by its sheer size and proximity also threatened the regional balance of Niger since the Centre–East region of Niger was an economic satellite to Kano in Northern Nigeria. On the other hand, without close ties with Nigeria or France, Niger's economic growth, already slow, would become even slower.

Reformulating the Niger *problèmatique* in *eclectic* terms, we find that this is an obvious trade-off between 'good and good', the perceived good of economic growth versus the quaternary commodities c-independence and c-unity. As usual, the economists would tend to discount the quaternary commodities in favour of economic growth and the more political–social-minded observers would favour the opposite ruling. To deal with the problem we indicated the incompatibilities to the authorities, pointing out that the cost of independence was slower growth, and that the cost of faster growth was less independence.

The need for eclectics is also evident when the planning takes the form of utopian model design. With the acceleration of change we become more and more aware of what we are against and less and less aware of what we are for. The identification of quaternary commodities and their use in an eclectic model would permit meaningful positive thinking. Witness the following course-description found in two Free University catalogues in the US:

(1) The course will be divided into two parts. In the first there will be an opening crying session in which we will knock present day America and indulge in many New Left clichés. Next we will attempt to answer the arch-typical parent's remark, "so what do you want for Christ's sake!" After seeing if we can agree to some notion of a society we want to move toward, we will do some power-structure analysis to see who is keeping us from getting there. Finally if we get this far, we may discuss what tactics have some hope of success and which of the others are fun and irrelevant.

(2) Seminar for those who are tired of capitalism but uncertain and fearful of what may replace it. Can capitalism be junked without violence. Is it possible to secure both the form and substance of democracy under socialism or would it destroy the human potential? Do the Soviet Union, Czechoslovakia, China or Cuba offer guidelines for bettering N. American society...[8]

To construct utopias (and the whole branch of future studies dealing with normative forecasting is directly or indirectly involved with utopian thought), we must fully understand behaviour. Assumption of 'man is inherently good' or 'man is inherently evil' must be treated with circumspection. A full identification of quaternary commodities will help to avoid such tempting pitfalls and allow reasoned planning with full knowledge of the total nature of man.

CONCLUSION

By way of summary I would like to restate the essential points made in this article. First it must be recognized that I am actually reporting work in progress and not offering a finished product—which because of the complexity of the issues involved must take the form of a book. The outline presented here represents more a series of questions, a *problèmatique*, as it were, rather than a series of answers. These questions seem to be meaningful and fertile. They are connected with an all-encompassing view of scarcity and a suspicion that stems from subjectively perceived scarcity. A busy executive under stress, a married man envisioning divorce, a nation at odds with itself—all are experiencing scarcity and the agony of choice between 'good' and 'good', the most difficult choice of all. What the alternatives in this choice really are is the subject matter of eclectics, which is economics plus socio-politico-anthropologico-psychology.

Second, in progressing along our chosen avenue towards a full methodology for futures studies, we must pause before certain obstacles of great importance. These are, the nature of felicity functions, the nature of quaternary commodities and their possibility of aggregation, and finally the nature of the measurement problem. Once these have been solved 'the base' will be well known and the actual forecasting of future states will be a relatively simple endeavour.

In dealing with felicity functions we must delve far into psychology and the theory of motivation. Perhaps some kind of psychological homeostasis may be identified, akin to the biochemical homeostasis in our bodies. Perhaps, too, there is not one felicity function but two. The *authentic* complete felicity function may be hidden in the most private recesses of our unconscious. It would then take a most proficient psychoanalyst to act as midwife and explicate our felicity function for us. In addition, at the conscious level there may be an explicit preference-function easily identified by interview and questionnaire. The direct questions, 'do you like X?', 'why do you like Y?' can have direct answers—sometimes. But when we obtain the frequent 'I really don't know why' response we have to repair back to the *authentic* felicity function of the unconscious. The *overt* preference function is like the tip of the iceberg; it is partial, spotty, incomplete, and rare is the person 'who knows himself', as the Buddhists advise. The overt function may in fact be inconsistent because the real motives are not recognized. One way or the other, much work is needed on the psychology of motivation and also on the psychology of 'pleasure' or 'happiness'. This appears to be a grossly underdeveloped field of study within psychology itself. An eclectics team must do fundamental work in this direction before proceeding further.

The identification of quaternary commodities is a second obstacle along the road requiring the wholehearted assistance of sociologists and anthropologists in addition to the psychologist. What it really involves is a programme of naming, defining and analysing.

There are those of course who would rather not raise these issues. To live in a 'world without names', a world without categories, is indeed a worthy aesthetic goal. Such a world should best be expressed, if expressed at all, by art forms, the literary, poetic, cinematic or musical genres. The scientific method, for good or ill, is taxonomy, categorizing, non-contradiction and logical inference. If man is to study himself by using science he must investigate his behaviour systemically. This implies naming, sub-naming and sub-sub-naming. The tyranny of language is with us anyway, whether we have read Wittgenstein or not. To define is to understand, even if understanding is perhaps anticlimactic in that it eliminates suspense and analysis. However, the stakes are sufficiently high to make the study most interesting and useful. If indeed we want to construct a transdisciplinary language, we must build a meaningful vocabulary.

Finally the last obstacle, but strangely enough the least formidable, once the other two have been surmounted, is formal modelling into theorems of choice describing actual situations. Here the economist, with the close assistance of the political scientist, can digest the inputs and construct decision alternatives with some degree of quantification. Whether this quantification is ordinal or fully cardinal is not the issue, provided that some quantification is realized. Once we have the raw material there are sufficient sophisticated techniques in decision theory, game theory and conflict theory to come up with the full range of alternatives. Then the decision maker—whether an individual choosing between chess and movies, a nation choosing nationalism or internationalism, or human society choosing a conservation ethic or a consumerist ethic—will make informed choices. To predict or to plan we must get away from naive assumptions about the nature of man and encounter the implications of (mega)-scarcity head on. 'Good versus good' must be tackled and an iterative process developed. 'Eclectics' is one of many starting points. But rather than pass the buck and dismiss what we do not understand, we must instead perceive the order that lies in apparent chaos. For it is the basic tenet of the systems view of the universe or indeed of science that there is really no such thing as irrationality. Only ignorance of motives!

Discussion

Waddington: We must be able to think in multidimensional terms, and universities must teach these modes of thought. They will have to show how to go beyond linear cause-and-effect thinking, and the idea that there is one measure of all things. No biologist wanting to differentiate between two species dreams of being able to get one index that will do it; he measures a hundred or more differences. Similarly, there will be not one felicity, but a hundred different felicities, and somehow we have to get used to taking account of all of them.

Dror: I am strongly in sympathy with the fundamental search for ways of dealing with the issues presented here. We need some integrated prescriptive approach which permits us to order our knowledge so that we can make recommendations for future action. Ideas developed in decision theory, micro-economics and systems engineering can, among others, be helpful—if suitably reworked. Indeed the complexity of problems calls for some redundancy or overlapping approaches, so that we have an arsenal of methods and approaches which can be used to reduce bias and ignorance. Neither economics nor operations research nor management sciences in their classical form can deal with the basic societal problems, unless developed into a kind of 'policy science'. Also, in reality we are faced in most situations with a choice not between good and good but between bad and bad. Our main need is therefore often to design new alternatives, not screening tools which can only help us to identify the best of the available alternatives or the less bad amongst the available ones.

Few of the approaches at present available handle the continuous feedback problem, though there are some cybernetic beginnings, which stress that we are dealing with a continuous learning process rather than with determining how to make decision A, then decision B, and then decision C. The classical decision approaches do not usually handle institutional aspects, and cannot handle them. Thus, in the face of real uncertainty, the only way to do something is to improve crisis management, which is an institutional feature quite distinct from comparing alternatives. Another institutional aspect is that even though all political ideologies favour transparent goal decisions, the dynamics of political systems—the need to maintain a consensus—makes opaque decisions much more useful. How to reduce the political barriers to decision improvement is another problem which cannot be handled by classical decision theory. Therefore I agree with your basic search but I think we need a much broader approach to the provision of a systematic intellectual basis for improving decision-making.

Waddington: Decision theory seems to me a rather misty term; I don't know just what it includes. For practical decisions, it is most important to arrange for adequate feedback. In complex situations which we don't understand, it doesn't much matter what you do first, so long as you get adequate feedback on what the results are and react to those. Many situations have certain stability characteristics. They form what I call an epigenetic landscape; that is, they can go in various directions, but once they start to go in a certain direction it is difficult to shift them to another one. They tend to go on and on; but after a bit they will reach their stability limits and break down into two other branches. If there are several pathways of change of this kind, they form a landscape.

You often find yourself confronting a situation which you know has some definite general character, but you have no idea of the shape of the landscape. Gelfand and Tsitsin said it was as though you had landed by parachute in thick fog in a strange landscape and you wanted to discover what the landscape was like. So you make small steps in all possible directions out from where you landed. You find that in some directions you are going uphill and in others downhill, and so you will eventually discover what the slope is in that immediate locality. You then make quite a big jump, not straight downhill or straight uphill and not straight along the horizontal, but down some sort of slope. That is where you have to judge how to jump and in which direction. Testing around by small steps again you may find that you are still obviously on the slope of the same bank. So you then make a bigger jump, and find yourself at the other side of the valley, with the slope going in the opposite direction. It is a combination of little probing movements with adequate feedback, and then a biggish jump, and again little probing movements with feedback. This has always struck me as a convincing recipe for making decisions in unknown situations.

Valaskakis: The eclectics procedure that I have been describing actually stands or falls on two issues. The first is: is there directive goal-seeking—i.e. cybernetic mechanisms in behaviour—or is it haphazard? Are actions purposive—do they tend towards an objective, implicit or explicit—or not? If behaviour is not haphazard but mechanistic (i.e. the billiard-ball metaphor where we predict future behaviour by observing the path of the first billiard ball which hits the second, and so on and so forth), then it is explainable by the laws of physics. If on the other hand behaviour is purposive then there is an entity, X, that we are seeking. Whether we reach it or not is immaterial. In either case it would be possible to identify some of its elements. If we accept that there is such a magnitude, the next thing on which this approach stands or falls would be on the identification of all the elements of this entity X, including what I call the quaternary commodities in the 'felicity function'. The felicity function would conceivably change every hour, but there is reason to believe that it is reasonably stable over time. This stability I suspect is reinforced by *culture*, which teaches people to like the same things, more or less. The trouble I have had so far in trying to convince people of the usefulness of the concept of quaternary commodities is twofold. Economists recognize commodities but they say that I should forget about the quaternary aspect. They say 'Let's talk in terms of guns and butter and shoes and ships, because we know what these are'. Other social scientists say 'Sure, there are also kinship, leisure, prestige, but why call them commodities?' I think the two words are important, 'commodity' because of the cost element—the fact that you can't have prestige for nothing, you can't even have leisure for nothing, in fact there is almost nothing you can actually have for nothing. And the word 'quaternary' emphasizes the abstract nature of certain things we desire that are neither visible nor tangible. I agree with Professor Waddington that there are many individual felicity functions. But, as I just mentioned, anthropologists claim that there is a family resemblance between individual happiness functions in the same culture, and that within the same culture and subculture one can identify similar goals. A middle-class British university professor probably has a lot in common with other middle-class university professors, and so on and so forth. What people want may not be such a great mystery after all.

Waddington: This is what I mean by cluster analysis. I think you will probably find clusters in your multidimensional space.

Jevons: Are there any guidelines to indicate how the coefficients or weighting factors that you applied to the commodities in the felicity function will change over time? Professor Eldredge suggested earlier that there might be such a thing as a theory of cultural change. Of what would such a theory consist?

Kumar: Exchange theory in anthropology tries to take into account things like love, hate, affection, and so on. What seemed to be missing in your methodology, Dr Valaskakis, was a political dimension, which is also part of the problem with some of the other things we have been talking about. We are talking about searching for a common vocabulary, and we want this vocabulary to include values and alternatives and so on. That seems to me to be talking about a political philosophy. Although you mentioned the Quebec Separatists, you didn't really discuss the political dimension. A British example is the third London Airport, where the Roskill Commission went in for something like your exercise, trying to quantify the unquantifiable by putting a value on a Norman church, for example. The whole exercise was absolute nonsense, and it was admitted to be so in the end. This was partly because they were trying to make a decision at a national level for a local community. If that kind of mix of variables had been localized there might have been some kind of rational strategy. As it was, no matter how sophisticated the social science was that went into it, there couldn't possibly have been a satisfactory outcome. In your notion of eclectics, have you got some kind of political contouring or level or scale on which these kinds of calculations ought to be made?

Valaskakis: I would bring in political science very simply through the quaternary commodity of power and all its derivatives—influence and so on and so forth. Power can be viewed as a capital commodity or a capital good, that is as a means to an end, or it can be viewed as a *final consumption* good, in other words as one that would produce direct satisfaction. You could then make a power analysis at the individual or at the subcultural level—whether at a regional level, a class level, a sexist level or whatever—and look at the commodity power as it is effectively desired and do some kind of behaviouristic analysis to ascertain its competitiveness with other commodities.

When I mentioned quantifying the unquantifiable I meant it in terms of an ordinal rather than a cardinal ranking. Economic theory has allowed us to treat such a thing as 'utility' or 'felicity' without having to specify what units it is measured in. We only need to say that we rank a situation, alpha, higher than beta, and beta higher than gamma, but not necessarily alpha higher than gamma. The relationship doesn't even have to be transitive in the overt preference function. Quantifying the unquantifiable is merely using the technique of opportunity-cost and saying that the cost of nationalism is so and so, the cost of so and so is something else, and so on. The cost of Britain leaving the EEC could possibly be measured in terms of other quaternary commodities and other conventional commodities, and vice versa.

It is ridiculous of course to give a monetary value to a Norman church. But if it can be shown that demolishing the church will allow the building of, say, a hospital (and it is wartime and no other possibilities are open), then we must trade off the very real cultural and aesthetic value of the church (which would probably get my vote) against the immediate concern with the wounded and the dying. Such a trade-off is admittedly far-fetched but it dramatizes my main point: it is as misleading to assign an infinite value to a Norman church as it is to assign such a value to an airport. There is a human cost element always to be reckoned with.

Eldredge: We seem to be talking a slightly different language. I begin to recognize felicity functions as similar to what we call social indicators, which have a long and not as yet very successful tradition in what has been termed trans-economic cost–benefit analysis. I prefer the phrase 'societal' indicators because that includes a whole lot more than social indicators, unless you are a sociologist and understand that social means the whole complex of human society and culture.

The System Dynamic Center at MIT uses a completely cybernetic system in decision-making for urban planning which may be relevant here. For the city of Lowell, which I mentioned in my paper, they assigned arbitrary numbers to certain types of goods. They found that it didn't matter much how arbitrary the numbers were, since they showed the interrelationship in their dynamic model and helped people to make decisions.

Valaskakis: My case is that we should adopt the methodology of choice theory which was developed via economics. I accept entirely your point about social indicators. My argument against them is that we don't know what they indicate. What does a newspaper per thousand inhabitants really mean? If we want to go towards meaningful social indicators we must try and find out what is behind them. This is where we come back to felicity functions and quaternary commodities.

Eldredge: I was trying to marry your phraseology to quality of life. I have made an economic analysis where I concluded that heroin was more important to the inhabitants of New York than the Metropolitan Opera, in terms of money spent on the two commodities.

Shane: I met some Montreal businessmen in 1974 who were involved in a controversy about the teaching of French in the schools. They insisted that it should be taught even though the teaching time was at the cost of other fields of study. How do you cope with people like these who were striving to have French required in the schools, to the loss of those students seeking other more general educational benefits? The Montreal spokesmen for French instruction said frankly in newspaper interviews that they thought it would help to strengthen the ascendancy of the French in local business affairs, in competition with the non-French.

Valaskakis: I can give you an even better example than this on multicultural problems. Belgium like Canada has two primary languages, which makes things extremely expensive because everything has to be translated. One person suggested, tongue-in-cheek, that if one language has to be given up and the other adopted as the national language, the people whose language was chosen should pay all the income tax. People would then have to make a choice. The introduction of cost is the key thing in this analysis. Teaching in French in Quebec universities is extremely costly, in terms of having to translate so many new things that appear in English. There is a time lag of many months if not years before the new material is available. Yet it is something people are quite willing to pay for.

Shane: Perhaps what you have to do is to accept the happy assumption that people will be reasonable.

Ziman: Implicit in Dr Valaskakis's approach there is a model of man. We ought to be very worried about such a model becoming too dominant in our thinking. Anthropological evidence for exchange functions etc. was mentioned but that example does not show that this model of man is correct. On the contrary it shows that this metaphor of commodity, which implies exchange equivalence and so on, is forced by anthropologists onto the groups of people that they study. It is by no means clear that this is the full description of human social relations. If you want to start all this, you must first take account of what the poets and other writers have been saying. If I want to discuss the rationality of irrational action, I would turn to Stendhal or to Doris Lessing. Doris Lessing discusses the whole process of what people want and what they haven't got in their personal lives in ways that just don't seem to me to depend on a hidden utility or felicity function, a 'goal function'. What is missing from the Valaskakis model is the notion that everybody, every community, is itself a historical process. Life isn't a steady state, with each person trying to maximize his or her utility function. People arrive in the world with all sorts of backgrounds. If you are going to find what this felicity function is, you must use your analysis to *discover* it, not hypothesize it as a hidden variable. You have to go right into the heart of the lives of each individual in this society. In other words what you are trying to achieve would need far more than a mathematical or logical model that you can deal with in some sort of analytical way. In the end, you are making a model of the whole; you are trying to reconstruct reality. We must face that and not try to push it aside. With horizon analysis you are doing something that is not so bad in this sense, because there you are envisaging certain types of steady state. You are abstracting them from their history, in conditions where certain exchanges, trade-offs, etc., are credible. Classical economics talks about the steady state but doesn't really talk about change, or dynamics. Perhaps that is the use of it; but I don't see how your method is going to deal with getting from here to there and beyond.

Valaskakis: Dynamics is in fact a well-developed branch of economics, at least in the mathematical sense, and I would not fault the discipline on this specific point. Let me express my confidence in the 'eclectics' approach by saying that even the most difficult of behavioural problems could be dealt with successfully through this approach: Hamlet's felicity function could well be discovered through critical examination of his words and deeds—for, like Polonius, I feel there was a method to the madness—and too often we dismiss what we do not understand as not understandable (by anyone).

References cited

[1] VALASKAKIS, K. (1975) Prospective, rétrospective et perspective. *Actualité Economique*, August

[2] QUERILY, J. (1965) *Economic Thought, A Historical Anthology*, Random House, New York

[3] SCHAFFER, H. G. (ed.) (1967) in *The Communist World*, p.99, Appleton-Century-Crofts, New York

4 CLARK, C. (1957) *Conditions of Economic Progress*, 3rd edn., Macmillan, London
5 ROTHSCHILD, K. W. (ed.) (1971) *Power in Economics*, Penguin, Baltimore, Maryland
6 ISARD, W. *et al.* (1969) *General Theory: Social, Political Economic & Regional*, MIT Press, Cambridge, Mass.
7 MCLELLAND, D. C. (1967) *The Achieving Society*, Free Press/Macmillan, New York
8 BRONFENBRENNER, M. (1972) A review of radical economics. *Journal of Economic Literature*

Additional reading

BOULDING, K. E. (ed.) (1970) *Economics as a Science*, McGraw-Hill, New York
BOULDING, K. E. (1973) *The Economy of Love and Fear*, Wadsworth, Belmont, California
DEUTSCH, K. W. (1953) *Nationalism and Social Communication: An Inquiry into the Foundations of Nationality*, MIT Press, Cambridge, Mass.
FROMM, E. (1971) *Escape from Freedom*, Avon, New York
GARDINER, W. L. (1973) *An Invitation to Cognitive Psychology*, Brooks-Cole/Wadsworth, Monterey, California
MASLOW, A. H. (1954) *Motivation and Personality*, Harper & Row, New York
MUNDELL, R. (1968) *Man and Economics*, McGraw-Hill, New York
VALASKAKIS, K. (1971) *Quaternary Commodities*, Cahier de l'Université de Montréal/Sciences Economiques

Some fundamental philosophical, psychological and intellectual assumptions of futures studies

YEHEZKEL DROR

Department of Political Science, The Hebrew University of Jerusalem; and The London School of Economics and Political Science

Abstract Futures studies have three operational bases, each supported by a number of assumptions or premises.

The first basis is that something ought to be known about the future. This is based on two assumptions: (1) the future should be known, as a goal or value in itself; (2) knowledge about the future is useful for achieving other values and goals.

The second basis is that something can be known about the future. It is based on four assumptions: (1) the past can serve as a basis for predicting the future because society has some stability or ultra-stability; (2) special senses permit predictions that are independent of the past; (3) the human mind is capable, directly or indirectly, of recognizing stability or ultra-stability and basing predictions on it; (4) knowledge-distorting effects of intense values, emotions and interests can be overcome.

The third basis is that 'futures studies' as a specific endeavour are a preferable frame for producing desirable knowledge about the future. It is supported by three assumptions: (1) futures studies have shared characteristics; (2) the shared features of futures studies are unique; (3) the unique features of 'futures studies' are best developed within a distinct frame.

Altogether, futures studies seem to be based on nine assumptions which are mixed philosophical, psychological and intellectual. Critical examination of these nine premises seems to indicate that most of them can be supported by some parts of futures studies. These subdivisions can, therefore, constitute the elements of an academic–professional discipline or sub-discipline of 'futures studies'.

Interest in the future may well have accompanied humanity since its very beginnings. Certainly, organized societies have had future-probing institutions from early history, such as seers, prophets, fate-questioning devices, oracles, etc.[1,2] Whether motivated by curiosity or caused by the dependence of all conscious decision-making processes on contingency predictions, attempts to foresee the future are nothing new. Therefore, if indeed contemporary futures studies belong to a different species of endeavours, the distinctions must be sought not in subject matter but in methodology and paradigms and their underlying foundations (for the term futures studies see ref. 3, p.45).

The problem is made all the more difficult by possible differences between appearance and reality. A superficial look at contemporary futures studies reveals many features of modernity, of professionalism and of scientism, all of them recent. A large and rapidly growing professional literature, international and national associations and conferences, special research organizations, university chairs and teaching programmes, special units in private and public organizations, and a large set of tools, techniques and methods—all these characterize contemporary futures studies. These characteristics seem to set futures studies in their modern form apart from their historic ancestors and present a *prima facie* case of scientific–professional legitimacy. The trouble is that alchemy and demonology could develop similar features, given suitable support and interest. External symptoms and presenting signs must not, therefore, be relied upon when one is diagnosing the validity and usefulness of futures studies: a more thorough examination is needed.

Evaluation of the quality of an intellectual endeavour such as futures studies can proceed on different levels, with the help of a variety of criteria. In particular, three levels of investigation are relevant: (a) the pragmatic; (b) the paradigmatic and (c) that of basic assumptions. For futures studies to be accepted as a valid scientific–professional endeavour, or at least as a worthwhile intellectual activity, some criteria for all three dimensions must be satisfied. At the very least, the endeavour must meet requirements on one of these levels.

The trouble with futures studies is that both pragmatic and paradigmatic tests are hard to apply. At the pragmatic level, the utility of futures studies outputs (never mind how arrived at) has to be examined. But this is unproductive for the following reasons. (1) Predictions on complex issues are probabilistic and open-ended; therefore, often actual events cannot prove or disprove the validity of the predictions in the absence of statistically significant sets of similar events, which usually do not exist for socially important phenomena. (2) Human action is influenced by images of the future, which in turn are influenced by futures studies; self-fulfilling or self-negating effects of predictions may be among the useful outputs of futures studies, but they are hard to identify and they distort the objective validity of the predictions themselves. (3) Long-range predictions are among the important concerns of futures studies, but their accuracy cannot be evaluated for a long time. (4) The youth of futures studies may be one of the reasons why they do not meet the pragmatic tests, rather than any inherent defects. (5) To disagreements among those working on futures studies about desired outputs and even about the qualifications needed for engaging in futures studies must be added the difficulty of applying the concept of 'objective knowledge'[4] to the domain of futures studies.

I do not want to overstate my argument. Any good book on futures studies methods (e.g. Martino[5]) includes some pragmatic evidence on the usefulness of some techniques and tools. But for futures studies as a whole, pragmatic tests are in part inappropriate and in part impossible or too difficult to apply at present.

The paradigmatic level of investigation, too, seems inappropriate for futures studies. It involves evaluation of the paradigms used in futures studies in terms of those of other sciences or of contemporary sciences as a whole.[6] But, as I have argued elsewhere at length,[7] futures studies can, and perhaps should, be regarded as part of a 'scientific revolution' which involves substantive changes in their paradigms. Therefore, the paradigms unique to futures studies (on which there is a lot of disagreement) cannot be evaluated through comparison with other sets of paradigms but must be examined and justified in terms of their own foundations.

Medicine, engineering, applied physics, chemistry—these and other disciplines registered significant progress in terms of pragmatic results before achieving validated paradigms and before improving the assumptions on which they were based (though validated paradigms and improved bases became essential for their advancement into the post-pragmatic stage). Futures studies cannot follow a similar road, because the pragmatic and paradigmatic tests cannot be applied or are inappropriate. Validated assumptions are, it follows, already essential for futures studies while they are in their *status nascendi*. This conclusion is all the more important because this dimension has been neglected in published futures studies and is disliked by many of the mission-driven scholars and advocates of futures studies.

Futures studies, in all their varieties, have three operational bases:

(1) Something *ought* to be known about the future.
(2) Something *can* be known about the future.
(3) 'Futures studies' as a specific endeavour are a preferable frame for producing desirable knowledge about the future.

To justify futures studies and, indeed, everything concerned with 'the future as an academic discipline', these bases must, in the main, be supported by viable philosophical, psychological and intellectual assumptions.

Without trying to distinguish strictly between 'philosophical', 'psychological' and 'intellectual' facets, I would like to turn now to a critical, though concise, examination of some such main assumptions of futures studies.

(1) THE FUTURE SHOULD BE KNOWN, AS A GOAL OR VALUE IN ITSELF

Behaviourally, curiosity about the future is a widespread phenomenon, though not a universal one. For example, various primitive societies without time perspectives, or with different time perspectives, show little curiosity about the future. Similarly, fatalistic *Weltanschauungen* and perhaps some existentialistic variations may tend towards non-interest in the future. But, in most contemporary and many historic societies, curiosity about the future is intense.

Independently of the distribution of interest in the future among various populations, every scientist must choose for himself, value-wise, his own area of interest.[8] If one accepts the ideology of the autonomy of science from society and social needs, knowledge about the future is as valid a value for pure-science concern as any other subject. If one introduces considerations of social utility of knowledge of the 'technology assessment' type, the next assumption is reached.

(2) KNOWLEDGE ABOUT THE FUTURE IS USEFUL FOR ACHIEVING OTHER VALUES AND GOALS

In this assumption, knowledge about the future is seen as instrumental for achieving other, undefined, values and goals. This assumption is closely tied in with assumptions about decision-making. Clearly, every conscious and goal-oriented decision-making process depends on knowledge about the future when the probable results of different alternatives have to be compared (ref. 9, chapter 12). Therefore, if such decision-making is accepted as possible and desirable, the assumption about knowledge of the future being instrumentally useful is acceptable. Decision-making itself can be negated either by an extreme deterministic and steady-state point of view or by doubts about the capacity of the human mind to achieve more good than bad through decisions. Also, if one regards human decisions in any case as being incapable of warding off some terrible future, then ignorance about that future can perhaps be regarded as useful, under some conditions.

Another instrumental argument against futures studies relates to their self-fulfilling potentials. Predicting possible undesirable scenarios, so the argument may go, increases their probability of occurring. This, for instance, was a main line of argument against strategic studies dealing with the possibilities of survival during and after a nuclear war.[10,11]

To meet such objections, one can either rely on existing consensus among many scientists on the possibilities of improving human fate through conscious decisions,[12,13] or allow that both positions are equally plausible, so leaving each scholar free to choose sides on the basis of extra-rational beliefs. A stoic philosophy which demands that we try our best, whether it helps or not, can also serve as a foundation for futures studies, as part of policy sciences as a whole.[7]

The first operational basis of futures studies, that something *should* be known about the future, seems therefore well based on philosophical and other assumptions. These assumptions are open to doubts, but not more so than those of most sciences and disciplines.

To continue with the main assumptions of futures studies, we reach now a few that are relevant for the second operational basis of futures studies.

(3) THE PAST CAN SERVE AS A BASIS FOR PREDICTING THE FUTURE BECAUSE OF SOME STABILITY OR ULTRA-STABILITY OF RELEVANT PHENOMENA

Without some regularity of phenomena no nomographic rules can exist, and such rules, in various ways, constitute the base for predictions. In other words, without continuity in the time dimension, no futures studies are possible. Continuity does not have to be deterministic, linear and fixed: probabilistic dynamics, complex continuities, ultra-stability with constant change and even a limited amount of discontinuities—all these can be handled by sophisticated prediction methods. Nevertheless, all knowledge (with one hypothetical exception, to be discussed under the next heading) is based on the past and can, therefore, serve to probe the future only in so far as the future is in continuity with the past.

This is so important an assumption as to justify some further clarifications:

(*a*) Dependence on the past is obvious in the simpler prediction methods, such as extrapolation. But more advanced methods also depend on the past, because models and theories have been verified in the past.

(*b*) Intuition, on which the Delphi method relies, also depends on experience and tacit knowledge accumulated in the past.

(*c*) Even utopian schools of futures studies depend on the past, which shaped concepts and ideas and limited the domain of imagination. Some imaginative creativity may escape these fetters—but, however important for prophetic activities and artistic expression, creativity cannot by itself serve as a main basis for futures studies.

The assumption of continuity in the time dimension is shared by all scientific knowledge related to the physical world and creates few difficulties in the physical sciences, where regularity is assumed on a cosmic scale. In life sciences and medicine there is more awareness of possible non-continuous changes in the objects of inquiry. When we come to the social domain, discontinuities appear frequently and may become dominant during the approaching epoch. Paradoxically, it is the accelerated rate of change itself which pushed the development of futures studies as an aid to dealing with increasing uncertainties, while simultaneously imposing rigid limits on the domain of predictability open to futures studies.

Again, overstatement must be avoided. When we are dealing with short time spans and limited sets of phenomena, sufficient continuity exists to permit predictions, at least if they are in stochastic form and open-ended. Also, explication of the limits of predictability can be helpful by leading to the adoption of uncertainty-absorbing (as distinguished from uncertainty-reducing or uncertainty-patterning) modes of decision-making, such as planning for uncertainty[14] and institutionalized learning.[15,16,17] Nevertheless, dependency upon continuity and past-based knowledge imposes limits on futures studies of non-stable phenomena, so reducing the usefulness and feasibility of futures studies as a whole. Another implication is that futures studies need to be tied in with uncertainty-absorbing modes of decision-making and therefore at least parts of futures studies should be integrated into policy sciences as a whole (ref. 3, chapter 5).

(4) SPECIAL SENSES PERMIT PREDICTIONS INDEPENDENT FROM THE PAST

A logical, but unacceptable, alternative to assumption (3) is a belief in precognition. Even people who accept some parapsychological phenomena as true reject precognition, which contradicts assumptions fundamental to all sciences and to most philosophical systems about time, the cosmos and the nature of human life. Therefore, such an assumption must be rejected, though some persons active in futures studies seem tacitly to believe in precognition, without saying that this is the basis for what they are saying.

(5) THE HUMAN MIND IS CAPABLE, DIRECTLY OR INDIRECTLY, OF RECOGNIZING STABILITY OR ULTRA-STABILITY AND BASING PREDICTIONS ON IT

Within the domain of validity of assumption (3), futures studies are in principle possible if and as far as assumption (5) is also correct. It is not enough that some continuity in the time dimension exists—we must be able to recognize it (either directly or indirectly, e.g. with the help of pattern-recognizing computers) and utilize it for futures studies.

This assumption is related in part to epistemological considerations, in part to psychology, especially the psychology of thinking and perception theory, and in part to intellectual considerations concerning the availability of scientific methodologies and their limitations. Full consideration of these issues would lead us too deep into the philosophy of science, where they have been quite fully considered[4,18,19] though not applied to the specific problems of futures studies. Let me, therefore, limit myself to a few comments.

(*a*) Subjects which futures studies share with other disciplines present no special problems for this assumption.

(*b*) When we are dealing with complex phenomena, such as social macro-change, we begin to doubt our ability at present to arrive at valid perception and understanding of the phenomenon. Less ambitious attempts, in the social sciences, to explain specific cases of social macro-change have not so far been very successful, which raises doubts about the capacity of futures studies (which depend on knowledge of different subjects supplied by appropriate disciplines) to do much better in the near future.

(*c*) Nevertheless, futures studies may do better than expected, thanks to novel packages and methodologies able to handle dynamic, complex and non-deterministic phenomena—such as scenarios, alternative futures, unexpected occurrences, structured imagination, and others.[5,20]

(*d*) There is no clear and immediate limit to human capacity for understanding complexity, if necessary with the help of intelligence-amplifying devices. Even if an absolute limit exists, futures studies still have a long way to go before it is reached, as demonstrated by ongoing advances in methodologies for futures studies.

(*e*) Even if an optimistic view of human ability to develop futures studies is adopted, the many difficulties in doing so must be acknowledged. As a minimum, methodological care and sophistication are needed. Simple tools and naive images cannot be expected to go far in futures studies.

Subject to these observations and reservations, assumption (5) seems to be, in the main, acceptable. But a strong barrier, relevant to (5) as well as to (3) and (4), remains: futures studies deal with a subject that is emotional, intensely value-loaded and related to vested interests. Therefore, the need for assumption (6).

(6) KNOWLEDGE-DISTORTING EFFECTS OF INTENSE VALUES, EMOTIONS AND INTERESTS CAN BE OVERCOME

Futures studies deal with a highly emotion-sensitive, value-sensitive and interest-sensitive subject—the shape of the future. All of us have values, the only hope for realization of which lies in the future; all of us have emotions which shape our perception of the future; and many of us have interests whose present fate may depend on accepted images of the future. If the self-fulfilling and self-defying effects of images of the future are added to the above-mentioned forces, then the strength of their distorting effects on futures studies is clear. This effect is fully shown by the present state of much of futures studies, in which hopes for the future, hopes for the present, emotions about both the future and the present, and efforts at identification of probable and possible futures, are often completely mixed up. (This situation is fully reflected in the proceedings of the various international and special world conferences on futures research. For detailed discussion of such weaknesses of futures studies, as reflected in the world conferences, see refs. 21 and 22).

The present state of much of futures studies, therefore, does not supply much factual evidence for the validity of this assumption. But, although psychological factors undermine this assumption, intellectually it is tenable: modern methodology for value analysis permits some separation between futures studies and emotions, interests and values;[23] explicit methods for futures studies help this separation to be made[5] (e.g. see the many methodological articles in the two professional futures studies journals in English, *Futures*[24] and *Technological Forecasting and Social Change*[25]); suitable institutional arrangements can push this separation beyond psychological barriers, through pluralism, positive redundancy and mutual set-offs. Therefore, the conclusion seems to be that in principle assumption (6) will be sustained if—and it is an important 'if'—futures studies in fact are methodologically sophisticated and evolve within a suitable structural setting.

From the combined examination of assumptions (3), (4), (5) and (6) it seems that the second operational basis of futures studies, namely that something *can* be known about the future, can be supported conditionally. The conditions involve some characteristics of futures studies that lead directly into the third operational basis for futures studies, namely that futures studies as a specific endeavour are a suitable frame for producing desirable knowledge about the future.

This operational basis in turn depends on three assumptions, to the examination of which we now turn.

(7) FUTURES STUDIES HAVE SHARED CHARACTERISTICS

The very use of the term 'futures studies' in the plural demonstrates my image of pluralistic features of this activity. Indeed, books, articles and ideas presented under the flag of 'futures studies' have many divergent elements, which do not form a meaningful mosaic. Revolutionary exhortations, utopian and anti-utopian prophecies and plain hallucinations can be found hand-in-hand with careful studies of possible futures, design of desirable and feasible futures, and stimulating counter-probabilistic scenarios. (In addition to the already-mentioned conferences and journals, the more popular monthly *The Futurist*[26] provides a good sample of the various elements that go under the name of 'futures studies'.)

Behaviourally, the seventh assumption is, therefore, not too well supported. Only if one excludes from the legitimate domain of futures studies some of the fringe activities, including—in addition to those already mentioned—strong 'action-oriented' quasi-political activities aggregating around the standard of futures studies, can one identify a meaningful shared characteristic that can serve as a basis for a 'futures studies' frame. Interest in the future by itself is not a meaningful characteristic, being much too diffuse. The shared characteristic of those futures interests which can constitute elements of a discipline, inter-discipline, subdiscipline, supradiscipline, of futures studies etc., must be that they have an explicit methodology for dealing with the future. This common denominator of futures studies returns us, in part, to assumption (5). As indicated there, a methodology for futures studies is possible and, in fact, already exists in part.

(8) THE SHARED FEATURES OF FUTURES STUDIES ARE UNIQUE TO THOSE STUDIES

To justify a specific frame for futures studies, it is necessary to show both (*a*) that there is a common denominator, as considered just now; and (*b*) that this denominator is unique, at least in some aspects. All disciplines of knowledge are interested in the future, prediction being a main test of a valid theory or model. The question is whether predictions and futures studies, and their methodologies, have something special which justifies their advancement as a distinct endeavour.

This question can probably be answered positively. No existing discipline focuses mainly on predictions and futures treatment as such. If one includes all the special features of methodologies for futures studies (e.g. utilization of intuition, important role of futures invention with the help of creativity and imagination, special relation to planning and policy-making, and others), 'futures studies' seem to have a unique domain of concern, which is specific but not exclusive.

(9) THE UNIQUE FEATURES OF FUTURES STUDIES ARE BEST
DEVELOPED WITHIN A DISTINCT FRAME

Given the features of the organization of knowledge and the structure of
universities and of research, the need for distinct frames in which futures studies
can develop seems both reasonable and experience-based. The analogue of the
dependence of policy studies on novel institutions which fit their special characteristics seems quite convincing (see ref. 7, especially Part Four). The differences
between some of the methodological features of futures studies and those of
most 'normal' academic endeavours reinforce the conclusion that distinct
frames are needed for futures studies. This does not imply that those frames
must be separate and unique for futures studies. Perhaps, some parts at least
of futures studies have a better chance of developing in conjunction with policy
sciences or policy studies as a whole—never mind the name. But the requirement for a distinct frame for futures studies seems well enough supported
to justify at least some serious experimentation with it.

In the aggregate, assumptions (7), (8) and (9) seem to support the third
operational basis, at least in respect to some sorts of futures studies, which in
turn should be open-ended and innovative but not completely anarchic.

To sum up this examination of the nine main assumptions on which futures
studies rest, it seems that for parts of futures studies, as constituted now, these
assumptions are sufficiently well supported to justify a *prima facie* case for
'futures studies' as an academic–professional endeavour. But, if they are to
live up to the assumptions of this ambition and claim, futures studies must
transform themselves and upgrade their qualities. For actual moves in these
directions, suitable institutionalization, designed to build up the foundations
of futures studies, is necessary, as discussed in this paper. The details of appropriate institutionalization need separate enquiry.

Discussion

Waddington: In the academic context, futures studies should be compared
with the discipline of history. Nobody really pretends that history leads us to
an exact definition of the facts, or an account of all the facts. History is a normative exercise. The evidence is never complete, and the best historians give a
personal interpretation of the way people were feeling and the way they were
acting. Historians are, of course, constrained by what facts are known, but the
best historians are also great moralists. The sort of truth they are aiming at is
not the same as scientific truth, and even scientific truth is not absolute truth.

I am sure that students of the future should not be regarded as simple seekers after the truth. I don't believe in futuristics as prediction: they have always turned out to be wrong.

One characteristic of futures studies is that, in today's immediate context, they are much more multidimensional than most other types of studies. Just looking at telecommunications and asking how soon we are going to get the video-telephone isn't 'futures study'—it is the future of a specific technology. Futures studies must be as totally multidimensional as they can be, trying to look at everything. That is a distinct difference from nearly everything else in the academic world now. The academic world has gone through a hundred years of sub-division, and it is fairly difficult to find anybody anywhere who really looks at the world in a multidimensional way. Historians perhaps do so, and lawyers to some extent, but it is against the general trend of academia in the last hundred years.

The practical justification of futures studies is that they are an attempt to draw a picture of the present, from the point of view that the present is not just the existing instant but really consists of processes. We can't have a picture of the present without knowing what has been going on for the last thirty years—in fact we may have to go back to Magna Carta to get some of the relevant dimensions—and we also need to look ahead five, ten, twenty or thirty years. Futures studies are an attempt to draw a picture of the stage on which we are going to take the next step; and the next step must carry us away from where we are now towards somewhere. Futures studies try to give us some idea of whether we are going to fall down a chasm in the next few years or not. And this has to be done in a multidimensional sense, not just two-dimensional.

Those seem to me to be the three major characteristics of futures studies: they can only aim at the sort of truth historians aim at—a truth involving a great element of normative moralizing; they must be exceedingly multidimensional and their basic relevance is as a dynamic analysis of today.

Platt: It is worth remembering that three different kinds of problem-solving were needed in evolution. The first is problem-solving by survival: the creatures that didn't solve the problems died off. That kind is encoded in the DNA. The second is problem-solving by learning, with the nervous system. That kind is encoded in the neurons: you don't have to fall over the cliff before you draw back. The third is problem-solving by anticipation; this can only come with science, with the knowledge of laws and regularities, so that one can predict things that have never happened. The Sputnik is a good example of these differences. The first Sputnik was not one of ten thousand that were shot up at random and only one survived; nor was it something which flew too high and then too low until it learned the right orbit. No: it was designed by anticipation—programmed with a feedback-stabilization program to go into the right orbit on the first try.

In the same way, the human race collectively is now encountering families of hard problems that have never been encountered before. We cannot solve them by learning because it would require living through them; and we cannot solve them by survival, because we have in a sense only one world for one trip. We must therefore solve them by anticipation. This requires us to understand the laws of social dynamics so that we can anticipate all sorts of things that have never happened before. It will require many sensitive little feedbacks all along the way: tiny indicators, fluctuations which show whether we have got the rules right or whether they are going astray, advance warnings or 'feed-forwards'. We will need all sorts of special little methods that give us indications short of catastrophe to help us to go rapidly but as cautiously as possible in solving this global problem that has never existed before.

Nevertheless, there is another sense in which knowledge of the future is impossible, simply because of its interaction with our choices. Here the analogy I would suggest is something like the steering of a bus. For this, we need not a narrow knowledge of one single possible path or rut, but knowledge of the total visual field, the total set of alternative paths, so that you see the old ruts here and the good roadway there, and the dangers somewhere else. You choose among them in a cybernetic way and the result is that you cannot predict your own choices until you know what the whole field is, and it continues to change as your vision changes, and your choices as you move along.

The role of futures studies, it seems to me, is to describe this total visual field, this total multidimensional family of alternatives within which we choose. It is, in Harvey Cox's sense,[27] a prophecy—that is, it is an 'if–then' procedure rather than 'prediction'. Prediction says that we *will* do so and so, at least with a certain probability. Cox says, on the other hand, that what we need instead is the Judaeo-Christian tradition of prophecy, not probabilistic but *conditional: if* you make love to your neighbour's wife, *then* you will roast in hell; but *if* you love God, *then* you can create the Kingdom of Heaven around you. The old prophets were never predictors but made prophecies in this conditional sense. So a view of futures knowledge, it seems to me, is a description of conditional knowledge—that is, of a range of alternatives such that *if* you do this, *then* with fair probability *that* will happen. This makes it very operational, but different from the deterministic findings of science, not like physics but cybernetics.

Oldfield: Even after Professor Dror's interesting philosophical, psychological and intellectual analysis of futures studies I am still very much the worried outsider. As an empirical ecologist and certainly not a philosopher, I find it difficult to express the problems that I see, but there are at least five aspects of futures studies which worry me. I think I would label them identity, cost, shift of mode, the question of responsibility or escapism, and the question of positive feedback.

Identity—Professor Waddington encouraged us to think in terms of history, so let us think briefly of African history. Until recently this was essentially colonial history, with which the African had little identity. I fear that some futures studies are perhaps tending towards an even more worrying and more dangerous kind of intellectual neocolonialism in which the majority become alienated not merely from the real experiences of the past but from all the alternative articulated images of the future.

Cost—scenario models cost money and I think they are usually funded by people who have cash and a belief that they have options. People who have neither, don't or can't fund them.

Shift of mode—when we contemplate the idea of the future as an academic discipline, I think we are saying by implication that we can study the past and we can study the future. But 'study' means such different things in those two contexts, different in terms both of what is available for our empirical examination and different in terms of what is amenable to change. In practice there seems to be, within futures studies, an emphasis on the positive evaluation of methodology, no bad thing in itself. However, I suspect that it is a self-generating thing, that it heightens mystique and jargon, and that it helps to diminish communication outside the subject.

Escapism—some of the points I suppose are McLuhanesque and they are by way of saying that the study of the future is a different medium. Therefore I suspect that it will be perceived and decoded by people outside the study in ways which we might find difficult to anticipate. My fear is that, all too often, it will tend to promote despair or irresponsibility or escapism. T. S. Eliot, who said wiser and more beautiful things about time than any of us, said that 'humankind cannot bear very much reality'. For myself I am forced to wonder in what sense, if any, it is still possible to affirm that the future is not something to be predicted or anticipated, but to be worked for?

Feedback—my final point is that I suspect, partly from the little reading that I have done and partly from our discussions, that it is going to be difficult for futures study to avoid reinforcing the great socioeconomic disparities in the world. I think it is difficult for it ever to become a vehicle for doing the reverse. It is more likely to be a mechanism for positive feedback in socio-economic divergencies and disparities.

I am not trying to discredit futures studies. I am merely expressing a lot of worries and I would be happier if some of these things were discussed in a meeting of this kind.

Waddington: Why do you think futures studies are necessarily going to encourage the development of disparity in different parts of the world?

Oldfield: I suspect that by revealing the range of possibilities and the range of choice they will be most clearly perceived and acted upon by those who can profit from the range of alternatives presented.

King: Like all knowledge?

Oldfield: Sadly, yes.

Dror: Edmund Burke, I think, said that the present is a bridge between the past and the future. In this sense I certainly agree with Professor Waddington. But I think there are radical differences between futures studies and studies of the past. Thus, there is one past but many alternative futures.

Waddington: Are you sure there is only one past?

Dror: There are different perceptions of the past, but there is only one past.

I agree that in principle anticipation and learning must be tied in but the problem is more complex. For example, even though few areas of learning from information have received such large inputs of money and high quality manpower as military defence intelligence—which certainly has had much more attention than social indicators—the history of military intelligence is full of extreme failures because all data were perceived in the mirrors of the past. A main danger is, therefore, that even when the future already gives warning symptoms we cannot recognize what is going to happen. Therefore, one main problem of futures studies is how to jump out of our own skins, how to broaden our perception of the future. This is a main intellectual challenge which leads us to the question of learning, anticipation and so forth.

I would completely disagree with what Professor Oldfield said about methodology (p. 157). Methodology is difficult for those who don't study it. Indeed, in a new endeavour where we can't test the results the only thing we can do is to test the methods and the underlying assumptions.

If the Zionist movement had had an excellent institute for futures study sixty years ago, it would probably have failed. In a movement that was trying to do the nearly impossible, the knowledge that it was nearly impossible would have made it completely impossible. It is different in Israel today, where good futures studies are very necessary. Futures studies are useful for most societies today, but for some types of social movements they are dysfunctional.

Oldfield: I didn't want to imply that a careful regard for methodology is bad. I was saying that a preoccupation with methodology has certain sorts of implications for people outside the methodology.

Waddington: Nobody could possibly deny that professional futurologists have invented some pretty awe-inspiring jargon, which inspires more awe than the subject can really carry off. Some of the methodologies are definitely useful, but there has been, as you said, too great a proliferation of methodology, and the promises held out have been too great. Delphi sounds a wonderful method, but it is simply systematized guessing, though it sometimes pretends it is a lot more.

Eldredge: Futures studies are really a problem-oriented field. I have worked in a number of problem-oriented areas, and we never did like the word 'discipline' because it suggests a body of knowledge, with well-worked-out theory and methodologies. 'Field', on the other hand, suggests an area of interest that hasn't yet grown up; moreover it doesn't sound quite so pretentious. One of the worst things that futures studies at this point can do is act in a pretentious fashion. We don't use the term 'discipline' for urban studies, which are very interdisciplinary, or for women's studies or black studies.

Waddington: You are possibly right but I would say that, on your definition, history should be a field.

Ashby: I think the opportunity costs which Dr Valaskakis discussed are relevant to the main theme of our discussion. I am uneasy about their use, for various reasons. First, it tempts the worker to put a money value on something which many people believe can't be measured, and then to slip the money value into a cost–benefit equation as though it were as valid as the other numerical data. This is exactly what was done by the Roskill commission; they did a cost–benefit analysis for the third London airport at a cost of £1 million, and its conclusion—to put the airport in Buckinghamshire—was promptly rejected by the Minister. The only relevant question about opportunity costs for our discussion is: can you use this technique, and are you prepared to do so, to estimate what people are prepared to give up in the way of present benefits for the benefit of their great-grandchildren. The relevance of discussions about the future, in so far as they bear on policy-making, depends on how much we are prepared to sacrifice now for the benefit of coming generations. Without knowing how we stand on that question, we cannot be clear about what kind of future we want for people not yet born. A future of the kind we want now may not be at all what our great-grandchildren would want. They might not even want to go around in cars. There might be quite different means of inter-communication then, and people might not want much to travel. I think we have to distinguish the study of the future—which is immensely interesting and which has great potentialities—from the application of the study of the future to present political policies. I am suspicious of those who are tempted to calculate numerical discounts on the future.

Valaskakis: I shall resist the temptation you referred to. Opportunity–cost has in essence nothing to do with money, because one can measure opportunity–cost with this idea of felicity without mentioning money at all.

Another example shows that money does not have to enter into the subject at all. The sociologists say that we seem to be moving towards a singles life-style as opposed to a married life-style. Many people argue about this but they can't seem to explain why. If we could identify not the material but the abstract advantages of the marriage situation, including some form of emotional security, and then trade this off against the liberty or freedom that is perceived in the so-called 'singles' situation, then we would have the quaternary commodity trade-off that I am talking about. No money enters into the picture, but what seems to happen is that people make changing choices: they have alternative goals depending on their position in life. In the Californian model, a person marries six or seven times in a lifetime because of a continuous change in the hierarchy of values. At times the need for emotional security seems to be stronger than the need for so-called freedom, and vice versa. I shall give yet another example of non-monetary opportunity cost as an explanation of behaviour. Kenneth Boulding has written a fascinating book called *The Economy of Love and Fear*[28] where he substitutes for the notion of exchange the notion of grants, which are unilateral movements of goods with no counterpart. It is the *quid* without the *quo*. Implicit grants occur when such a transfer of commodities arises as a by-product of certain actions. If we deplete non-renewable natural resources, we are actually exacting a tribute or an implicit grant from future generations to ourselves, because we are reducing the anticipated felicities of future generations. This is not measurable in any cardinal terms, but we could speak in terms of orders of magnitude, or of the magnitude of anticipated effects. To deplete this now is to help our grandchildren at the cost of lower present consumption. The opportunity-cost tool thus helps us to decide.

Waddington: This opportunity-cost argument doesn't necessarily apply only to the future. It applies also today. You are loading onto the shoulders of the people doing futures studies one of the insoluble problems of today. It is today that you ask a man living in Berkeley, would he go to Los Angeles for so many thousand dollars more? The problem of comparing incomparables is a present-day problem. Of course, it is also a problem that arises in the future, but it is not the responsibility of the future to raise it: it is a problem of today.

I am much more modest than Lord Ashby about what I would give up for my great-grandchildren. I am worried enough about what I would give up for my own present-day children. I don't think I can see the future for the whole of their lives, let alone their children's lives, or their children's children's lives. You are a terrific optimist if you think you could get much idea of what your great-grandchildren will want.

Ashby: I am not optimistic at all. I am dealing with the need to approach the problem as objectively as possible. To do that, one has to minimize personal involvement. One can do that for one's grandchildren, not for one's own children.

Waddington: The point I wanted to make is that with futures studies one can hope to say what sort of things are going to be the important variables—the non-comparable variables, I am sure. But one of the things to explore is, what sort of questions will you be asked? That is by no means obvious. I don't think we can get more than indications of it.

Valaskakis: An excellent common denominator which is much better than money is time. Time is a scarce commodity. If we think in terms of an evening out where we have a choice between the theatre and a concert, money need not enter into the picture. The two tickets cost the same. It is at the felicity level that we compare either allocation of time.

Shane: Studies of interventions in the future are present realities—at least in the sense that a great deal of money is being spent on plans for new commercial products. Could you list some practical reasons that you feel are valid ones for deciding quickly whether futures studies should be deemed to be a discipline, Professor Dror?

Dror: If I were given a few million pounds to do something to improve human capacity for influencing the future, I would establish integrated policy research institutes with comprehensive interdisciplinary teams. These would work for a number of years, say between five and ten, on the main problems, with predictions constituting an integral part of the analysis as a whole. If I had to decide on a new programme at a university I would establish demanding and advanced programmes for graduate and postgraduate students, preparing them for dealing professionally with complex decisions.

Woodroofe: Ought one in the first instance to concentrate studies of the future on the short term rather than on the long term, and then proceed at some later date to the long term? If we concentrate on the short term, we can validate some of the methodology and so have a firm base. We talked about looking back and saying that most of the predictions were wrong, and we also say that the purpose of looking at the future is to make our decisions better. If, then, our predictions in the past have been bad, we must have been taking bad decisions. If we now concentrate on the long-term future which we are not able to validate, we may continue to excite interest in this particular area, making predictions which are wrong and taking wrong decisions. Why not work on the short-term scale, say five years, and validate; then work on a ten-year scale and so on; and proceed in that way?

Shane: The US Office of Education had an interesting experience in that line when they commissioned two educational policy centres. Within eighteen months they had moved from a focus on developments thirty years hence to a focus on immediate future developments.

Dror: That certainly should be done, but the prediction problems are even more serious for three to six years ahead, because one cannot assume linear continuity. Also, for many decisions the lead time needed to have any impact on reality is rather long. It takes two to four years, and sometimes much more, just to start changing something complex like a transit system or an educational system.

Woodroofe: Some years ago I asked my staff what they could do about telling me about the next five years. They said the next five years were difficult but they could be much more confident about the next twenty-five years!

Francis: The renewal of the capital stock, for example, on which our society depends, can't be achieved on that kind of time scale, given the constraints as we now see them. The reason that we can be so certain is because there is a great deal of inertia already incorporated in the present system. I really don't understand how you can suggest that there is such a wide spectrum of possibilities and that these possibilities still exist in an open-ended way, Professor Dror.

Dror: It depends on the time stream. The longer the time stream, the more hypothetical the possibilities are, and the more uncertainties there are. This is the basic dilemma. A main problem in top-level decision-making is that good predictions replace subjective certainty with objective uncertainty. If the decision maker has to consider what the Soviet Union will do, he may think A, B or C are possible, so he calls in his prediction experts. The prediction experts will probably say—after suitable studies—no to A, B is possible, C is possible and D, E, F, G are other possibilities which the decision maker forgot. Most decision makers will then kick the experts out of the door. Therefore, for applied purposes, as aids to decision-making, futures studies or predictions are of little use unless they are tied in with uncertainty-absorbing decision methods. For this, different and new modes of decision-making are needed; classical decision-making patterns which assumed a lot of certainty are hopeless and even counter-productive under contemporary and future conditions.

Waddington: In operational research in the war, cost was a major factor. Was it worth changing a weapon, say, and retraining and re-equiping a squadron?

Woodroofe: This also applies to information. You can improve your decisions by getting more and more information, but information costs money and there comes a time when it costs more to get the information than an improved decision is worth.

Perry: I can only go along with cost–benefit analysis when we are talking economics. I can't see how we can relate all values by such means. We can do it, perhaps, with those values which money can buy, but it can't buy all the values that are built into a felicity index, either now or in the future. I come to a complete impasse there.

Waddington: The trouble is, we relate values all the time. We decide we want to go to the opera or have dinner.

Perry: But if it is to be an academic discipline, we can't compare like with unlike. A decision to go to the opera is a political decision, not an academic or a scientific decision.

Ziman: If there is to be a rationale of decision-making in terms of futures, it must displace some other way of taking decisions or acting. Human beings have taken actions and made decisions throughout the whole of history, and we want to be very careful that we do not displace a not very good method by a worse one. Intuition based on experience, which cannot be rationalized in a formal way, should not necessarily be replaced by something that is mechanized.

Waddington: Aren't all students in universities now told that it can be?

Ziman: I am saying that this is a folly. For example, a good general knows that up to a certain point he can trust his staff plans; but to carry that trust too far is dangerous. Such misplaced confidence produces bad generals.

Dror: I agree. It is a question of adding to intuition so that better decisions have a higher probability of being made. Decisions by many generals and other decision makers in the past show a history of stupidity, ignorance and mistakes. Most methods for improving decision-making are not very good. But the strong justification for using them is that most real-life decision-making is even worse.

Woodroofe: One ultimately makes decisions on the basis of judgement, after getting as much information as possible, including predictions about things likely to happen in the future. At the end of that, there is still a large element of uncertainty.

Ziman: Is it justified to hope that the stupid generals will make better decisions if they have better staff plans?

Dror: No. The decisions will only be better if the decision structure of the army is changed. It is not enough to give the same person, if he is no good, more information.

Ziman: They might be better generals if they read a great deal of the history of war.

Waddington: You make better generals by giving them feedback, as the results of operational research.

Dror: If they are not very good, even though they are aided by suitable structures, they don't learn correctly. Learning is a very complex process which cannot be relied on as spontaneously successful.

Eldredge: An interesting aspect of technological forecasting is where one knows more or less surely that something is going to appear, but not quite how it is going to appear. We knew that the speed of transportation was going to increase before we knew about jet engines or rockets. In 1946 Ogburn[29] thought it would be possible soon for aircraft to fly under imperfect conditions and at night. He spoke of using fog dispellers, flares and fog-piercing lights, but he didn't then know about radar, although he believed that it was pretty certain to happen. That is technical technology forecasting. I think there is now going to be trans-economic cost–benefit analysis (societal technology). Nobody yet knows how to do this, but it is so important that someone is going to find a way. Trans-economic cost–benefit analysis will not be very reliable initially but it will be better than some of today's intuitive guesses. In planning, one has to value any loss of amenities against economic costs. The aircraft industry in the 1930s had to get those unlikely miserable crates up and down on runways. We have to find some method for decision-making which helps us to weigh apples against opera. I really feel that someone is going to break through within the next few decades in a cost–benefit analysis which will be trans-economic. This is an act of faith. This is an umbrella curve—technological forecasting in societal technology.

Waddington: Work is going on on that sort of question in evolutionary biology. How do species cope with having two or three different environments making different demands on them for natural selection? There is quite a lot of theoretical or mathematical work on how they do it. It depends on the scale of the mix—is it a big-scale mosaic or a small-scale mosaic of different environments? It is the beginning of an intellectual mathematical analysis of adaptation to disparate demands. Something will eventually come out, which will provide more understanding of what can be done about it. I don't think we will get a prescription to tell us how to solve the problem. I think what we will get will be more understanding of the logic of the situation.

References cited

[1] DAVID, F. N. (1962) *Games, Gods and Gambling*, Hafner, New York

[2] LEWINSOHN, R. (1961) *Science, Prophecy and Prediction*, Harper, New York

[3] DROR, Y. (1971) *Ventures in Policy Sciences*, American Elsevier, New York

[4] POPPER, K. R. (1972) *Objective Knowledge*, Clarendon Press, Oxford

[5] MARTINO, J. P. (1972) *Technological Forecasting for Decisionmaking*, American Elsevier, New York

[6] KUHN, T. S. (1962) *The Structure of Scientific Revolutions*, University of Chicago Press, Chicago

[7] DROR, Y. (1971) *Design for Policy Sciences*, American Elsevier, New York

[8] POLANYI, M. (1962) The Republic of Science. *Minerva*, *1*, 54 ff.

[9] DROR, Y. (1968) *Public Policymaking Reexamined*, Intertext, New York

[10] GREEN, P. (1966) *Deadly Logic*, Ohio State University Press, Ohio

[11] KAPLAN, M. A. (1973) *Strategic Thinking and Its Moral Implications*, University of Chicago Press, Chicago
[12] ETZIONI, A. (1968) *The Active Society*, Free Press, New York
[13] LASSWELL, H. D. (1971) *A Pre-View of Policy Sciences*, American Elsevier, New York
[14] MACK, R. (1971) *Planning on Uncertainty*, Wiley, New York
[15] BEER, S. (1975) *Platform for Change*, Wiley, Chichester
[16] SCHON, A. D. (1971) *Beyond the Stable State*, Temple Smith, London
[17] DUNN, E. S., Jr. (1971) *Economic and Social Development: A Process of Social Learning*, Johns Hopkins University Press, Baltimore, Md., and London
[18] POLANYI, M. (1958) *Personal Knowledge*, Routledge & Kegan Paul, London
[19] NAGEL, E. *et al.* (eds.) (1962) *Logic, Methodology and Philosophy of Science*, Stanford University Press, Stanford, California
[20] KAHN, H. & WIENER, A. J. (1967) *The Year 2000*, Macmillan, New York
[21] DROR, Y. (1973) A third look at futures study. *Technological Forecasting and Social Change*, 5, 109–112
[22] DROR, Y. (1974) Future studies—quo vadis? in *Human Futures*, pp. 169–176, IPC Press, Guildford
[23] DROR, Y. (1973) Scientific aid to value judgment, in *Modern Science and Moral Values*, pp. 257–264, International Cultural Foundation, New York
[24] *Futures: the journal of forecasting and planning*, IPC Science and Technology Press, Guildford, Surrey
[25] *Technological Forecasting and Social Change*, American Elsevier, New York
[26] *The Futurist*, World Future Society, Washington, D.C.
[27] COX, H. (1968) *On Not Leaving it to the Snake*, Macmillan, New York
[28] BOULDING, K. E. (1973) *The Economy of Love and Fear*, Wadsworth, Belmont, California
[29] OGBURN, W. F. (1946) *The Social Effects of Aviation*, Houghton Mifflin, Boston

Universities as nerve centres of society

JOHN PLATT

Mental Health Research Institute, University of Michigan, Ann Arbor

Abstract The smartest brain is made of ignorant cells. They achieve intelligence and complex differentiated responses by multiple inputs, parallel processing, extensive cross-connection with common biochemical excitation, hierarchical stages of abstraction and differentiated parallel output, and feedback restimulation for goal-seeking. The parallels with effective action for a national or global society deserve exploration.

Television is the adrenaline of the body politic, producing instant outrage, instant imitation and instant demands. In a high-education society with free news media and participatory checks and balances, this can lead to immediate expert debate and the creation of interest groups and pressure groups in any area of information, forecast and concern. 'Social lag' turns to social pressure for change, with revaluing and restructuring—often with technological lag instead. This constitutes a new form of revolution—informational and structural rather than military.

The universities, as the primary repositories and transmitters of knowledge, become abstracting centres and catalytic combination and forecasting centres, offering information as desired to the community, farmers, industry, business, government, policy makers and change agents, the young, the curious, and the leisured, often through their mutual interests in participatory action. The universities will expand problem-oriented research and their interconnected network-outputs of research reports, news organs, radio, television, and community education.

THE ELECTRONIC SURROUND: HOW IT CHANGES SOCIAL INFORMATION AND ACTION PATTERNS

In the course of evolution, every change in the mode or speed of communication has led to a step-function jump in the organization and competence of organisms in relation to themselves and to their environment. We see successive steps of this kind in the development of the chordate nervous system; in encephalization, with the grouping of sensory and decision functions into a brain; in collective signalling; in symbolic language and speech; in the invention of

167

writing; in mass printing of books and newspapers; in the compression of knowledge by mathematical symbolism and scientific laws; in photography; and today, in the invention that has given us for the first time simultaneous global aggregate consciousness—television.

This is what Marshall McLuhan in recent discussions has called the Electronic Surround. Probably neither he nor anyone else of this generation has realized or can realize how this new medium will change our view of reality, our habits of mind, our intellectual and social development, and our mode and success of interaction into more integrated or more differentiated human organization. But in the United States and other nations with almost universal television, we can see some of the changes already and we can see the probable lines along which further changes will carry us.

The first of these changes is that television eliminates distance and direction. The same news commentator is two metres away, in the direction of the box, whether we are on the top floor in Seattle or rocking in a boat in a Miami marina. This will also be true of videocassettes, just as it is true now for electronically amplified rock-music concerts or for self-chosen stereo records or quadraphonic tapes in the home. 'I am *inside* the music', Janis Joplin said.

This is just the beginning of the ways in which television eliminates reality, or rather, changes what we have called reality to another and more public reality, simultaneous for everybody. We all watch the late-night murder movie together, and it becomes more real than the murder in the street outside our window, because we can validate it the next day in conversation with a dozen people. We all share the nation's or the world's grief and joy, not only with shared in-jokes that every stewardess knows, but with going to the Kennedy funeral together, walking on the moon together, and seeing the Olympic games in Munich together, and the terrorist murders there. It has been estimated that 1500 million people, or 38 per cent of the world's population, saw those Olympic games and their aftermath by simultaneous or delayed satellite broadcasts.

Television expands to fill the available leisure time. This is a corollary of Parkinson's law of the expansion of work. Surveys show that the average set in the United States is on for more than six hours a day. Even allowing for different viewers at different times in the same family, this may represent well over half of the available free-choice time for the average person. With good programming, this could even be good—a collective and enlarging experience for all, as dancing once was, and epic myths and poetry, when we watched and listened around the fire in the cave.

Television will spread quickly to the poorest corners of the world, because it is the cheapest way of spending time that the human race has ever invented.

The total cost, including sets, power and programming, is about two cents per person per day, even at American prices; that is, hundreds of times cheaper than a car and a thousand times cheaper than a schoolteacher. Indeed it is the poorest countries that may find television the cheapest investment for rapid economic growth, because it can bring literacy, rural and urban skills, family planning knowledge and images, weather reports, and government exhortations and plans, and hope. For these reasons, it seems likely that 80 per cent or more of the world's population may be linked together, at least by village television, by about 1980. The effect on global consciousness and global unity of these steady daily messages shared by everybody cannot help but be immense.

For McLuhan is right again, in saying that the medium is the message. Just as automobiles transform road systems and cities and food distribution and family structure, regardless of the economic system and the design of the cars, so television will transform consciousness and human interaction in many of these ways, regardless of the programming. Yes, it is better not to have continual violence or raw government propaganda or censorship; but even with these, the medium—the flashing box itself—is saying: There *is* high technology; There is human communication and organization and planning; These ideas, like these weather fronts, may cross all boundaries; There is one world and one set of human problems; and Those people live like *that*, so why don't you? It is no wonder that closed societies fear television.

For television is the real revolutionary of our times. It produces instant outrage, instant imitation, and instant demands. The conventional intellectual view, that belittles television as an idiot box, offering mainly football or late-night movies to passive beer-drinkers who are taken in by the advertising, is only partly true. For many viewers who are concerned people, it is not a pacifying or coercing medium, but an activating medium. My own scanning of television programmes in the San Francisco Bay area in 1973 indicated that a large fraction of programmes implied responsive action by the viewers, such as setting-up exercises, yoga, TV auctions, French cooking, Japanese brush-painting, language learning, and Sesame Street with the children dancing and singing around the box. In addition, political activism in the news or problem-analysis can lead to 100 000 letters to Congress the next morning, or to thousands of people going down to help picket City Hall. The only way to talk back to the box—so that it becomes two-way *communication*—is to exert political pressure or to get out in the streets so that you get on television yourself.

The somewhat surprising result has been not uniformitarianism but the sudden development of powerful differentiated movements, with group images and group communication leading to group unity for protests or demands.

These include the civil rights movement, the student movement, ecology, consumerism, birth control, black power, the ethnic movements, the anti-war movement, women's liberation, and the limits to growth, as well as the political pressures connected with Watergate, all in the last decade or so. Each of these movements, of course, had its own special causes and dynamics and timing, but I believe that it was television in a high-education society that gave each of them a national simultaneity, spread, speed of development, and impact, that went considerably beyond the effects of the older media of the press and the radio.

And I think television gave these movements their 'participatory democracy', with none of them being directed by a single central committee, but with leaders and issues springing up in a hundred cities at once. Television becomes the adrenaline of the body politic, so to speak, exciting the concerned groups to put immense pressure on policy makers and administrators for a change of attitudes and the correction of old inequities. The old hierarchical methods of government and business direction and planning by managers and manipulators, 'the best and the brightest' of the Kennedy and Johnson and Nixon administrations, with their technological élitism—pro-male, pro-natalist, progrowth, pro-hierarchy, pro-Vietnam War, pro-supersonic transport, pro-auto —have gone down again and again before the power of these new movements of consciousness. It is a new politics of shared consciousness that is loose in the world.

This ferment has made television the primary educator for adults. Today, in the United States, there are probably several millions of people who could give good lectures on ecology or Watergate and the US political process or on world population or world food or energy problems or on the limits to growth or women's rights, yet who never learned about these subjects in college. By a good lecture, I mean one that includes material and arguments that professors themselves did not know five years ago. These are all subjects which are not usually taught, even now, to university undergraduates, but which are vital for democratic voting and policy making and for the world's future. How did we all learn them?—By television debates that called in the concerned and the expert for public confrontation. It has taught not only adults but young students, who frequently know more than their teachers now, and who transform the classrooms as a result.

Such an analysis of the role of television in powering these new movements of consciousness must not neglect the supportive and analytical role played by other recent inventions, such as photocopying and cheap lithoprinting and university FM radio and even the jet plane. Television may generate the simultaneous emotion and concern, but it is print and the lecture circuit that give the structural details and subtleties of analysis and action. Tens of millions of Americans have been so disgusted by the admitted lies and 'inoperative' statements of government and the establishment media that they will believe any opposing statements of counter-cultural media and critics, even sometimes when they are no more accurate. This creates a receptive seed-bed for thousands of alternative communications, counter-cultural newspapers, house organs, movement magazines, pamphlets from small mailing groups, books, and lectures on FM radio, with movement leaders and speakers flying continually between centres. In many Californian cities today, a downtown street corner may have fifteen or more newspaper vending machines representing competing political opinions and social interests.

These alternative media get read and analysed by local groups in all kinds of mass meetings, retreats, or Tuesday evening consciousness-raising sessions. The result is probably a more widespread, diverse and critical assessment of society and of our alternative futures than any society has ever had. This is much of what the French observer, Jean-François Revel, talked about in his 1971 book *Without Marx or Jesus: The New American Revolution Has Begun.*[1]

These new technologies, with this new consciousness and political interaction, have led to a remarkably rapid reversal of the attitudes and laws of many decades or centuries. The reason for the reversals has been described by Jonas Salk in his book, *The Survival of the Wisest.*[2] He points out that when exponential growth approaches limits and begins to level off—passing the 'watershed', where we take our foot off the gas and put it on the brakes, so to speak—then our ethics and attitudes must also turn around in many areas. In population, for example, the injunction of the Bible to 'go forth, be fruitful, and multiply' must change to 'Zero Population Growth' if we are not to destroy ourselves. The increase of energy consumption and the use of non-renewable resources was good in the growth phase, because it got rid of slavery and gave leisure and new potentialities. But it becomes bad when it leads to the overheating of all our cities or the dispersal of resources our children will need to make a decent life.

What is remarkable is the speed and number of these reversals today. I believe that more than forty major changes of this kind can be demonstrated in the United States and in significant new world structures since, say, 1968. They include

— several détente agreements ending the Cold War;
— the first international money not based on gold or a national currency;
— new national and international laws and organizations for pollution control and ecological protection, with the banning of such disruptive

developments as the SST and new jetports for the first time in western technological history;

— the changes in sex laws, in the US, Italy and France, on homosexuality, pornography, abortion and contraception, with more permissiveness for sexual acts between consenting adults than in western Christian history;

— the reduction of birth rates to 'replacement level' or below, in the US and eleven other countries, through the free choice of tens of millions of families;

— and the reversal of numerous other laws, decriminalizing drunkenness, auto accidents, and divorce, and increasing the rights of prisoners and the mentally ill.

There is also

— the greatest reform in the universities, in the treatment of students as adults, since the early 1900s;

— the greatest reform in western religions since the Protestant Reformation, according to several observers;

— the greatest reform in the rights and opportunities of minority groups and women in several generations;

— the greatest reform in American politics, in election laws and accountability, in this century;

— and a turnaround in attitudes towards (*a*) science, (*b*) energy, (*c*) space exploration, (*d*) the global future in the next century, (*e*) the limits to growth, and (*f*) systems analysis studies of global problems and alternative futures.

These are the fastest and most extensive peacetime reversals of attitudes in the whole intellectual history of humanity. It all makes this the most responsive society ever known. It is a new kind of revolution, an information and consciousness revolution that works by changing ideas rather than by killing off the old leaders.

It is worth looking at the dynamic sequence of some of these reversals to see how they happen and how fast. A classic example is the ecology movement. In its current form, it started essentially with the 1962 book by Rachel Carson, *Silent Spring*,[3] which put together, in a readable and gripping way, many of the trends and threats to air, water, land, the network of plant and animal life, and human survival. This can be called catalytic analysis, because of its self-multiplying power as others take up the same concern. But many such analyses, even true ones, are neglected by the public because they are not related to real and obvious events. Carson's book, however, was followed by a series of catalytic crises that came to public attention, such as DDT in the rivers, the California oil spills, and the increasing Los Angeles smog. The term refers to crises that are not quite catastrophic, but are dramatic and important enough to mobilize human concern and the money, time, and energy to do something about it. When such crises erupt, people organize picket lines and study groups and call for lecturers and pass around the book, saying, This shows why it happened and what we have to do about it. The fastest way to radicalize a Republican rose gardener is to put an oil spill on the doorstep.

So concerned constituencies build up rapidly, like the Sierra Club and the rest of the ecology movement, and they elect legislators and throw out 'The Dirty Dozen'. The *New York Times* identified ecology as the main ideological issue affecting the elections in 1970, 1972 and 1974. By 1974, of course, the new laws had been passed, the new agencies such as the Environmental Protection Agency had been set up, and they were in the Federal Bureau phase, with all the ongoing checks and balances of the Federal power structure. The transition from catalytic analysis, isolated and derided, to an established government structure to deal with the problems in an ongoing way took about ten years. We can see an exactly similar but even faster chain of events in several other areas. These include the sequence of action starting with Ralph Nader's *Unsafe at Any Speed*[4] in 1965 and going on to the major auto safety and pollution-control laws of 1972; and a large-scale consumer movement by that time with hundreds of activist lawyers. Another sequence is that beginning with Paul Ehrlich's *The Population Bomb*[5] in 1968, and his Zero Population Growth [ZPG] campaign, which may have accelerated the downturn in birth rates, so that they dropped below replacement levels in 1971, 1972 and 1973. (Note that this very rapid change did not require centralized or radical government birth control measures, but only many independent democratic consciousness-raisings and decisions in tens of millions of families.) The fastest case of all is the sequence starting from the MIT–Club of Rome book, *The Limits to Growth*,[6] by Donella Meadows and coworkers in 1972, and going on to a city-wide, nation-wide and world-wide recognition of such limits, especially in oil and energy and other resources, by 1974.

We see that for this responsive society, when analysis is coupled to dramatic evidence of the need for change—evidence most compellingly presented through television—the turnaround times for old ideas and laws are now in the range of two to ten years. This reverses not only our old ideas of revolution, but our conventional ideas of 'social lag'. In the 1920s, the sociologists of social lag supposed that society took twenty-five years to adapt to the electric light or the automobile because the old people with the old ideas had to die off. But for this present high-education television society, the ideas turn around suddenly and simultaneously in young and old alike ('co-figurative learning', as Margaret Mead calls it); and it is technology that now lags, with pleas that it will take twenty years or more for improved contraceptives, or mass transportation, or fusion or breeder power, or coal gasification, or solar energy. But this is what is to be expected in a cybernetic society which is consciously choosing its own values and steering its own future and shaping its own research and development, instead of being helplessly overrun by the technological juggernaut of greedy companies or unheeding inventors.

It is interesting to show the close parallel between these sequences of rapid change and the revolutionary sequence of proletarian revolution as outlined by Karl Marx. The catalytic analysis is done by the Intellectual Vanguard, who have knowledge, concern, and leisure to study, but who are traitors to their class. Their writings are then used to awaken the proletariat when oppression, or catalytic crises or confrontations occur. The workers are further educated by reactionary responses from the system when they attack it. Even when they have to go underground, the movement grows. But the old structure is rotten at the core and is unable to solve its problems or to keep the allegiance of its own people or to go on opposing the workers' movement; so that finally the workers take over easily, although they must go on fighting the bourgeois remnant who are sabotaging the new structure for selfish purposes.

Ecologists will find some glee in these parallels. The difference is that the socialist revolutions, with underground pamphlets, took a lifetime; while these television revolutions of consciousness and laws have achieved major structural rearrangements in a decade or less.

It seems probable that many of these rearrangements of attitudes and laws in the United States are now approaching a limit. There is still an extensive process of consolidation to be carried out in all these areas, but further changes on the same scale may be rarer in the future, unless some more encompassing war occurs, or some larger revolution in philosophy and belief systems, comparable in scope, say, to the Maoist revolutions in China.

Except for such dramatic deep changes, the next step today may simply be the extension of many of these new characteristics of social innovation and action to other societies as rapidly as they get universal television. This may rapidly change many patterns of elections and the structure of democracies and dictatorships. The potentiality for such sudden changes in response to perceived problems and inequities will continue indefinitely into the future as long as we have instantaneous global video electronics of any kind.

In the last two years, many of the high-speed and participatory-pressure aspects of these television-induced movements could be seen in such countries as Italy and Japan, in their debates over political accountability and ecology and pollution; and in Italy and France in the reversals of divorce and abortion and contraceptive laws. In dozens of countries, the sudden awareness of limits to growth is a typical consciousness-raising process that was made possible by the standard sequence of events: the confirmation of the catalytic-analysis book on *Limits*[6] by the catalytic crisis of the rise in oil prices, which seemed to prove the thesis.

Nevertheless, the change in global laws and policy-making among the 150 countries of the world will not be as easy or fast as the change within individual countries. National differences and slanting of television presentations will support self-righteous national differences on policy, and all the dilemmas of non-zero-sum game theory and the Tragedy of the Commons will hinder agreement or solution. It is in this context that the role of the multinational corporations must be seen as useful and even benevolent, since they will exert a steady pressure for common television programmes and parallel interest groups in many countries, easing a parallel approach to global problems. Even when such approaches are not concordant with the larger world interest or human interest, the competition between multinationals will make such discrepancies visible and will spur the growth of television debates and of multinational labour movements, consumer movements, ecology movements, and multinational-control movements. The success of the new movements in the United States, in changing policies and laws, will be a powerful example for similar interest groups in other countries, especially since these laws now apply to the head-quarters operations of the largest of the multinationals. Because of these various considerations, the rate of change in reversing old and dangerous nation-state policies and in getting more effective solutions of global problems is hard to predict, but it may be much faster than is generally supposed, and it could lead to massive transformation of world management structures in the decade of the 1980s.

Note that many of the futurist electronic innovations frequently proposed, such as shopping by cable television, or instantaneous electronic voting, are either irrelevant or dangerous for the participatory debates and consciousness movements described here. They may need careful watching and anticipatory control.

THE ROLE OF UNIVERSITIES IN A GLOBAL ELECTRONIC SOCIETY

To understand the role of the colleges and universities in the kind of national and global television-informed society which we see developing, it may be helpful to think of the systems-theory analogy between society and the human brain. The smartest brain is made of ignorant cells. How do those cells achieve collective intelligence? The answers are not all in, but it is clear experimentally

and theoretically that they involve several major features, such as
— multiple sensory inputs with parallel processing and intercomparison;
— extensive cross-connection with common neural and biochemical excitation of many centres at once, depending on the body's overall state
   of deprivation or excitation;
— hierarchical stages of abstraction, with higher centres controlling the
   goals and feedback-settings of lower-order sub-goals;
— differentiated parallel output, with coordinated sequences and cycles
   of action in thousands of glandular and motor outputs; and
— feedback restimulation or reafferent stimulation for fine-tuning and
   success in overall goal-seeking.

It is always dangerous to apply such systems-parallels too literally between
a biological body and the body social or the body politic, or between the brain
and our collective intellectual and social enterprise of information, values,
decision and action, but the parallels nevertheless raise questions that are
suggestive and that deserve exploration.

In the total intellectual enterprise of human society, it is clear that the universities are the primary repositories of available knowledge, the centres of analysis
of that knowledge, and the generators of basic or abstract new knowledge. This
is particularly true in the twentieth century, since the time when science and
basic research and development were brought into the universities, although
government bureaus and laboratories and industrial and agricultural research
groups also play a major role in the generation of new and practical knowledge.

When all of its historical and recent functions are added up, the university
comes to be a sort of five-legged animal. The left hind leg could be thought of
as traditional scholarship, the knowledge and library storage of everything that
humanity has known or said or thought. The left front leg is then traditional
teaching, the communication of this organized and filtered knowledge to the
next generation. The right hind leg would be the creation of new thought or
knowledge, basic studies in the natural and biological and social sciences on
how the world works, its laws and predictions. The right front leg is then the
transmission of this knowledge for human use, with writing or consulting or
broadcasting to farm and industry and business and government and the community.

(Note however that the humanistic creation of fiction, poetry, plays, art or
music, is not usually located at universities except in token form, being more
individualist and more closely tied to outlets in publishing or the entertainment
industry. If four great creators, Michelangelo, Shakespeare, Newton and Mo-
zart, were living today, only Newton would be likely to work regularly at a

university. Of the humanists, only the philosophers, the critics and the teachers have been university-based—typically being derided by the creative humanists, from Chaucer to Goethe and Browning.)

The fifth leg of the university is then the trunk of this wise elephant, so to speak, grasping the future. It is the seminal creation of world-changing inventions or paradigms or critiques, such as cybernetics or atomic energy or feedback theory or ecology or the negative income tax or the concept of limits to growth. These are not merely services to industry or government in the existing structure, but fundamental intellectual and operational reorganizations that change the whole structure. They have been major sources of funding and influence for the universities in the last forty years. Nevertheless they tend to be 'in the university but not of it', using its resources of expertise, libraries and laboratories and leisure, but located outside regular departments, in more project-oriented centres such as the Manhattan Project, or the MIT Research Laboratory of Electronics, or the Sloan Institute of Management.

These five functions are fully displayed only at a few of the great universities, such as Harvard and MIT, but the functions support each other, and schools which are lacking two or more of them frequently find themselves in financial or operational difficulties. Thus the schools that only teach, without research opportunities, cannot attract strong science faculties; while the schools that specialize in research to the neglect of teaching often have disaffected students as well as weak public or alumni support. And schools that make no contribution to the fifth leg, to catalytic analysis and invention that can change large-scale social problems, now find themselves less and less relevant to government and the community, and less and less interacting with the rest of the active university network and the intellectual community.

One further point needs to be noted, namely the scale of college and university operations in a high-information society such as the United States. At present there are some nine million college students, nearly 50 per cent of all the 18- to 21-year-olds in the US. Together with their three-quarters of a million teachers, and supporting staffs of some two million and their families, they make up a much larger group than the family farm population. It is no accident that for the last couple of decades, American politicians have made their major policy addresses at universities, with their audiences of professional experts and with this great body of young adult students, relatively uncommitted politically and with time and energy for grass-roots political effort. Over 70 per cent of male high-school graduates now go to college, and the figure is over 80 per cent in the high-income states, and over 95 per cent in the Jewish community. These numbers are near saturation, at least for males, and will probably come down as higher education is postponed or fitted into longer-range life objectives, but they make an order-of-magnitude change from the 5 per cent college population of the 1930s, and a correspondingly enormous change in every aspect of American leadership, democracy, business and government, decision, management and policy, as well as culture. The revolutionary changes of the last ten years, already noted, were surely due to the impact of television—yes, but especially to its impact on this tremendous new group of college-educated adults who already had a larger vision and more training for leadership than their local high school provided.

Looking back at the comparison between our social intellectual networks and the brain, therefore, we can see the university as, not a small social organ, but a large and influential one, an organ having a role somewhat like those higher nerve centres in abstracting and combining and analysing and reassessing all the other information of the society—in short, in *thinking*. The schools are now centres for the development of novel concepts and the examination of goals and values, which can persuade the other segments of society by illuminating what they are doing and what the consequences are. They are lookout centres for warnings and for the development of alternative policy options. Traditionalists may object that these functions are not the primary business of the teaching university, or that they are too programme-oriented and not basic enough, and that they should be left to other groups, such as business or industry or government. But knowledge is for use, as Bacon said, and as the pragmatic Americans have always recognized, and should we let it 'fust in us unused'? What other group than that of the universities has the breadth of vision, or the libraries, the laboratories and the leisure for analysis, to look at the concerns and needs and goals of the *whole* of society rather than some narrower sector of profit or bureaucratic concern? Society will and must use the universities for this integrative and future-directed purpose, even if it goes beyond traditional roles—just because no other agencies have yet been created to do it. And even if such separate and specialized agencies were created, they would generally have to be placed close to great universities for all the reasons just given.

The result is that alongside their traditional disciplinary education, the universities will probably expand their social research-and-development centres. This will inevitably feed back into more problem-oriented education which for students may become much more involving, more integrative, and more like a practical apprenticeship for adult participatory leadership and management.

In addition to these changes in university structure and functions and methods, there will surely be radical changes in their range of community services for the high-education television-consciousness society we have been describing. For one thing, the age range being served by the schools will change, and there are already strong pressures to provide education from age 2 to 82, coextensive with life. Schools of education will probaby expand into still more extensive university experimental programmes and nursery schools for small children. At a higher level, they already run their own experimental grade schools and high schools, and they may begin to compete commercially for running such schools in other communities on commission or contract, with performance-testing of their educational success.

For adults over 18, there are developing already increasing numbers of community colleges specializing in part-time or night-school education. An increasing number of older adults may come back for summer courses or one-year sabbaticals, for 'retreading' and getting up to date again in teaching and business and engineering and biology, where information and methods are changing very rapidly. With increased leisure or unemployment, other numbers of adults may come for courses or lecture series on global problems or personal development or general culture. In some communities in the United States, 5 to 20 per cent of the adults over 25 years already are enrolled in such night-school programmes or lecture series—more than half of the college enrolment.

The universities may also continue and expand their recent roles in generating and disseminating new information and analyses for farmers, industry, business and government, whether this is done by published research reports or by part-time private consulting by the faculty and staff. The élitist role of this kind of advice and expertise, or its possible controversial advocacy, may have to be examined more carefully than in the past, if there is not to be widespread political backlash against these activities.

A solution to this problem of the narrowness or special interests of the experts may be the development of 'adversary science' by university scientists and consultants, as a kind of parallel to adversary law. The idea would be that major public issues, such as environmental or energy decisions, frequently have public pros and cons, related to the values of different groups in the society. Scientific experts on a problem, either for policy decisions or judicial decisions, might then come to be hired by the opposing sides, as lawyers are, with each group attempting to make the best possible case for their clients, although they might be arguing on the opposite side in the next case. This kind of semi-public or public confrontation might be expected to lead to better-informed decisions, which could find ways around the objections and dangers more successfully than our present partisan and often secretive decision methods.

The development of improved ways of this kind for bringing all of our knowledge to bear on our problems could also lead to the rapid development of new clienteles for the universities. These could include more public policy makers, plus international civil servants and designers of new international structures, as well as change agents and leaders in the new movements and pressure groups. All these groups that work with large-scale social problems are struggling with the lack of complete and coherent and relevant information, and they always seem to benefit from work at short-time university conferences or permanent conference centres.

It is worth emphasizing that these knowledge-services to society and its sub-groups are not simply retrieval problems from a computerized data bank in the sense of information sciences. Our great public decisions today have to be made on the basis of incomplete and uncertain data, by fallible and emotional decision makers often limited by old habit, but guided by feedback consequences —like the brain itself. This gives a human and humane and ongoing cybernetic character to our social decisions, with continual re-evaluation and often a change of fundamental values as new consequences become more apparent, and it makes the role of the universities and their knowledge in such decisions more involving than that of input–output data-processing or search and retrieval, even of the most sophisticated kind.

In addition to all these direct services to students and clients, the universities have a more general role in raising the consciousness and culture of their whole communities. There is a level where their research reports or new discoveries are of general interest, and new channels may be found to reach an interested audience, from journalists and businessmen to factory workers, farmers and housewives. They operate newspapers and radio and television stations, and this, combined with their more traditional lecture courses and public lecture series, can make a continuous dialogue for the enrichment of a very large public, like the Chatauqua lecture-series and networks that educated adult audiences throughout the United States a hundred years ago. There are more than 2300 colleges and universities in the United States, and about 1000 of these are the principal industry of their city or town, so that almost all of the US population could be within radio or television range of university cultural programmes. Rightly used, this could be as valuable an audience for public support of enlarged university programmes as the commercial audience is for the support of broadcasters and advertisers. This is not to say that all these schools will be or should be in agreement on their knowledge or their advocacy, but that most such programmes are likely to be a contribution to raising the level of dispassionate discussion and understanding of any problem.

In all this, it should not be forgotten that the universities are all part of a closely linked network of knowledge. It is 'the great university in the sky', as some of the jet-set professors call it. They are linked not only by real computer networks and telephone networks, but also by widely distributed cassette and videotape exchanges of lectures, and art-film exchanges, as well as by the lecture and music series of the academic and cultural lecture bureaus, the inheritors of the real Chatauqua network of a hundred years ago. What is even more important with respect to the growth and utilization of knowledge is their linkage through the hundreds of 'invisible colleges' of the various academic disciplines. It is these in-groups of close friends and competitors who telephone daily across the country, who share the prepublication reports fresh off the typewriter in a hundred photocopies, and who are continually visiting each others' laboratories and lecturing to and hiring each others' graduate students. In large US universities in the 1960s, one-third of the scientists would be out of town on any given weekday, while an equal number were presumably visiting from elsewhere. In most such cases, the business of this travel was the business of the invisible college, whether lecturing or consulting or on sabbatical leave at some other colleague's laboratory, writing a book.

These networks and invisible colleges of knowledge have always been international. Their contribution to shared knowledge and culture and concerns and decision-making around the globe may be as great in the intellectual sphere as the contribution of the multinational corporations is in commerce. And when the leaders of a dozen major countries have been educated at the London School of Economics or Harvard or MIT or Stanford, these intellectual networks resonate at the political level. The networks carrying new ideas become, and are, worldwide channels of change.

What finally clinches this change role for the universities is that they are now seeing themselves, and being seen by governments, as the primary place where those catalytic analyses of present and forthcoming problems must be carried out. Some 80 million dollars, one-third of the research budget of the National Science Foundation, now go into project RANN—Research Applied to National Needs—of which the larger part is being done in the universities. Rachel Carson and Paul Ehrlich were academic biologists with a side concern with ecology and population problems. The Limits to Growth[6] was a computer study at MIT. The Academy for Contemporary Problems in Columbus, Ohio, is a joint venture between Battelle and Ohio State University. Once such university studies have pointed the way, other bureaus and institutes and foundations may take up the work and diversify and improve it, like the sixteen-nation International Institute of Applied Systems Analysis (IIASA) in Austria. But these groups with a well-defined mission have usually not been as flexible as university groups in identifying and working on new problems on the horizon. It follows that it is to the universities that society and the world must turn for major lookout and warning functions, except for the occasional cases when self-appointed groups like the Club of Rome take voluntary action. And when the warnings have been raised, it may be only the universities that can do the tedious work of analysis of alternative futures and the consequences of policy decisions or game-playing, in the detached and careful and complete way that is necessary for success. In the near future, academic and research departments may come to spend a good deal of their time making needed studies of this kind.

These intellectual networks of thought and change will interact in a powerful and symbiotic way with the consciousness-raising role of television, with which I began this paper. The universities, like the higher abstract nerve centres of the brain, collect their information and feedback monitoring from thousands of parallel inputs, but their resultant conclusions are then fed simultaneously by television to millions of output actors, to make the analogy very crude. How does this happen? By the expert analysis and debate which is called forth by television within a few hours after any problem or concern becomes visible and important. Who are the movement speakers, who fly from one group to another, worrying and explaining? Frequently they are the university researchers or synthesizers who have been in the forefront of analysis or concern. Even when the concern is initiated from outside the universities, as it has been in the black power and ethnic movements, the women's movement, the Nader auto safety and consumer movement, and the Club of Rome limits-to-growth debate, it now leads quickly to responses within the universities, such as black studies programmes and women's programmes, or poor-law programmes, or academic computer programs; and a hundred academic hands take up the cause, because they are the ones whose knowledge and analysis are needed.

All this is a rather tentative description of the interplay of these complex groups and forces for change in our time. It is uncertain and has to be pieced out by theories and guesses, because this fluid and participatory information-interplay in the new electronic surround has little precedent in the rather fixed institutions and hierarchical management structures of a low-education society. There will be room for debate over how far these trends will continue, especially under the disasters of the next decade, with famine and oil wars, and terrorist Hiroshima bombs, and back-lash dictatorships and censorship and television barriers, and possibly violent anti-scientific and anti-intellectual movements. But, as H. G. Wells said, 'Civilization is a race between education and catastrophe' and if the trends I have identified are real and can continue and expand, and if these disasters can be anticipated or postponed or contained a little bit, then there is a chance that these forces may yet move us into a more participatory and democratic and humanely conscious global future before the next century. Progress is being made, I think, and we must work with those forces to extend it in the next few years as fast as we can.

Discussion

Valaskakis: You said that the technological–social gap had been reversed, with society now asking for things and technology reacting, but some people might distort that to mean something other than what you have in mind. Before the limits-to-growth controversy the traditional and orthodox economist would have said that if the price system were allowed to react to whatever scarcities or whatever shortages occurred, i.e. if prices rose when there were shortages, people would automatically take corrective action by consuming less. However if we are dealing with an overshoot and collapse system we cannot take corrective action in time. When the signal has been identified it is too late to do anything about it. You seem to be suggesting that with television we can quickly identify certain problems like pollution, and that our reaction time is so fast that there is no such thing as social lag. This might lead to some unintended optimism about the possibilities of solving our problems, which I am sure you are not advocating.

Platt: I think a 'man on horseback' with the right kind of charisma, another Hitler, could leap in and use the medium in the same way. But so far the medium has been part of the checks and balances in the US. It was television that brought McCarthy down in 1953, and it was really television of the Watergate investigation that brought Nixon down. On the whole I think its influence has been helpful and healthy in politics rather than the reverse. But somebody who knows how to use it more subtly, or has a better organized pressure group, could perhaps use these fast time-constants for a disastrous outcome. On the other hand it does seem to bring us both sides, in controversies and debates. Once some influential person stands up and says 'A', then there will be a thousand people in the community and in the universities who will jump up and say 'not-A'. Television, at least in the US where it is relatively free of government censorship, will bring this debate to people and will inform them because they can see the confrontation before their eyes.

Klimes: The use of television as a communications medium and as a new tool for societal engineering depends, obviously, on social conditions. The projections you made are based on a certain kind of society that is relatively open and free. In another kind of society the same technology can be used to halt, slow down or otherwise manipulate social change. A much more important question about this new communications medium is, who controls it? How is it manipulated?

Platt: This is a real and important fear. But in fact it is 'closed societies' that fear television; and the reason is that while the first-order effects may be directly manipulatable and damaging, this is fairly visible manipulation. The second-order effect is criticism and at least some private reply, on subjects that are now opened for discussion, so that in some important sense the medium is the message, as McLuhan said, and as I tried to show in my paper.

Dror: You underrate the capacity of governments for controlling television. If Nazi Germany had had television its propaganda would have been even more effective. A free global broadcasting network might operate more as you say, but as long as television can be controlled technically, it will be used in a totalitarian country to indoctrinate people. In a free society television may help to perpetuate freedom. In a totalitarian society it will probably reinforce the totalitarian system. In other words television *per se* may not lead to a specific form of society; it depends on the starting point.

Platt: This is the conventional view but there are things to be said on the other side. Television is dangerous for a totalitarian society. People see how other people live. It raises questions and changes goals. Just to show a sports event, with athletes from other countries or races, just to show the dictator arriving in his Cadillac or Zis, is to spread ferment and revolution.

Dror: In a totalitarian country they show what they want to show, not what you like them to see.

Klimes: This illustrates to me how some projections, even if they aim at presenting a global picture with a generally valid view of the future, are just based on one particular kind of imagination corresponding to the sociocultural environment of its originator. While I agree entirely that as the information system opens things up, it won't actually be possible to keep any information absolutely closed, the point is that regardless of the technology employed, there is a certain dialectical contradiction in the use of information, and consequently in the types of information society. Can we identify that contradiction? Can we see both sides so that we can point out the dangers?

Shane: About two years ago I worked on a television programme, a 90-minute special in the US called 'Give Us The Children'. The young man responsible for directing this presentation had a large sum of money to spend on it, yet he felt that he was responsible to no one for the programme content. When I asked who did determine policies for the network, the 24-year-old director and his 26-year-old associate assured me that the owners of the television station were concerned with advertising, with mollifying customers, and with new accounts. The persons who presented the newscasts had their material prepared for them. In short, a group of 'unknowns' working like gnomes seemed to be making policy as their judgement dictated. Presumably they were not responsible to anyone—but they often do a great deal to shape what goes out on television. Do you see that as a threat to our culture, and is it something we can take steps to remedy?

Platt: I see this as a great danger. I dislike much television programming. I was just making the additional point that beyond the programming itself there is another message, a meta-message, the message of the medium. This produces effects beyond and counter to any direct attempts at manipulation of the programming, at least for some thoughtful and concerned sections of the population.

Shane: Then you will agree that, when a news commentator says 'And that's the way it was today', that the 'news' really was what a group of TV people decided was most interesting or important to show during the brief time available on the screen. In the Selma, Alabama, Freedom Marches, for example, a number of persons who had been rather dispiritedly walking along at the end of the day began behaving in a most lively fashion as the television cameras turned on them. Thus an image is created on the television screen that is or can be distinctly different from what actually existed or took place. I wonder how great a danger it is, and how we can whip it.

Waddington: Professor Platt has brought out the importance of catalytic crises. It is no use writing *Silent Spring*[3] unless something happens to bring it home to the public mind. There happened to be an oil spill in Santa Barbara, just where it would catch the public mind and would have to get on television; it would be a very dictatorial state indeed that could keep it off. But it might have been something quite different—many books could be as catalytic as *Silent Spring*, if a catalytic crisis happened to bring a particular event to the fore. You can't get a great public movement unless a body of public opinion can be mobilized about something, but which movement happens at which time depends on very chancy events.

Oldfield: I accept that the medium is a message, but I think that the television medium is perceived in different ways by different people. With our ethnocentric viewpoint we tend to underemphasize the different ways in which it is perceived by people who can neither generate nor control what they see. The metaphor of the global village is a soothing one for us, but most people must feel more as if they were in a global aquarium. In a public aquarium, a limited number of people control what a much larger range of organisms see. In a village the intervisibility is more mutual. In an aquarium many barriers inhibit the passage from one condition to the other perceived and unperceived conditions.

Waddington: The metaphor of a zoo might be better. In a zoo the animals are in cages while in an aquarium one gets at first the exact opposite impression; an aquarium is normally transparent, with no opaque walls. I think you are suggesting that the world system is closely controlled, and that people are not absolutely free to move in all possible directions.

Francis: Your thesis seems to imply that an accepted principle of universality comes out of these levels of prophecy, Professor Platt. Instead it seems to me, particularly from my own experience when travelling in Asia, that there is a wall of resistance against exactly these viewpoints. Virtually everything you illustrated was based exclusively on North American experience. How long is it going to take for universities in developing countries to achieve their own catalytic analysis and become receptive in the way you have described? Any real change will take much longer than the three to ten years that you have given for the current North American experience, and that situation has benefited from the consolidated experience of the universities.

Platt: Some countries will move up the path of development at one time and others will move up it later. Some countries will already be facing the problems of saturation, the turnaround and so on, while others are still in the growth phase. But the time between them is now coming down into the five- to ten-year range. For example, Italy has reversed its divorce law. Who would have thought this possible two years ago? France reversed the open sale of contraceptives, and the old abortion law. Who would have thought this two years ago? In Japan and Italy the major themes in the last two years on non-political radio and TV programmes have been ecology and pollution. The fall of Tanaka over financial accountability was probably assisted by the parallel to the US-Nixon Watergate case which they had followed on television. The spread happens just as fast as television arrives.

Francis: Those are all industrialized countries.

Platt: Yes, because they are the first in this; but when there is village television in India I think they will also begin to have television-type awareness. I guess I should emphasize, as I did in the paper, that my opinions and insights here are not dogmatic or final, and are presented more hesitantly than perhaps I sound; but I felt it worth while to try to state clearly a different point of view that may offer some useful corrections to the more conventional ideas.

Francis: I think you are dismissing the cultural elements too lightly, particularly in Asia, which I believe is much more resistant to television than North America.

Waddington: Television brings a revolution of expectations, though this may come more from the movies than from television. You see people living in the style of the affluent industrial society, and you think, why the devil shouldn't we live in something like that? Surely that has had an enormous effect in the whole of Asia.

Oldfield: Professor Platt said that in an affluent society pollution is a catalytic crisis that can promote a sensible response. But in a poor society starvation is a catalytic crisis that can promote death. I don't see how what is essentially a sigmoid curve for population growth, which is density-regulated, can be used as a basis for so many (to my mind) ethnocentric generalizations about crisis and response in the whole of the contemporary world.

Ziman: The Italian divorce laws are fifty years behind the times, by any Anglo-Saxon standards. Relating the change in that law to television seems to be a misplaced historical analysis of the situation.

Eldredge: It is much easier to construct a gadget than it is to construct a societal structure. Societal structure today still cannot cope, even remotely, with the gadgets of nuclear fission and fusion which made a spectacular entrance on the world scene in 1945. The original rather primitive atomic bomb has given rise to a whole family of nuclear weapons, with $n+1$ countries having the bomb and reactors proliferating all over the place. Professor Platt has taught me that public opinion can be mobilized concerning some fringe societal technologies, but I don't really believe that television can produce real détente. There are certainly no institutions to ensure détente, though there are public speeches lauding progress and so forth. I don't see any societal institutions in the immediate future that will cope with the technology of taking oil out of the North Sea and balancing that against oil from the Persian Gulf! Hiroshima happened in 1945 and in 1975 we are in a much more dangerous situation—in a noisy spring rather than a silent one. I am a societal technologist, but I don't think that societal technology is remotely capable of coping with those dreadful technical technologies that keep spewing out new gadgets which I simply don't know how to cope with.

Platt: One thing that amuses me about this particular kind of analysis-and-change sequence is the parallel I mentioned in my paper with the old Marxist analysis of revolutionary change—but moved into a high information society. But in this kind of high-education television society it is not a bloody revolution, but an information revolution, a revolution that is consciousness-raising, and it takes place in this short time of ten years instead of in a century. It is not a revolution in the streets but in the minds, including the minds of cabinet members and Boards of Directors. Our methods of revolution today are as changed from those of a hundred years ago as our methods of television are from print.

Eldredge: But so is the counter-revolution, which is also a part of our society.

Waddington: Some technical changes have been easier for society to cope with than others. It is easier to pass anti-pollution laws than to know what to do about nuclear power. Eldredge has a good point when he says that we have been aware of the nuclear power problem for a long time without having decided what society should do about it. Pollution has been with us for a much shorter time but it is much easier to deal with.

Dror: Political science had quite a lot of published work, usually pessimistic, on the idea of the mass society before television came along. Most writers thought that technological devices permitting rapid mobilization of mass support would work more for the bad than for the good. I wouldn't go as far as that but the question must be put. You say that if television represents a balanced point of view, pro and con, the population will adopt a balanced view. Behind that idea is the underlying or tacit model of citizens having a reasonable pattern of behaviour. I don't see any reason why the mobilization of mass opinion should work for the better rather than for the worse. In some cases it may be for the better, but in other types of situations, such as crisis— an energy crisis, a nuclear war crisis—a different kind of culture may result from the same mass mechanism, one turning in what you and I would regard as a negative direction. This may be partly because, as Professor Eldredge indicated, television communication mechanisms change the message and the speed but don't change the institutions. That is, the interfaces between public opinion and political institutions are not basically changed. Different messages flow through the channels but the channels themselves are not changed. I don't see the evidence for your thesis that the very existence of television assures a radical change for the better in the institutions themselves.

Platt: Yes, we have, and have had, a group of manipulators and would-be manipulators, in Washington and in the military and in industry—manager-manipulators, the best and the brightest. They operate on the old hierarchical system, the old pyramid, the idea that there is a small group at the top who know what is best for the people and who can manage and direct any plan. But I tried to say in the paper that in the last ten years, these managers and manipulators have gone down again and again before the power of these new movements of consciousness, these participatory movements. Somebody in San Francisco sees Germaine Greer and says 'We can do that too'. The result is that a hundred centres spring up all over the country, on women's liberation or black power and so on. The managers and manipulators don't know what the score is. It is a new political phenomenon in the United States. The only person from abroad who saw it coming was Revel, with his book *Without Marx or Jesus*.[1] He saw this as a revolution of communications in the United States which would produce a political, cultural and social revolution. He is right on target: these old structures with the managers and manipulators will have to change their pattern towards participation and decentralization and diversity under the pressure of this new form of power.

Dror: But your underlying assumption is that this new consciousness will always be for the better. What historical or psychological evidence do you have for that?

Platt: More information *is* for the better! More sharing of consciousness between people *is* for the better!—At least, on the average!

Dror: It may be for the better if we absorb and understand it correctly.

Eldredge: That is simplistic eighteenth century rationalism, Professor Platt. One must do better than that!

Platt: It is *human* rationalism—an interconnected brain, a set of eyes seeing the alternative futures, is being created instead of the human race crawling along like disconnected amoebas.

Valaskakis: Your underlying value assumption that change itself is a good thing is probably shared by all of us at this meeting, but it is by no means self-evident. You might have a heated argument with an anthropologist on that count. For example, according to some anthropologists, television has had a disruptive effect on Eskimo societies in northern Canada, where it has produced the kind of social change or catalytic transformation that you have been talking about. It has been successful in creating discontent by providing models that cannot be achieved or approximated by the indigenous Eskimo population. It seems to have destroyed the native culture without replacing it with a viable alternative paradigm. I tend to share the idea that change is a good thing in itself, and that if television accelerates the process of change then television is good. But I feel nevertheless that it is a very western culture-bound idea that is by no means universally accepted.

Eldredge: The 'managers' will soon learn how to manipulate the development of consciousness for good or evil. This is an interim period, while they learn how to manipulate the new types of organization.

References cited

1 REVEL, JEAN-FRANÇOIS (1971) *Without Marx or Jesus: The New American Revolution Has Begun*, Doubleday, New York
2 SALK, JONAS (1973) *The Survival of the Wisest*, Harper & Row, New York
3 CARSON, RACHEL (1962) *Silent Spring*, Houghton Mifflin, Boston
4 NADER, RALPH (1965) *Unsafe at Any Speed*, Grossman, New York
5 EHRLICH, PAUL (1968) *The Population Bomb*, Sierra Club, New York
6 MEADOWS, DONELLA H., MEADOWS, DENNIS L., RANDERS, JØRGEN & BEHRENS, WILLIAM W., III (1972) *The Limits to Growth*, Universe, New York; Earth Island, London

Patterns of education for the future

SIR WALTER PERRY

The Open University, Milton Keynes

Abstract There are three facets to the probable role of universities in the future: maintaining scholarship, providing general courses for students and the general community, providing continuing education. Whereas scholarship requires a permanent structure based on discipline groups, general courses are best produced by 'course teams' as pioneered by the Open University. These teams bring together subject-matter experts in related fields, educational technologists and media specialists; although making great personal demands, as well as demands on time and resources, the resultant course is of high quality.

A speculative pattern for future education might include a shorter, general school education followed by a period of work to develop self-reliance; then a basic degree and a second interval of service to the community, of a vocational kind. Return could then be made to a second period of university education in a specialized field. Finally there would be specific refresher programmes.

The question of 'The Future as an Academic Discipline' within such a framework can be considered either from a research and advanced teaching viewpoint, based on individuals and groups, or as service courses. Here one of the important functions of basic degrees should be to introduce complex problems which are the stuff of futures studies. Such courses can best be produced by the creation of course teams. A balanced view is then presented, resulting in an increased awareness among the community. Thus the university indirectly affects national political processes, through the constituents.

To be the last speaker in a symposium of this kind offers the great advantage that one has heard all that has gone before; but there may, of course, be a countervailing disadvantage in that all that one had hoped to say has already been said! Thus, in some respects, my contribution will be a summary of what has gone before.

I would like to consider, first, what the role of universities in the future is likely to be; second to suggest a possible pattern of education provision for the future; and, finally, to look at the subject of this symposium

'The Future as an Academic Discipline' within the context of that pattern.

THE ROLE OF UNIVERSITIES IN THE FUTURE

There are, I think, three main facets to the probable role of the universities in the future:

(1) The traditional role of the universities in maintaining and nurturing scholarship through research and advanced teaching (honours and postgraduate) must, I believe, continue. It is vital that what Ashby has called 'the thin clear stream of excellence' be provided for in this way; and that provision is made thereby for the preservation of values through whatever political vicissitudes may lie in the future. Universities have an honourable record of preserving values through just such vicissitudes in the past.

To maintain and nurture scholarship requires, I believe, a continuation within the universities of a permanent structure that is firmly based upon disciplinary groups, although new disciplines may emerge and some older ones may disappear. There are a number of reasons underlying this assertion. In the first place any attempt to abolish a structure based upon disciplines is in a very real sense self-defeating; mathematicians will consort with other mathematicians however dispersed they may be by an alternative structure. Second, it is both necessary and desirable to use a senior mathematician to recruit junior mathematicians. Third, if there is anything that defines a 'discipline' it is, at least on the scientific side, a common body of research technique; so that, over quite a wide range, research activities can be adequately funded only for a disciplinary group and not for individual workers. Finally, the ultimate goal of advanced teaching is the reproduction of one's own kind; and only mathematical scholars can breed a new generation of mathematical scholars. It therefore follows that disciplines must be the permanent organizational units in a university that is adequately to fill this first role in the future.

(2) On the other hand, disciplines are already faced in the university by the necessity of providing 'service' courses for students who require an elementary grounding in the discipline; and such students greatly outnumber those who are being trained as the next generation of scholars. This second role of the universities is likely to increase, as a proportion of the total effort of universities, in the future. 'Service' courses will be needed for an increasing number of undergraduates and, in addition, for the general community through the growth of external or extramural teaching.

My second assertion is that the provision of such 'service' courses should *not* be controlled by the disciplines themselves. This assertion cuts right across the normal customs of most universities and I must clearly justify it. I shall try to do so first on general grounds and then by reference to our practice in the Open University.

On general grounds

(*a*) Courses prepared and delivered by one man can be splendid when it is the right man and horrid when it is not.

(*b*) Even when the right man is chosen from the point of view both of academic excellence and of brilliance in presentation, the course may tend to be too inward-looking—stressing the development of scholars in the discipline rather than looking outwards towards the actual needs of the students.

(*c*) 'Service' courses tend to be regarded by many academics as dull chores. Thus even members of a faculty of medicine may regard the course for dental students as a punishment rather than a challenge.

(*d*) There is, as has been pointed out many times at this meeting, a very real problem in mounting any real interdisciplinary course when the control of all courses is vested in the individual disciplines.

By reference to practice in the Open University

Our courses are all produced by groups which we have called 'Course Teams' and I think that the concept of the course team is possibly the most notable of all our innovatory ideas. A course team consists of the academic staff, from one or more disciplines, who are experts in the subject matter of the course, together with academics from related disciplines by whom the course may be used as a 'service' course. The course team also has, as full members, first, experts in educational technology who can advise on such matters as the definition of the course objectives, the methods of assessing whether the students have attained these objectives, and the manner of presentation of the course materials; and, second, experts in the media through which the course will be presented—in our case the radio and television producers who will create the audiovisual course materials. Each team is created *ad hoc* by the Senate, is given control of the content and structure of the course, and is disbanded when its task is completed. The academic members then return to their permanent homes within their discipline.

The course team approach makes considerable demands upon the individual members of its team, and, indeed, upon the institution. It is justified, I believe, by the high quality of the resulting courses and by their suitability for acceptance by the target student audience.

Among the demands that are made are:

(*a*) The primary loyalty of the members to the aims and objectives of the institution: In our experience it is very difficult for even distinguished academics to make as efficient a contribution if they are on a part-time seconded basis from other universities to which their primary loyalty is naturally given.

(*b*) The commitment of a long period of time to the preparation of the course: It requires a minimum of fifteen months, and preferably much longer, to create a high-quality course lasting thirty-four weeks and occupying a student roughly half-time. In the early months there is a necessary period of settling down and getting to know one another—a sort of group dynamic must be evolved. Later there can be a severe level of criticism from colleagues in the team, more often of the presentation than of the content of material. I once met a Professor of the Open University looking rather woebegone. It turned out that he had just been sent away by his course team to write certain material for the seventh time. Perhaps even more significant than the fact that he had been asked to do it was that he was going to do it!

(*c*) The resultant commitment of a lot of resources: Our courses are very expensive to create, compared with traditional university courses, largely because of the number of people involved in the team and the length of time that is spent. This cost is increased, of course, by our use of the mass media, which involves heavy production costs. This heavy initial cost is, of course, offset by the large number of students we serve; but it presents a formidable difficulty to smaller institutions.

(*d*) The loss of complete academic freedom implicit in the course team concept: It is clear that no individual academic can teach exactly what he wants in exactly the way he wants if the control of courses is given to a team. (It is, of course, true that, in the context of the Open University where the courses are transmitted on open circuits and in the bookshops to a public much wider than the students in a closed class-room, this demand of the course team concept offers certain safeguards.)

I would conclude from these arguments that the course team approach is the right one for all service 'courses' and that such courses should not be controlled by individual disciplines. I would further argue that only a course team approach can produce good quality interdisciplinary courses. In respect of the inevitably high cost of the course team approach, I would suggest that there is a strong case for the exchange of courses between institutions in order to spread the cost more widely. While I would be the first to resist any move towards a dull level of uniformity in the teaching programmes of the universities, I believe that the exchange and consequent sharing of 'service' courses would do little to invoke this. Such courses require the interpretation of individual tutors for credit in individual institutions and this in itself would obviate uniformity; and the quality of 'service' teaching would undoubtedly rise.

(3) The third role that I envisage for the universities in the future is that of providing for programmes of continuing education rather than just for initial education. I have developed this argument at length elsewhere.[1] Initial education has been the pattern from time immemorial. It is based on the idea that a man can be fitted for a lifetime in his chosen career and this was largely true until comparatively recent times. It is still true of the small band of natural scholars. For all the rest, the large majority, it is no longer adequate as an overall educational pattern. The quantity of knowledge is now so large that our young are almost middle-aged before they emerge from the ghettoes of education to be of service to the community; and, even worse, the pace of acquisition of new knowledge is now so fast that, even then, their initial education is out-of-date when they are in mid-career.

Most authorities now pay lip-service to the idea that a new pattern of continuing education must come, but little actually happens. This seems to me to be for three main reasons which make the introduction of continuing education very difficult:

(a) We cannot spare people from productive work to go back for further spells of full-time education.

(b) There is bound to be a shortage of teachers competent to deal with new knowledge and those who are available are wholly occupied with initial education.

(c) There is an enormous vested interest in the maintenance of the present pattern of initial education, which calls for such a vast expenditure that little resource is available to add to it the provision of continuing education.

The Open University offers one way of overcoming all these difficulties to a limited extent; it could therefore act as a catalyst to the introduction of the new pattern of continuing education. Further development will require a concomitant reduction in the provision of initial education.

A POSSIBLE EDUCATIONAL PATTERN FOR THE FUTURE

I would like now to take a speculative look at what might be a desirable
overall pattern of education in the future. I will not stick my neck out quite
so far as to suggest the possible duration in years of the various phases of such
a pattern, but will content myself with giving general indications. Thus there
might be six phases in the new pattern, namely:

	Duration of education	Duration of interval
(1) Initial school education	X	
(2) 'Deschooling'—experience of life		A
(3) Basic higher education—'general'	Y	
(4) Service to community		B
(5) Specialist higher education (honours and postgraduate)	Z	
(6) Periodic updating courses		

I would like to see a move to compress phase (1) into a shorter period—primarily by removing from it the element of specialized studies designed as a
preparation for the usual type of English honours degree. Thus there would
be a move away from the 'A-level' pattern of school education which forces
decisions about career patterns far too soon for the majority of children. For
a few natural scholars rapid progress at school should, however, be possible;
but these are themselves the very people whose rate of progress is currently
retarded to the pace of the slower members in their classes and who, a priori,
might be expected to complete more advanced work within the shorter, more
compressed, phase (1). I am very conscious of the difficulty of the problems
associated with such 'streaming'; but I am certain that, in any new pattern of
education that caters better for the needs of the majority, provision must be
made for the needs of the minority who comprise the 'thin clear stream of
excellence'.

There has been a great deal of discussion of the idea of 'deschooling'—which
is, in itself, a horrid word; but the idea is far from horrid. There is a great deal
to be said for the argument that higher education is of much greater value to
people whose experience embraces not only a period of school education but
also a period of work in a wholly different ambience where self-reliance is
more important than group activity. Furthermore, motivation amongst students
is, by common consent, intensified by such experience, as is evidenced both in the
Open University and amongst ex-service students.

Phase (3) would consist of a basic degree programme of a very 'general' character. I am not here suggesting a programme *common* to all students but a series of general programmes each pertinent to, say, one particular faculty. Thus, as I have argued elsewhere, a basic medical degree leading to a limited licence to practice under supervision in hospital or in general practice could be a highly vocational example.[1] General programmes within science or within the humanities are other examples more akin to the current degree programmes of the Open University.

Phase (4) would represent a second interval between periods of education, an interval of service to the community. Such service would be of a vocational kind, as suggested in the field of medicine, or of a much more general kind, as, for example, where those trained basically in the humanities could spend a period of time in industry, commerce, or in the public services. As a result of such a period of active work, some would discover a particular field in which they wished to make their careers. They would then return, in phase (5), for a second period of university education in that specialized field. To pursue my two examples, the doctor with a limited licence might discover or reinforce an interest in surgery and return for a specialized training therein (but avoiding any specialized training in all the other branches of medicine), while the graduate in humanities might discover an interest in management studies or in school teaching of history or in librarianship or in any other of a host of possibilities and return to pursue such a specialized course. Finally, phase (6) represents the periodic updating refresher programmes that I have already discussed as a necessary feature of future education.

This whole schematic pattern is, as I said, wildly speculative. It would, I believe, offer great advantages both to individuals in relation to their personal fulfilment and satisfaction and to society in the gains that it would make. There are, however, two enormous practical difficulties. The first, which I have already mentioned, is the need of the minority, of the scholars of the future. Clearly they do not require the intervals from study built into phases (2) and (4); and there must therefore be bridges between phases (1), (3) and (5) that they can cross. There must also be bridges that allow for the late development of scholarship, but most of these are provided within the suggested new pattern itself. The second practical problem is that any educational pattern of this kind requires radical changes in employment practices to enable a proper utilization of the manpower available from the introduction of the intervals of phases (2) and (4). Otherwise these intervals become meaningless and wasteful. If for no other reason, it will be clear that this suggested pattern can only be achieved by a national programme devised to achieve the goal.

THE FUTURE AS AN ACADEMIC DISCIPLINE

Finally, I would like to turn to the question of 'The Future as an Academic Discipline' *within* a future pattern of educational provision of the kind I have described. There seem to be two main ways in which this can be considered:

(1) *Research and advanced teaching in futures studies*

There are, I think, three ways in which the universities of the future could become involved in research and advanced teaching in futures studies:

(*a*) Within a permanent structure based upon individual disciplines, each discipline could indulge in futures studies; but these, as has been pointed out, could be of great depth but of limited width. Perhaps even more important, however, is the fact that individual members of the staff of the universities could, as they do now, continue to serve on external groups created to study specific problems. Such 'think tanks' offer one way in which an individual can affect the processes of decision-making at a political level. The idea that a university, as an institution, can affect decision-making in this way is one that I feel should be resisted. Universities are after all communities of scholars and should have room for all shades of political opinion; they should not seek to promote institutional political policies.

(*b*) On the other hand, within the universities, *ad hoc* groups to study particular problems can always be set up; but they should not be part of the permanent structure of the universities. Views expressed by such *ad hoc* groups should not, as the views of individuals should not, be represented as institutional views.

(*c*) Possibly futures studies will emerge as a new discipline in its own right but, at the moment, I think that the time is not yet ripe for such a development.

(2) *Service courses*

I believe that one major and important function of basic university degrees (my phase 3) should be to introduce students to the complexity of the global problems which are the stuff of futures studies. It is also true that such an introduction would be more valuable and more easily comprehensible after some experience of life during phase (2) of the educational pattern.

Such basic service courses in futures studies, being necessarily interdisciplinary, can best be produced by the creation of course teams created *ad hoc* for the purpose. This is a very expensive way of providing courses in individual small universities; and the need for the exchange and sharing of such service courses between many institutions becomes paramount.

There is also a clear need to involve a wider public in the community at large by attracting them into service courses of this kind. Because the courses would be produced by course teams they would tend to present a balanced view of the complex problems; and in producing an increased awareness of the nature of these problems among the community in general, the university, as an institution, would be indirectly affecting the political processes of decision-making: for it is ultimately the constituents, educated and aware or not, who determine the shape of all political decisions. This is one ultimate and valid goal of a university.

Discussion

Waddington: One of the most important functions of futures study is at the service level in the university. Certainly such a service course ought to be provided by a team, but how does one get the team? The Open University has a mechanism for getting a group together, for funding them, and for allowing them to generate their own enthusiasm in the time that is necessary to produce a good course. In an ordinary university, there is no real mechanism for liberating people's interests sufficiently for a course team to function like your teams do. My one-man course was written simply to provoke somebody else to do something better. It was the only practical way for getting anything done.

Shane: Is the old saying 'the hungry dog hunts best' relevant to the search for the right teams? How do you motivate people so that they do not feel submerged when they become part of a team? Many of our young American assistant professors and associate professors are struggling valiantly to stand for something for which they can be known among their colleagues. Would there be in the Open University a potential submerging of the people who have drive and who struggle for identity? Or do you see the Open University as a launching pad from which they move to some other academic arena?

Perry: I think the answer is both. I would hate it not to be a launching pad because staff can perform a catalytic function by carrying these ideas to other places. I don't think they lose their identity. They are quite free to express their own views, even as polemic if they want to, within the course material. The course team seldom say 'You musn't do that'. All they say is 'We must have somebody else with an opposite view' or 'You must put your views in context'.

I don't think they are stultified in that sense. I think the people in our teams are carried forward primarily by the sheer excitement of doing something that is innovative. A very real problem looming on the horizon is that after something has been done for the first time it it not quite so exciting the next time. The best way of meeting that problem is by exchange and by bringing in new people. That is not easy with the present low mobility of academic staff.

Black: You touched on academic freedom. The view that academic staff can teach what they like, how they like, when they like and if they like isn't a recipe for academic freedom but one for academic anarchy. Academic freedom is only freedom within the constraints of some loyalty to the institution and to the objects of the courses taught, however these may be manifested. I was not in the least worried when you spoke about abrogating some academic freedom because in the situation you outlined you are not really abrogating it but building it in, by substituting a loyalty to the wider concept of your course structure. This means more to me than a rather abstract academic freedom.

Francis: As a teacher at the Open University it seems to me that one functional level has been missed out, perhaps understandably. The course team in Buckinghamshire certainly puts the course together competently and efficiently, but there is an element of good will in the teaching itself. The course is taken as a package by a group of students and then it has to be seen virtually through the eyes of one person who has contact with the students in the teaching situation, who has to get them over their hurdles and has to integrate the package. The package as it comes out through the media is essentially a linear programme and there is still the problem of overcoming the individual idiosyncrasies and difficulties of students. Sometimes the teacher is dealing with broadly based courses of the kind that a futures course might represent. Often the tutor is the least qualified person in the group on certain aspects of the course. In fact, self-help becomes an important element of the teaching process, as I said earlier. Often in my tutorials somebody with considerable industrial experience can take over the class at a certain point because they have far more experience of the point that is being communicated in the group. I don't know how much this is taken for granted.

Waddington: You are saying that however much the high technology media are used, an input of personality remains. But would you wish to eliminate the input of personality?

Perry: I wouldn't. This is the safeguard, as it were—the way the dead hand of uniformity is avoided. Otherwise we would be back in one room with closed walls. Somebody can say precisely what his interpretation is and that is a good thing. The student at least has a balanced view for judging that opinion, and if he is any good he is going to take it with a grain of salt.

Lundberg: You said that the courses cannot afford to be polemical, and it is easy to see why. But isn't there an inherent danger in this in the long run?

Perry: There are inherent dangers in both directions, of course. If we indulge in courses which are not balanced, which are more polemical, we run the risk of evoking government interference because we are a public institution. Governments could close down and impose their will on any of the universities tomorrow. They have the power but by convention they don't use it. We could upset that convention because we use the power of the mass media. I don't think we can take the risk. On the other hand, there is an undoubted inherent risk of just becoming dull, flat and uninteresting.

Lundberg: Isn't there a built-in polemical element?

Perry: Many of the courses have material, written by one man, which is straight polemic, but attached and bound into the same volume is somebody giving the opposite view. You just can't put polemic in on its own and not bother about it.

Platt: In the US, as I said in my paper, we are beginning to have something called 'adversary science', where scientists speak on public issues, doing their best, like lawyers, for a particular side, and then in a later case perhaps doing their best for the opposite side. The hope is that in this kind of open confrontation, as in a court of law, one comes closer to the truth than by having just accidents of committee structure or unanswered polemics decide the matter.

Waddington: I would strongly oppose that as a way of advancing science.

Platt: But somebody should make the total case for a nuclear plant, and somebody should make the total case against the plant for environmental reasons, so that we can see all of both sides before we decide.

Dror: Why shouldn't the two sides make two balanced presentations for and against? Why total? The judge is highly professional and trained to understand the lawyers. This does not hold for the amateur audience, which cannot draw correct conclusions from extreme positions. The analogy of the judicial adversary process is completely misleading. The jury system applies only to limited questions, is controlled by the judge, and is very doubtful.

Platt: Do you know a better system?

Dror: Yes, reliance on professional judges in courts; and careful policy analysis on television for the public.

Platt: Who judges the judges?

Dror: Who judges the juries?

Waddington: That is a piece of politics, not a piece of learning. Learning is not advanced by legal procedures.

Perry: The courses that we are talking about in science don't get to that advanced level of judgement. In futures courses you are dealing with issues of judgement because you are dealing with global problems. A confrontation situation should be expressed within that course material but is not usually necessary in the elementary science that we are teaching.

Eldredge: Could you do specialist or advanced work in the Open University?

Perry: We can in the liberal arts, but I don't think we can in science. I don't think it is possible to teach nuclear physics by the media. We can teach advanced mathematics.

Valaskakis: How would you and Dr Black treat professors who are truly outstanding, innovative and perhaps even geniuses—somebody like an Einstein or a Wittgenstein—but who at the same time are bad teachers? It is said that Wittgenstein never taught in a classroom but always at home, and that if he happened to be inspired he would go on inexhaustibly for hours, while if he happened not to be inspired he would just dismiss the class and declare: 'I have nothing to say'. If the university demands too much from these undisciplined professors, the dynamic elements that they represent might be lost to the university.

Perry: I would have them in the university.

Waddington: I don't think Wittgenstein would have taken a job with the Open University.

Perry: I would like a Wittgenstein as a part-time tutor.

Black: If a university is so rigid in its procedures that it can't take into account the waywardness of such people, then it is really on the way out.

Lundberg: In Sweden there is now strong emphasis on mid-career university education at the expense of initial education. It is probably fair to state that a large section of the academic community favoured initial education. Nonetheless the politically enforced new education policy has been very quickly accepted.

Waddington: The general view of academia until quite recently was that its purpose was producing scholars. It is only gradually sinking into the minds of university staffs that in the present world 80 to 90 per cent of their task consists essentially of providing service courses. Many people regard this as a downgrading of the function of the pure university scholar, but of course one can see it instead as an up-grading of the university's service to the community. But people don't change their minds very fast, so they are bound to oppose it for some time.

Woodroofe: In business we look at what the assumptions are about the future and what kind of world we are going to be working in. We have objectives and priorities about how we carry them out. Do universities ever set down their objectives? You are already saying that some think the main objective is teaching, others say it is advanced studies, research and so on. And there is much talk about academic freedom and little about common objectives, but why should academics be free? Nobody else is.

Waddington: I have rarely heard objectives being discussed by a university senate. I have heard them continuously discussed by groups of individual academics.

Ashby: My answer is that the purpose of a university should be directed to the students, not to the possible jobs awaiting them. It should be concerned with men, not manpower. It should give one student the chance to become a historian, another a doctor, another a psychologist, if these are the disciplines they are interested in, even if there aren't any jobs awaiting them. It was Mark Pattison in Oxford who declared that his aim as a tutor was to produce 'not a book, but a man'.

Waddington: Some people who work in universities would say that, but many others would not.

Woodroofe: That might be a good objective for three universities. I am not sure that it is the right objective for forty-seven universities in a country the size of the United Kingdom.

Perry: We have to differentiate between the overall objectives, and what academics are actually doing from day to day. We need a much more closely defined set of objectives within those overall objectives. That is what is missing.

Waddington: The tradition so far has been that universities don't, as organizations, have overall objectives. The universities consist of conglomerates of individuals, and different individuals have different objectives. Many people in universities say that their reason for being in the university (their objective) is that it gives them the best position for pursuing their own research. For a historian there is probably nowhere else where he can pursue his research, and that is his objective. Other people would say that their objective is to improve individual people according to their desires. Yet others would say their objective is to serve society by turning out the specialists that the society needs. Walter Perry's argument is that universities should have much more defined overall objectives and a certain amount of freedom within those objectives. I am not quite clear whether they need to have those objectives.

Perry: Clear institutional objectives are recommended in the charters of those universities which have charters. Oxford and Cambridge don't have charters.

Waddington: 'Education, religion, learning and research' was the accepted formula when I was at Cambridge.

Woodroofe: Universities also have responsibilities. If we are to have more university education, the idea is not just to improve the fullness of life for the people who go through university but also to make a contribution to the community. A community can afford to have a certain number of scholars searching for knowledge for the sake of knowledge, but it can't afford to have all the scholars of forty-seven universities doing that. They must contribute to the community. In present economic conditions the universities are going to suffer. For their own preservation they should be thinking about making a greater contribution to the community.

Waddington: You don't think universities serve the community sufficiently simply by keeping young people out of labour exchanges?

Robson: I really must protest at this suggestion that disorganized anarchy is the normal state of universities. In this country all forty-seven universities at regular five-yearly intervals have to be extremely specific about what they are doing, what they propose to do, and what they have done. Statistics on university activities are published in great detail, to an extent which is unknown in industry. People in this country can get every piece of information they could possibly want about what universities are doing. If they don't know what that information is, it is simply because they have not read it!

Platt: In my analogy (p. 176) of the university as a five-legged animal, the fifth 'leg' of this wise elephant is its trunk, which is the grasp on the future. As I said in my paper, those universities which neglect futures studies are dropping out of the total network of discussion of world problems and failing to contribute what they might to the total society. And I think there might be useful parallels here, or anticipations, of the futures-role of other universities in other countries.

Waddington: Admittedly the whole university system has to deal with all these functions. But we must find an ideal mix—or can we leave this to work itself out by the forces of interplay between the universities and society?

King: There is no single uniform mix. It must depend on the particular university.

Shane: If you were looking forward to a next step which was as significant a break-away from the present situation as the Open University was thirteen years ago, what would you suggest that this next dramatic step beyond the Open University might be, Sir Walter?

Perry: I see another step for the Open University, and I see another step in the whole pattern of education in Britain. The really deprived people who are not ready for the Open University need an open system of pre-university teaching. I don't think the Open University itself can do it but it ought to be done. Secondly, we haven't even begun to break into the continuing educational field properly. We can do a lot of short courses for periodic 'retreading' that other people can't do. This catalytic move towards continuing education is an exciting prospect for the future, but it hasn't really begun yet.

Eldredge: The 'futurized' part of your scheme for the Open University is excellent. After exploring all sorts of futures courses, I have come to the tentative conclusion that courses outside universities are doing a remarkable job in retreading or 'futurizing' the learning of lots of people and leading them to find their way in the Brave New World. Most people have high motivation when they come in for retreading. The World War II veterans whom I taught had magnificent motivation. We should explore fifty different ways of providing retreading, not necessarily through the university itself. There may be new types of institutions which are better at it.

Woodroofe: One type of retreading is that whereby university teachers come into particular companies in industry and take part in courses. This is beneficial for the people in industry. It is part of retreading. It is also beneficial for the university professor, because he gets contact with reality. Somebody in his audience may know more about some aspect of his subject than he does, and he gets this feedback.

Waddington: Could you explain a bit on the general relation between retreading, technological innovation and technological unemployment? Can retraining be regarded as a way of using people at a time when they have no definite jobs?

Woodroofe: I don't see it that way. I certainly see that the interrelationship between the universities and industry should grow stronger as time goes on, to the benefit of both. Obviously, the intake into industry in the management field comes largely from universities. Some of those people have had a generalized and not a specifically business-oriented education.

Waddington: That is in the management field, but in America there is a great intake of operatives from universities into industry. Are we going to get much more of that in this country?

Woodroofe: Industry would like it. In the US, college people become supervisors. The result is that, in the US, industry in general is less management-intensive than it is in this country—and this country is higher in its intensity of management than the rest of Europe. The reason is that in the US and elsewhere they delegate more power, so they need fewer layers of management. This would be fine, and with forty-seven universities in this country we ought to be doing the same. But the people who go to universities in this country expect to become managers, not supervisors. In many cases their expectations cannot be fulfilled.

Waddington: Dockworkers or miners now earn more than junior managers. With the change in wage patterns the purely financial inducements to go into management rather than operation must be less. Will students continue to expect to go into management?

Woodroofe: There are three features to that. First, there is concertina-ing of incomes all the time, from top to bottom, and it is much greater in this country than in any other. Secondly, a man who goes into management doesn't get paid the rate for the job immediately but he gets increases year by year until he reaches the full value for the job. That is the tradition. A man who becomes a dockworker gets his full rate for the job plus his overtime and all the other things straight away. Thirdly, if a man comes in as a manager, he comes in on the bottom rung of the ladder, but with the hope that he is going to climb up the management ladder to jobs of greater responsibility. So, although he might be on the same sort of level as a supervisor who has worked his way up from the shop floor, he will nevertheless when he gets further up the ladder be higher than that man. The problem of the compression of differentials in management pay is really getting quite intense. I think universities will experience the same problem.

Reference cited

[1] PERRY, W. (1975) *Higher Education for Adults: Where More Means Better (Rede Lecture 1974)*, Cambridge University Press, London

General discussion

Ziman: Views of the future are too important to be left to the futurists. Our view of the future is a dynamic image of life and of man. Futures studies as an academic discipline inevitably emphasize the analytical techniques. Part of being an academic discipline is that the things on which people can be made to agree by strongly persuasive arguments have to be talked about. It depends on sharp, formal, logical discourse—what we envisage, in the limit, as mathematical proof. That is at the expense of the informal imaginative view of the dynamics of life. This emphasis on analytical method transforms or modifies our view of life from the poetic towards the technocratic view. Because that view influences action, because the dynamics of life include the idea becoming practice, futurism tends to some extent towards a self-fulfilling prophecy. That is, there is a tendency to create a society which warps human life in the direction of the view seen by academic futurologists. The worry that I have in this whole discussion about the creation of departments, specialists and experts on the future, is that their view becomes the image of the future in the same sense that the physicist's image—his technical image—becomes the whole view of nature. The human view of nature should be much broader than the physicist's concepts and constants. Physicists are supposed to be the academics who have the duty of looking at nature as a whole, so everybody says that what the physicists have learned is 'reality'. This is not a deathbed repentance by a mathematical physicist! On the contrary, experience in mathematical physics has taught me the defects and difficulties of generalized mathematical modelling, even in the sphere of the natural sciences.

I want to give two examples of the sorts of things that can go wrong. In classical thermodynamics a maximizable function, the 'Gibbs' free energy', is the standard quantity from which all the properties of statistical mechanics can be derived. It is just like Dr Valaskakis's felicity function. But all theoretical physicists know that this is a very special property of the types of system that we are dealing with in thermodynamics. We know, for example, that the existence of such a function depends upon the intermolecular forces being conservative, and the whole system being very close to equilibrium. I do not see any proof that these conditions apply in the types of human systems we are discussing. This sort of analogy seems highly naive to the theoretical physicist, who knows how difficult it is to get to the genuine parameters and functional relations of a valid model. The theory that such a possibility exists is not proven. That doesn't mean to say that it is chaos. On the contrary, an assembly of atoms might be a perfectly deterministic system, with every particle in the system following its own course under the influence of the others, and yet there would still not be such a maximizable function from which the whole motion could be deduced by variation. I am talking technical mathematics, because this is precisely the sort of thing one has to get right.

The other example comes from the theory of plasma physics and the problems of controlled nuclear fusion.

Back in the 1950s people said that if we set up a system of a big tube containing a low density gas in a strong magnetic field, then we would get a stable electrical discharge at a high temperature. This is a simple system mathematically; the whole behaviour is described by three or four linked partial differential equations, all absolutely deterministic and straightforward. But when the switch was turned on something else happened. The experimental physicists asked the theoretical physicists what had gone wrong. They thought about it again, discovered their error, and suggested modifications in the experimental conditions. Alas, the plasma was still very unstable—more corrections had to be made in the mathematical analysis. There have been several cycles of that process; I am telling that story to show why I have no faith in mathematics as a system of calculating what is going to happen under circumstances where one hasn't already a fair idea of what to expect. They didn't know what the phenomena were—they hadn't done the experiment before—and that made it almost impossible to work it out in advance. Computational techniques have improved since then, but the systems to which they are to be applied are far more complex and poorly comprehended than a plasma discharge. So the worry I have in this whole meeting is simple enough: how are we going to bring a *poetic* view into the *problèmatique*?

Waddington: My suggestion originally was that the *problèmatique* should be treated as history, and we should bring in a few historians. When we talk about interdisciplinarity, why do we mean only inter-scientific disciplines? We need, as you say, to bring in the humanists too. (But, incidentally, the fact that mathematical theorists don't always get it right the first time, or even the

second or third time, is not a good argument for not letting them have a shot.)
I am a great believer in always having orthogonal views: never believe in a
thing unless you believe its opposite at the same time, or never adopt one
principle of ethics unless you adopt an orthogonal principle at the same time.

King: The Club of Rome has a new project being worked out now by Ervin
Laszlo on exactly the lines you have just indicated.

During this meeting my prejudices have perhaps become a little more rigid
than the reverse. We have come round to the fact that at undergraduate level
there is a good deal to be done, but I don't think it is futures studies and futures
teaching in the narrow sense. It is much broader than that. Your own book,
Professor Waddington,[1] is not exclusively on futures as such. There is a desper-
ate need to create a much deeper understanding of the nature of the world,
how the global system works, what its interactions are—the *problèmatique* if
you like, the question of complexity, the global problems, the need for local
participatory approaches in other ways. If we are going to succeed in the next
generation with the management of complexity, change and uncertainty there
has to be a great deal more understanding than we have now, and this has to
be greatly generalized. The political leaders with whom we have had discussions
in the Club of Rome apparently understand that many changes should be
made, but these would be extremely unpopular and they are unable to make
such changes until the general understanding of the world situation on the
part of the public is much greater than it is today. Therefore I think there is a
great deal to be done at the undergraduate level in universities. The prospective element, the futures element, is important but not the totality. To concentrate exclusively on the future as such is perhaps unwise at this level. At the
postgraduate level the needs are quite different. The needs of the decision
makers, the needs of society, the needs of our own search for new knowledge,
call for a great development of techniques and methodology, a great deal of
specific work. I am sure that Professor Dror is right in indicating that this has
a place in the university. Where it should be I couldn't say, but in many cases
it ought perhaps to be associated with policy science. The key to the utility
of futures studies lies first in the methodology, which requires a realistic understanding of the problems, and secondly in its applications. I would put great
stress on the need for communication between the universities and the decision
makers. From my own observations the decision makers are more open to this
than they have ever been before, out of desperation.

Lord Ashby brought in the question of how much we are willing to sacrifice
for our great-grandchildren. This raises the fundamental human problem of
the extent to which human beings, and their societies and governments, are
capable of acting in anticipation of events rather than merely reacting to them

post facto. One of the characteristics of *homo sapiens* is that he can look ahead. We can prepare for the winter just as well as the squirrels, perhaps a little better. We even prepare to some extent for our old age by taking out insurance policies, by supporting geriatrics and all kinds of things. We prepare for military onslaughts—not very well, because there is insufficient futurology in our thinking, so that we remain too traditional, constructing the Maginot Line generation after generation. Professor Dror has supported the idea of research on 'heresies', and I think it is very necessary to question the traditional. This is one part of the futures approach. There is however, also tradition in favour of anticipatory action. The classic example was Noah's Ark. Is there a possibility of a contemporary equivalent to that? I don't know, but I think that the rate of change brings in a new factor and makes anticipation even more necessary.

I am not sure that for the adoption of a futures approach to politics it is necessary to look as far ahead as to our great-grandchildren. In effect the speeding up in the rate of change means that long term has become medium term. So one of the reasons for taking an anticipatory approach is that we ourselves, or our children and people we know, may live long enough to see quite a number of difficulties which are already foreseeable. In other words, because of this shrinking of time, anticipation of difficulties becomes long-term self-interest. And where self-interest is still involved, there is a chance of people taking anticipatory precautions. This is less probable as the degree of self-interest is diluted by the time span from our children to our grandchildren and then to generations whom we don't know. In a period of rapid change such as the present, therefore, self-interest may drive us to anticipatory action to prevent disasters and, perhaps, to take painful decisions which will contribute to the survival of the human race.

Waddington: You are assuming that the rate of change will continue to accelerate. At the moment we don't know whether it will do so, or start slowing down. When Lord Ashby first mentioned them, I said I was not bothered about my great-grandchildren, but the time may come when we can again think about our great-grandchildren.

King: The prospective aspects of research and development are very important at present, particularly with regard to energy, conservation and the like. The lead time for R & D is very long and, taken together with the time required for capital accumulation, construction, etc., the general application of a major technological innovation takes up to thirty or forty years. With the present rapid rate of change, the time between two distinct sets of circumstances which represent radically different situations is now less than the lead time of R & D into production. The power of technology in solving many of the problems that we are up against therefore becomes very dubious. It could often come too late. It is implicit in much economic thinking that a technology 'fix' will in fact provide for a solution. The economists have always taken the view that technological innovation is essentially caused by the interaction of economic forces, which is the opposite point of view from that of the scientist. One of the biggest questions is whether there is time for the technological fixes to be developed. These matters are not properly appreciated in political and policy-making circles, where the time factor in change is seldom discussed. In France a quarter of a century elapsed between the first experimental pile going critical and the first power station opening. Yet France is relying on having nuclear energy within ten years so that a great number of major energy bottlenecks can be removed. The need to take decisions on quite long-term needs, because of this lead time for research and development, is very great, and seldom appreciated. An awful lot of nonsense has been talked in political circles about the energy question. There is a special need to take the prospective approach to research and development and to persuade the decision makers to make decisions now on major R & D projects whose results will be required thirty years from now.

Robson: I still have two basic anxieties. First, it is unlikely that the graph of any aspect of human affairs would be a smooth curve or a straight line. It would probably be a jerky line, with breaks and discontinuities. Major changes occur as a result of sudden and frequently unpredictable events. If groups of highly informed people in the past had tried to predict what was going to happen, I suspect that their success rate would have been extremely low. One can only predict on the basis of experience already experienced. The chances of predicting one of these massive discontinuities which switch the whole pathway of human affairs must be vanishingly small. People at a point in time don't have the information or the experience. If that is so, then futurology is clearly going to be not only difficult but only occasionally successful.

My second basic anxiety is that setting up futurology as a discipline is surely only one part of the equation and alone would be a sterile academic activity. If it is to have any value there must be some way of ensuring that the decision makers pay some attention to the predictions. At present, I see extremely little evidence that anybody would listen. Even if they did, how would they know which predictions were accurate?

King: I strongly disagree.

Robson: You mentioned Noah's Ark: I believe that according to legend somebody had to tell Noah to build his ark. People have been making predictions about population problems for years without anything being done.

Platt: Prediction alone is not enough. It has to be ratified by a reality principle—by a real and catalytic crisis—because that is when people begin to put in time, money, effort and organizational skills to meet the problem. It is important to make the prediction so that you have the intellectual tools in advance, as far as possible. It is important to do the homework and the critical analyses, but for society to get moving on these problems people have to come in contact with them in a real way.

Dror: Sometimes it is the other way round. Good analysis recognizes problems, while direct contact distorts understanding.

Waddington: Dr King mentioned that futurology in the sense of prediction is only one element in what we are talking about, and rather a minor element at that. I agree, but I find it difficult to know how any other word but 'futures' could act as a focus. Our interest is really in a dynamic analysis of the present, the present as a set of processes rather than as a state of affairs. It is difficult to express this in just one word without using some word like futures. Admittedly the word future has been largely spoilt for this use by the invention of things like futurology and futuristics, and by premature attempts to be more precise than is possible. Actual attempts to predict are not likely to be successful, and they are only a part of what one is interested in.

Another point was raised by Sir Hugh Robson—how do we get decision makers to pay any attention? Decisions of course are normally taken with some sort of future in mind. If one has to decide to invest in a plant for manufacturing something which will take years to build, one does this in relation to some idea of the future. Whether by studying the present as a dynamic system one can at all improve one's predictive power, is perhaps not so clear, but it is quite certain that among the people who are going to make predictions are the decision makers. They have to make them. Predicting is what decision-making essentially is.

Robson: They are going to base their assumptions on a continuation of the present.

Dror: Advisers say that top decision makers never listen to them. Decision makers say their advisers never say anything useful. Often, both claims are correct. One way to open up decision-making is by public pressure. Other decision makers feel the need for help because they feel uneasy, being unable to solve pressing problems. An additional way is to try and make predictions and other futures studies relevant to the concrete decision agenda of politicians. This requires a set of innovative structures in government itself.

Waddington: Let us consider Mrs Gandhi's problem when faced with the problem of the population of India. If she is to do anything about it at all, she has to do it in relation to the way the future seems to be unfolding. What she needs is not a more precise prediction, but an analysis of the dynamic factors affecting the population. The problem may be to reduce the desire for a family of more than two children: is that the major thing she has to do? Or has she got to disseminate birth control methods more widely and freely, or pay people to be sterilized? She needs a dynamic analysis of the situation much more than an actual prediction. But whatever she does, her decision must be taken in relation to the future.

Platt: It is important to emphasize that there is a historical process of change, or what was once called a dialectical process. The first dramatic presentation by a professor or a wild man or woman isn't enough; it isn't the end of the process. The ideas of those people need to be opposed and debated, because in many cases they will be false and dangerous prophets, whose warnings are simply wrong.

Many people do not understand or accept this historical process, these time constants for redirecting a big social system. For example, some people don't really believe in change at all, or progressive change. They are either young radicals who say the system is so rigid it will never change, or older conservatives who say that a system is going to go on because it has gone that way for all of human history. Then there is the kind of utopian who expects change immediately, as soon as the new truth has been proclaimed. All of these are wrong. Change occurs in a certain time scale, and in a first approximation the system won't change tomorrow or next year or the next. But in fifty years, and nowadays even in ten years, it may be totally different. We have to appreciate these time constants of change and what they really are today if we are to reconcile the different points of view of those who believe that change cannot happen, or that it will happen right away. On different time scales, both of them are entirely correct.

Valaskakis: I would like to expand on some of the points made by Professor Ziman and share some of the experiences I have had in doing interdisciplinary research with hard scientists, soft scientists and people from the humanities. In interdisciplinary teams I have found that it is the anthropologist, the sociologist, or perhaps even the literary critic, who argues for the computer, and it is the computer expert, the mathematical physicist, who argues against the computer, saying quite cogently that there is a 'garbage-in garbage-out' rule. My position would be that we should make sure that we do not feed garbage into the computer, rather than that we should necessarily junk the computer. Two concepts of the uses of mathematics are inherent here: the hard scientist sees mathematics as a tool for finding answers, while others see it as a way of defining problems in a heuristic and meaningful way. When I write an equation on the board I do not always expect to solve it. I am reminded of a billboard seen in the US Midwest with a giant 'Jesus is the Answer' on it. In much smaller graffiti was the irreverent rejoinder 'Yes, but what is the question?'

What we need are good questions even if good answers are not forthcoming. Mathematics can be one way of formulating questions. Insoluble equations measure our ignorance. Their absence makes our very ignorance incommensurable. There is much to be said for the notion of a '*problèmatique*'. Because what is in fact a *problèmatique*? In the technical sense the *problèmatique* is a hierarchy of questions and sub-questions, of problems and sub-problems. It is a systematic process, not a haphazard one, and it can benefit from formal mathematical expression. On the other hand I certainly think that the formal model should be tempered by the humanities. In our Montreal think tank we will endeavour to have a so-called 'scenarist in residence', a person who will produce scenarios. He will not be a physicist or an engineer but a playwright. He hopefully will take a societal model and develop human, rounded, realistic characters around it. This touch of humanity should, we hope, complement the formalism of theory.

Oldfield: For me this symposium has sharpened some personal dilemmas in education. I sense that a tension emerges between education for *adjustment* and education for rational, autonomous, *altruism*. The way in which one steers one's course between these poles depends on the relationship one sees between notions of positivism, questions of values, considerations of empirically knowable reality, and the power of the conceptual frameworks and theories which one uses. It still seems to me that futures study tends too often towards a dissociation between personal or collective value formation, and the generation or evaluation of projective images. It thus embraces a positivism which I still mistrust *vis-à-vis* the future. It tends to rely on theories, tools and concepts which are more impressive for their elegance, sophistication and precision than for their accuracy, validity or relationship to empirical reality. It becomes a sort of non-participatory mystique. Yet I am bound to confess that the frames of reference which I as a blinkered scientist find more authentic, valid and robust—for example, the ecosystem—are only partly integrative. The ecosystem is a powerful framework in empirical study as well as in pragmatic and normative terms. Thus one can try to use it as an axial concept in education for value formation, for judgement and, if you like, for democratic participation. However, working and thinking within an ecosystem framework, I am still forced to admit that I have developed only a partial perspective and I cannot fit it into a global, complex, holistic totality. Therefore I sense a tension between developing the holistic perspective and fostering realistic participation in democracy. That strikes me as being an uncomfortable point to recognize.

Waddington: You have put your finger on one of the difficulties of life. Life is not easy. But it is there and people have to cope with it.

Woodroofe: It seems to me that 'futurology' is a bad term and I would agree that the subject should be considered as the long-term implications of current activities. This is really what we are discussing. And I would again make the plea: let the time scale be as short as is practicable. If it is made long term it will be regarded as futurology in the worst sense and the community will not regard it as credible. Then, if the time scale is kept short, one can validate. Obviously one will have the discontinuities, the unexpected, but at least one will be able to tackle the unexpected better if these factors have been considered beforehand.

The effect of politics has not been thoroughly discussed here. The whole discussion was really on what are the long-term implications of what we are doing now. Politics on the other hand has a very short horizon. The politician has to get himself elected every five years or less. He has to promise goodies in order to get the vote, and he has to promise goodies which are often not achievable or which are borrowing from future generations, even from Eric Ashby's great-grandchildren. How do we get the political system as it is now, democracy as it is now, to agree to take decisions, in the interests of the long term, which are unpopular at the moment?

Perry: I wonder whether looking at the microcosm helps with the macrocosm. In 1969 and the few years afterwards I was having to make more decisions that would have a direct effect than anybody should ever have to make. Nearly all the decisions that I took about forming a new institution were wrong. It wasn't that the ideas or the policies were wrong, but the decisions, which were really not decisions of what policy was but of how to implement the policy, had no evidence to back them up. That applies to the macrocosmic decisions as well. Fortunately most of them are either reversible or, if not wholly reversible, modifiable by feedback. That kind of feedback may be where participatory democracy comes in. Can participatory democracy ever make the decisions through the democratic process or does it actually act as the feedback? Some decisions will be so wrong and so irreversible that they might have awful consequences for the preservation of scholarship. Maybe we should create universities so that they can be Noah's Arks through bad periods. It has happened historically and it may well happen again.

Francis: Universities have a caretaker function which is essentially complementary to that of the political process, and they provide an element of continuity that is not provided by other institutions. Although we have all stressed the essential value of an early warning system we haven't really talked about the assessment of risk, which has come up in a rather roundabout way when we have been talking about nuclear power or something like that. In many areas at present we are able to put down the equation: infinite potential equals infinite risk. We are tending to assume somehow that decisions made inside the political process involve the assessment of risk, and we are not sure how the politicians arrive at their assessment. This independent and complementary function can be provided, I believe, through the universities in their appraisal of the future, working in close contact with other institutions.

Reference cited

[1] WADDINGTON, C. H. (1975) *The Sources of the Man Made Future*, Cape & Paladin, London

Concluding remarks

C. H. WADDINGTON

As Walter Perry pointed out, he, being the last designated speaker in the symposium, had the opportunity to present something of a summary of all the previous contributions. He brought out several aspects of what has seemed to me a rather surprising consensus of opinion which has emerged during our meeting. We all seem to be agreed that universities are finding new responsibilities thrust upon them by the historical events of our present period, and that they will need to show a great deal more flexibility and a greater capacity for imaginative innovation, than they have been exhibiting in the last few decades. The days are long gone by when they could be contented to be mainly Noah's Arks preserving and handing on the wisdom of the past. Even if one adds to this the task, which they have gradually become accustomed to in the last hundred years, of making some modest contributions to the discovery of new knowledge, those two endeavours are by no means enough for the universities of the present day, though I think we can all agree that they remain essential aspects of university life which certainly should not be allowed to deteriorate.

Walter Perry drew particular attention to two further tasks. In the first place, universities have to provide a general background education, covering some broad fields not in great depth or detail, but sufficiently to provide a basis on which more thorough and narrower specialized studies can find a firm ground to stand on. Perhaps in the old days such background could be provided by the schools at pre-university age, or by informal communication between university students themselves. Nowadays the need has grown beyond the capacity of that type of instruction and calls for the provision of 'service' courses, specifically designed with this aim in view. Further, Walter Perry also stressed the important changes that have followed from the rapidity with which knowledge advances and older ideas or even alleged facts become out of date. Education, whether we like it or not, cannot be confined to an early period in life, but

217

must continue throughout the years of adult experience. Exactly what form this continuing education should take is still unclear, but it seems fairly certain that the universities must play an important part in it.

I should add, to these university functions, that of providing a forum for wide-ranging discussions between people who are interested in ideas and who bring with them differing points of view and background. I am not thinking only of discussions between academics of various disciplines, but of discussions between academics, industrialists, politicians, civil servants, trades union leaders, and the many other types of people in our world who feel the need to think things out and to learn other peoples' points of view. Again, of course, there are many such 'talking shops' which are not primarily connected with the universities, but it seems to me that the universities are in a favourable position to set them up and operate them.

It is against this background of the changing structure of university activities that we have been considering the relevance of the broad field which we have referred to as 'the future'. There seems to be a general agreement amongst us that it would not be sensible at present to think of this subject mainly in terms of specific prediction of what is going to happen, or even of a series of weighted bets on possible future situations or events. 'Futurology', in so far as it concerns itself with telling us what life is going to be like in the year 2000, is not robust enough to take any place in university concerns. It can at best provide a few vivid illustrations for arguments of a more firmly based character.

In fact there was, I think, general agreement that the 'futures' which might have relevance to universities would perhaps better be described as a multi-dimensional dynamic analysis of the present. It would be concerned with discovering the nature of the processes which are going on at the present time and how they interact with one another. This involves, of course, a consideration of the recent past, and also, since we are thinking of processes, a consideration of the near future. Woodroofe emphasized that the decision makers of today have, of course, to think in terms of processes of change which their decisions will effect; but at one point he was urging that we should keep our considerations to as short a term into the future as possible. Of course, if we never had to look any further ahead than one year, even in the present hectic times, one could hope things would not have changed too much in the interval. But, very often, policies take longer than that to come into effect; consider for instance the population problem. One cannot predict with any certainty what will happen in ten or twenty years' time in almost any field, but large-scale investors of capital, or initiators of major social policies, may in effect have to gamble on their hunches for periods of that time. What can be done, however, is to assess the character of the processes which are going to be operating. It seems to me that it is this aspect of the matter which is of interest to universities. Moreover we are realizing more and more the interrelatedness of the many factors involved. We are dealing with multidimensional interactions, many of which are non-linear and involve highly complex controlling systems of both positive and negative character. New disciplines of thought, such as cybernetics, are called for.

The impression I have received during these days is that there are at least four types of university activity in these fields, which many of us here feel to be valuable.

There is in the first place the straight research project. We have mentioned the designing of a world economic system as proposed by Jan Tinbergen, or the modelling of interactions on a world scale by Mesarovic and Pestel, as activities which are eminently suitable for the academic environment, and which through their interdisciplinary character may require that the environment should give up some of the rigidity of its conventional departmental organization.

Secondly, there is the provision of service courses, which would describe the existing state of knowledge about the processes affecting the main problems of the world—population, growth of cities, provision of food, transport, the natural environment, human aspirations and what people conceive of as 'the good life', and so on. As Walter Perry and John Francis have reminded us, the Open University has already organized a course of this kind and they are both deeply involved in it in different ways. I have myself written a book which I would like to believe could form a textbook for such a course, and I have attempted to organize this in Edinburgh, although still on an unofficial basis.

Thirdly, there is a different type of service course which would seem desirable, namely one which describes the newer types of thinking and theorizing about interacting complex systems. One hears a lot in the semi-popular press about cybernetics, information theory, control theory, decision theory, games theory, and a whole list of theoretical developments aimed at increasing our capacity to understand such matters. Sometimes I feel that the names are perhaps more impressive than the content, but even if one retains a healthy scepticism, one is bound to admit that considerable advances in understanding complex systems have, in fact, been made in the last few decades. Unfortunately most of them have not yet crept through into the general education of the ordinary educated citizen. They remain arcane secrets of mathematicians or the one or two specialist types of engineers who *have* to use them. I believe that here again a new type of service course should be made available to wide circles of the university population.

Finally, there is the possibility of the university acting as a focus and organizer

of discussions on the kind of topics we have referred to as futures, not only between different disciplines within the academic world, but between the academic
world and the many other interested parts of society. Here I think the University
of Göteborg has provided us with a wonderful example. Professor Lundberg
has described in some detail the great success they have had in using the university background to stimulate debate on such matters within Sweden. I think we
have all been very impressed with this, and I suspect that many of us share my
view that many other universities in Britain and elsewhere should try to follow
their example. This has, of course, already been done by many universities in the
United States, but my feeling is that, perhaps because Sweden is a smaller and
more coherent country, the Göteborg experiment is the most successful that
has yet been carried out along these lines.

Biographies of the participants

ERIC ASHBY (Lord Ashby of Brandon), born in 1904, is Master of Clare College, Cambridge. He was for 13 years Professor of Botany, in Sydney and Manchester, and for nine years Vice-Chancellor of the Queen's University, Belfast. He was chairman of the Royal Commission on Environmental Pollution in Britain. His books include *Technology and the Academics* (1958), *Adapting Universities to a Technological Society* (1974), and *Portrait of Haldane* (1974).

JOHN BLACK, born in 1922, is Principal of Bedford College, University of London. His academic career started in Agriculture, and has moved through Natural Resources, General Biology and Human Biology into university administration. He has written many papers and one book: *The Dominion of Man* (1970)

YEHEZKEL DROR, born in 1928, is Professor of Political Science and director of public administration programmes at the Hebrew University of Jerusalem. He is a policy consultant to governments and international organizations and a former senior staff member of the Rand Corporation, Santa Monica, California. His books include *Public Policymaking Reexamined* (1968), *Design for Policy Sciences* (1971), *Ventures in Policy Sciences* (1971) and *Crazy States* (1971)

H. WENTWORTH ELDREDGE, born in 1909, is Professor of Sociology Emeritus at Dartmouth College, Hanover, New Hampshire. An urban specialist, he is the editor of *Taming Megalopolis* (1967) and *World Capitals: Toward Guided Urbanization and Urbanism* (1975). Recently he has published a series of papers on long-range planning and futures study courses.

JOHN M. FRANCIS, born in 1939, is Senior Research Fellow in Energy Studies at the Heriot-Watt University in Edinburgh. He is currently also Director of the Society, Religion and Technology Project of the Church of Scotland and a consultant to the World Council of Churches. He is co-author of *Scotland in Turmoil* (1973)

FREDERIC R. JEVONS, born in 1929, is Professor of Liberal Studies in Science at the University of Manchester. His books include *The Biochemical Approach to Life* (1964), *The Teaching of Science* (1969), *Science Observed* (1973) and (with others) *Wealth from Knowledge* (1972)

ALEXANDER KING, born in 1909, is Chairman of the International Federation of Institutes of Advanced Study and was formerly Director-General for scientific affairs and education, OECD. He is a co-founder of the Club of Rome. He has written books and papers on physical chemistry, science policy and education.

IVAN KLIMES, born in 1935 in Prague, is the editor of *Futures: the journal of forecasting and planning*, and an associate editor of *Energy Policy* and *Science & Public Policy*. He has written *The Art of Criticism* (thesis, 1958), *A Young Theatre* (1960), *Via Exploratorium* (1964) and numerous articles and studies on literary criticism, history and science writing.

KRISHAN KUMAR, born 1942, is Lecturer in Sociology at the University of Kent at Canterbury. During 1972–3 he was a Talks Producer at the BBC. He has written *Revolution: The Theory and Practice of a European Idea* (1971), and is at present writing a book on the future of the industrial societies.

ANDERS P. LUNDBERG, born in 1930, is Professor of Physiology at the University of Göteborg and a member of the board of the Centre for Interdisciplinary Studies of the Human Condition, Göteborg. He is the author of many papers on neurophysiology.

FRANK OLDFIELD, born in 1936, is Director of the School of Independent Studies and Professor of Geography in the University of Lancaster. He has written articles on ecological themes.

SIR WALTER PERRY, born in 1921, is Vice-Chancellor of the Open University. He was formerly Professor of Pharmacology at the University of Edinburgh and has written numerous papers on pharmacological subjects.

JOHN PLATT, born in 1918, is a research scientist at the University of Michigan, and author of *The Excitement of Science* (1962), *The Step to Man* (1966), and *Perception and Change* (1970)

SIR HUGH ROBSON, born 1917, is Principal of the University of Edinburgh. Formerly Vice-Chancellor of the University of Sheffield, he was before that Professor of Medicine in the University of Adelaide.

HAROLD G. SHANE, born in 1914, is University Professor of Education, Indiana University, Bloomington. Among his 120 books are *Linguistics and the Classroom Teacher* (1967); (with Robert H. Anderson) *Bending the Twig* (1970); *Guiding Human Development* (1971); *The Educational Significance of The Future* (1973); (with Alvin Toffler et al.) *Learning for Tomorrow* (1974).

SIR FREDERICK STEWART, born in 1916, is Professor of Geology in the University of Edinburgh. After a period as Chairman of the Natural Environment Research Council he became Chairman of the Advisory Board of the Research Councils in 1973.

ROBERT D. UNDERWOOD, born in 1945, is research fellow at the School of the Man Made Future, University of Edinburgh.

K. VALASKAKIS, born in 1941, is Associate-Professor of Economics and director of GAMMA (an interuniversity futures-oriented think-tank of the University of Montreal and McGill University). He has written various papers and two books on economic development and futures studies in general.

C. H. WADDINGTON, born 1905, has been Buchanan Professor of Animal Genetics at the University of Edinburgh since 1947. After ten years as a Lecturer in Zoology at Cambridge, he did Operational Research for Coastal Command, Royal Air Force, from 1942–1945. He has published numerous scientific articles and books on embryological development and evolution, and also a number of books about the relations between science and society, addressed to the general reader, such as *The Scientific Attitude* (1941); *The Ethical Animal* (1960); *The Nature of Life* (1961); *Behind Appearance: The Study of Relations between Art and Science in this Century* (1970). Between 1969 and 1971 he spent two years as Einstein Professor in the State University of New York at Buffalo, and during this time devoted himself to considering how the university curriculum should be developed in relation to the present problems of the modern world, and in studying what is being done in this connection in American universities.

MAURICE WILKINS, born 1916, is Professor of Biophysics at Kings's College, University of London and Director of the Medical Research Council Cell Biophysics Unit. His Department provides various interdisciplinary undergraduate courses linking physics, biology and biochemistry, and has developed a student discussion course on social relations of biology. He is President of the British Society for Social Responsibility in Science. His research has been mainly on molecular biology, e.g. the structure of DNA (joint award of Nobel Prize 1962).

SIR ERNEST WOODROOFE, born in 1912, is a physicist turned businessman who in 1974 retired from the Chairmanship of Unilever Ltd., an international corporation. He has given a number of lectures on business economics and is a Visiting Fellow of Nuffield College, Oxford. He is a Trustee of the Leverhulme Trust.

JOHN ZIMAN, born in 1925, is a Professor of Theoretical Physics at the University of Bristol. He is also the author of *Public Knowledge* and a variety of articles on the sociology of science.

Index of Contributors

*Entries in **bold** type indicate papers; other entries refer to discussion contributions*

Indexes compiled by William Hill

225

Subject Index